Implementing Automated
Software Testing

Implementing Automated Software Testing

How to Save Time and Lower Costs While Raising Quality

Elfriede Dustin
Thom Garrett
Bernie Gauf

♦♦ Addison-Wesley

Upper Saddle River, NJ • Boston • Indianapolis • San Francisco
New York • Toronto • Montreal • London • Munich • Paris • Madrid
Capetown • Sydney • Tokyo • Singapore • Mexico City

The publisher offers excellent discounts on this book when ordered in quantity for bulk purchases or special sales, which may include electronic versions and/or custom covers and content particular to your business, training goals, marketing focus, and branding interests. For more information, please contact:

> U.S. Corporate and Government Sales
> (800) 382-3419
> corpsales@pearsontechgroup.com

For sales outside the United States please contact:

> International Sales
> international@pearson.com

Visit us on the Web: informit.com/aw

Library of Congress Cataloging-in-Publication Data

Dustin, Elfriede.
   Implementing automated software testing : how to save time and lower costs while raising quality / Elfriede Dustin, Thom Garrett, Bernie Gauf.
         p. cm.
   Includes bibliographical references and index.
   ISBN 0-321-58051-6 (pbk. : alk. paper)
   1. Computer software—Testing—Automation. I. Garrett, Thom. II. Gauf, Bernie. III. Title.

   QA76.76.T48D8744 2009
   005.1'4—dc22   2008055552

ISBN-13: 978- 0-321-58051-1
ISBN-10:   0-321-58051-6

Text printed in the United States on recycled paper at Courier in Stoughton, Massachusetts.
First printing, March 2009

Contents

Foreword by Admiral Edmund P. Giambastiani, Jr.   xv

Foreword by Dr. William Nylin, Jr.   xvii

Preface   xix

Acknowledgments   xxiii

About the Authors   xxv

I. What Is Automated Software Testing and Why Should We Automate?   1

  1. What Is Effective Automated Software Testing (AST)?   3

    1.1 Automated Software Testing Definition   4

    1.2 Automated Software Testing Recipes   5

    1.3 Advances in AST Technologies   8

    1.4 Automating Various Software Testing Types   11

    1.5 Providing AST-Based Production Support   16

      Support Troubleshooting the Production Issue, As Needed   16

      Support Identifying the Specific Program Components Affected by the Correction   16

      Verify the Accuracy and Quality of the Program Correction   17

      Support the Production STR Triage   17

    1.6 Automating Standards Assessments   18

    Summary   20

    Notes   21

  2. Why Automate?   23

    2.1 The Challenges of Testing Software Today   24

    2.2 Reducing the Time and Cost of Software Testing   26

      Automated Test Planning and Development—Initial Test Effort Increase   28

Test Data Generation—Test Effort/Schedule Decrease   28
Test Execution—Test Effort/Schedule Decrease   32
Test Results Analysis—Test Effort/Schedule Decrease   33
Error Status/Correction Monitoring—Test Effort/Schedule Decrease   35
Report Creation—Test Effort/Schedule Decrease   37
Other Mitigating Factors to Consider   37

2.3 Impacting Software Quality   38
2.4 Improvements to Your Software Test Program   42
Improved Build Verification Testing (Smoke Test)   43
Improved Regression Testing   43
Multiplatform and Configuration Compatibility Testing   44
Improved Execution of Mundane Tests   44
Improved Focus on Advanced Test Issues   44
Testing What Manual Testing Can't Accomplish   45
Ability to Reproduce Software Defects   45
Enhancement of System Expertise   45
After-Hours "Lights-Out" Testing   45
Improved Requirements Definition   46
Improved Performance Testing   46
Improved Stress and Endurance Testing   47
Quality Measurements and Test Optimization   47
Improved System Development Lifecycle   48
Improved Documentation and Traceability   48
Distributed Workload and Concurrency Testing   49

Summary   49
Notes   50

3. The Business Case   51

3.1 Definition of the Business Case   51
3.2 Identifying the Business Needs   53
Need for Speeding Up the Testing Effort and Increasing Efficiency 53
Need for Decreasing the Testing Cost   54
Need for Applying Test Team Member Skills Most Effectively   55
3.3 Justifying Automation in Terms of Cost and Benefits   55
Estimating ROI   55
Overall Test Automation Savings   57
Test Environment Setup Time Savings   57
Test Development Time Savings   59
Test Execution Time Savings   61
Test Evaluation/Diagnostics Time Savings   62
Other ROI Considerations   63
More ROI Metrics   65
3.4 Risks   65
3.5 Other Considerations   67

Summary 68

Notes 68

4. Why Automated Software Testing Fails and Pitfalls to Avoid 69

4.1 R&D Does Not Generally Focus on Automated or Manual
Testing Efforts 71

4.2 AST Myths and Realities 74
Automatic Test Plan Generation 74
Test Tool Fits All 75
Immediate Test Effort Reduction 76
Immediate Reduction in Schedule 77
Tool Ease of Use 77
Universal Application of AST 77
100% Test Coverage 79
Equating Capture/Playback to AST 80
AST Is a Manual Tester Activity 81
Losing Sight of the Testing Goal: Finding Defects 82
Focusing on System Test Automation and Not Automating Unit Tests 82

4.3 Lack of Software Development Considerations for AST 83
Build Testability into the Application 84
Adhere to Open Architecture Standards 86
Adhere to Standard Documentation Format 87
Document Test Cases in a Standard Way 88
Adhere to Coding Standards 89
Use of OMG's IDL 89
GUI Testing Recommendations 89
GUI Object Naming Standards 91
Library Concept of Code Reuse 91

4.4 The Forest for the Trees—Not Knowing Which Tool to Pick 91
How to Evaluate and Choose a Tool 92

4.5 Lack of Automation Standards across Tool Vendors 94
Sample Automated Test Tool Standards 95

4.6 Lack of Business Case 97
Summary 97
Notes 97

II. How to Automate: Top Six Keys for Automation Payoff 99

5. Key 1: Know Your Requirements 101

5.1 Understand the AST Support Requirements 102
AUT or SUT Requirements 103
AST Framework (ASTF) and Tool Requirements 105

		AST Data Requirements	105
		Test Environment Requirements	108
		AST Process Requirements	112
	5.2	Additional Information in Support of AST Requirements	114
		Manual Testing Procedure	114
		Design Documents	115
		Prototypes	115
	5.3	When Information Is Not Available	116
		Conducting Interviews	118
		Further Increasing Your Knowledge Base	120
		Developing Requirements Based on a Legacy Application or Legacy System	121
	5.4	Start Implementing Your Requirements Traceability Matrix (RTM)	124
		Information in an RTM	125
		Example RTM	125
		Summary	128
		Notes	128
6.		Key 2: Develop the Automated Test Strategy	129
	6.1	The AST Strategy Document	131
	6.2	Scope and Automated Test Objectives	132
		Deciding Which Tests to Automate	133
		Prioritize—Base Automation Requirements on a Prioritized Feature Schedule3	137
		Defining the Test Objectives: An Example	138
	6.3	Identify the Approach	139
		Designing and Developing the Test Cases	139
	6.4	Automated Software Test Framework (ASTF)	146
	6.5	AST Environment/Configuration	150
		Test Configurations	151
		Other Test Environment Automated Testing Requirements	153
		Automating the Test Environment Management—Automated CM	153
	6.6	Automating the RTM	159
		Require Standard Test Case Templates That Are Usable for Your Automation Framework	160
		Hyperlink the Test Cases	160
		Update the Test Case Steps to Include Pass/Fail Results	161
		Update the RTM to Include Pass/Fail Results	161
	6.7	Automated Defect Tracking	164
		Summary	164
		Notes	165

7. Key 3: Test the Automated Software Test Framework (ASTF)   167

   7.1   Verify That the ASTF Meets Specified Requirements and That
             Features Behave As Expected   169
             Verify That Effective ASTF Development Processes Have Been Applied   169

   7.2   Peer-Review All ASTF-Related Artifacts, Including Design,
             Development, and Test Cases   170
             Peer Review As Part of the Software Development Lifecycle   170
             Evaluate All ASTF Components   173
             Review Test Cases   173
             Review Test Logic   175
             Review Test Data   176
             Review Automated Test Code   178

   7.3   Verify Requirements and Coverage   182
             Traceability   182
             Coverage   183

   7.4   Hold a Customer Review   183

        Summary   184
        Notes   184

8. Key 4: Continuously Track Progress—and Adjust Accordingly   187

   8.1   AST Program Tracking and Defect Prevention   188
             Conduct Technical Interchanges and Walk-throughs   189
             Conduct Internal Inspections   189
             Examine Constraints and Associated Risks   189
             Implement Risk Mitigation Strategies   190
             Safeguard the Integrity of the AST Process and Environments   190
             Define, Communicate, and Track Schedules and Costs   191
             Track Actions, Issues, and Defects   192

   8.2   AST Metrics   192
             Percent Automatable or Automation Index   196
             Automation Progress   198
             Test Progress   199
             Percent of Automated Test Coverage   199
             Defect Density   201
             Defect Trend Analysis   202
             Defect Removal Efficiency   203
             Automated Software Testing ROI   204
             Other Software Testing Metrics   204

   8.3   Root Cause Analysis   205

        Summary   206
        Notes   207

9.   Key 5: Implement AST Processes   209

    9.1   AST Phases and Milestones   211

    9.2   AST Phase 1: Requirements Gathering—Analyze Automated
Testing Needs   212

    9.3   AST Phase 2: Test Case Design and Development   215

    9.4   AST Phase 3: Automated Software Testing Framework (ASTF)
and Test Script Development   216

    9.5   AST Phase 4: Automated Test Execution and Results Reporting   217

    9.6   AST Phase 5: Program Review and Assessment   218

    9.7   Virtual Quality Gates   219

    9.8   Process Measurement   220

        Summary   221

        Notes   222

10.   Key 6: Put the Right People on the Project—Know the Skill
Sets Required   223

        Soft Skills   231

   10.1   Program Management   232

        AST Phase 1: Requirements Gathering—Analyze Automated Testing Needs   233

        AST Phase 2: Test Case Design and Development   234

        AST Phase 3: Automated Software Testing Framework (ASTF) and Test Script Development   234

        AST Phase 4: Automated Test Execution and Results Reporting   235

        AST Phase 5: Program Review and Assessment   235

   10.2   Systems Engineering   236

        AST Phase 1: Requirements Gathering—Analyze Automated Testing Needs   236

        AST Phase 2: Test Case Design and Development   237

        AST Phase 3: Automated Software Testing Framework (ASTF) and Test Script Development   238

        AST Phase 4: Automated Test Execution and Results Reporting   238

        AST Phase 5: Program Review and Assessment   238

   10.3   Software Development   239

        AST Phase 1: Requirements Gathering—Analyze Automated Testing Needs   239

        AST Phase 2: Test Case Design and Development   240

        AST Phase 3: Automated Software Testing Framework (ASTF) and Test Script Development   240

        AST Phase 4: Automated Test Execution and Results Reporting   241

        AST Phase 5: Program Review and Assessment   241

   10.4   Configuration Management   242

        AST Phase 1: Requirements Gathering—Analyze Automated Testing Needs   242

AST Phase 2: Test Case Design and Development 243
AST Phase 3: Automated Software Testing Framework (ASTF) and Test Script Development 243
AST Phase 4: Automated Test Execution and Results Reporting 243
AST Phase 5: Program Review and Assessment 243

10.5 Quality Assurance 244
AST Phase 1: Requirements Gathering—Analyze Automated Testing Needs 244
AST Phase 2: Test Case Design and Development 244
AST Phase 3: Automated Software Testing Framework (ASTF) and Test Script Development 245
AST Phase 4: Automated Test Execution and Results Reporting 245
AST Phase 5: Program Review and Assessment 245

10.6 Subject Matter Experts (SMEs) 246
Training 246

Summary 247

Notes 248

Appendices 249

A. Process Checklist 251

A.1 AST Phase 1: Requirements Gathering—Analyze Automated Testing Needs 252
Checklist 252
Products 252

A.2 AST Phase 2: Test Case Design and Development 253
Checklist 253
Products 254

A.3 AST Phase 3: Automated Software Testing Framework (ASTF) and Test Script Development 254
Checklist 254
Products 255

A.4 AST Phase 4: Automated Test Execution and Results Reporting 255
Checklist 255
Products 256

A.5 AST Phase 5: Program Review and Assessment 256
Checklist 256
Products 256

B. AST Applied to Various Testing Types 257

B.1 Security Testing 257

B.2 Soak Testing 261

B.3 Concurrency Testing 263

B.4 Performance Testing   265

B.5 Code Coverage Testing   269

B.6 Unit Testing   271

Notes   274

C. The Right Tool for the Job   275

C.1 Requirements Management (RM)   276
Automating Requirements Management   278

C.2 Unit Testing Frameworks—Example Evaluation   281
How to Evaluate and Choose a Framework   281

C.3 Configuration Management—Example Evaluation   284
Benefits of Software Configuration Management (SCM)   285
The SCM Tools Evaluated   286

C.4 Defect Tracking—Example Evaluation   292
How to Evaluate and Choose a Defect Tracking Tool   292
Bugzilla versus Trac   296
Conclusion: Security Is Job 1   298

C.5 Security Testing   299
Static Analysis versus Dynamic Analysis   300
Source Analysis versus Binary Analysis   301
Application Footprinting   302
Fuzz Testing or Penetration Testing   302
Threat Modeling—Prioritizing Security Testing with Threat Modeling   303
Automated Regression Testing   303
Wireless Security Assessment Tools   303

C.6 Automated Software Testing Framework (ASTF)—
Example Evaluation   306
Test Case Development   307
High-Level Languages   307
Platform Support   307
Open-Source   307
Cost   308
Multiple Process Management   309
Capturing Test Case Results   309
Support of Distributed Environment   309
Future Execution Time   310
Scalable   310
Footprint on SUT   310
E-mail   311
Conclusion for ASTF   311
Automated Test Tool Example: Testplant's Eggplant   312

C.7   Other STL Support Tools   316
            Self-testable or Autonomic Computing   318
            Notes   319

D. Case Study: An Automated Software Testing Framework
        (ASTF) Example   321
   D.1   Key Design Features   323
   D.2   Test Manager   325
   D.3   More on Automated Test Case and Test Code Generation   326
   D.4   Results Reporting   328
   D.5   Automated Defect Reporting   328
            Notes   329

Contributing Authors   331

Index   333

Foreword

by Admiral Edmund P. Giambastiani, Jr.

Today, the world turns over so rapidly that you have to build in a culture of change and innovation on a day-to-day basis. Innovation is an every-single-day part of a soldier, sailor, airman, Marine, or Coast Guardsman's life. Over the course of my military career, I was fortunate to see and experience the dramatic impact innovation has on the war fighter. One area where there has been tremendous innovation is in the field of information technology. The systems that we deploy today are now comprised of millions of lines of software, computer processor speeds we thought were unimaginable a decade ago, and networks that provide extraordinary bandwidth.

Despite these innovations, the need to respond to emerging threats is greater than ever, and the time in which we need to respond continues to decrease. From an information technology perspective, this means we need to be able to make software changes and field the associated capability improvements more rapidly than ever before. Rapidly but effectively testing changes is vital; however, for many programs more than 50% of the schedule is currently devoted to testing.

Innovative Defense Technologies (IDT) has taken the lead on providing an innovative solution to testing that I believe is needed in order for us to keep pace with an ever changing threat. With this book, *Implementing Automated Software Testing,* they have developed a guide that can help implement successful automated software testing programs and efforts. This book includes experience-based case studies and a thorough dissection of automated software testing issues and solutions. This book articulates how to develop the business case for automated software testing and provides a lifecycle approach to automated software testing programs. With *Implementing Automated Software Testing,* IDT is

providing timely and necessary material that allows responsible parties to implement an effective automated software testing program.

Admiral Edmund P. Giambastiani, Jr.
United States Navy (Retired)
Vice Chairman, Joint Chiefs of Staff (2005–2007)

Foreword

by Dr. William Nylin, Jr.

When I first began developing software systems in the mid-1960s, testing was primarily a programmer's responsibility; end users validated a relatively small sample of test cases. During the next two decades, more time was spent on testing, but there was significant test case overlap between programming staff testing and end users or a specific testing group. The redundant testing was expensive and delayed project implementation. When errors were discovered, the time lag for correction and revalidation was expensive. Today, a significant portion of the time and cost to market for software products is spent on testing. With the increasing complexity and size of the software included in products, my expectation is that the amount of testing required in the future will only continue to increase. Vast improvements in testing technologies are required, and automated software testing is one of the most promising answers.

The purpose of automated software testing is to increase testing efficiencies via effective use of time and resources, to allow for increased test permutations and combinations, as needed, to avoid test execution redundancy while increasing test coverage, and to allow for automated results analysis, resulting in increased quality and reliability of the software within the same or a reduced testing time frame. IDT's book *Implementing Automated Software Testing* provides extensive technical guidance for implementing an effective automated software testing program. The book provides experience-based automated software testing recommendations and solutions applicable to software testing programs across the board. Applying the automated software testing best practices and guidelines provided in this book will help improve your testing program and ultimately support your business in delivering software products on time, on budget, and with the highest quality. In addition, the book gives practical and realistic advice on how to compute your return on investment for automated testing solutions. It helps the user understand where to best utilize automated testing and when it may not be cost-effective.

Finally, an additional advantage of automated software testing is the ability to formally audit the testing process. Section 404 of the Sarbanes-Oxley Act of 2002 (SOX 404) requires, as of 2004, that each annual report of a public company include a report by management on the company's internal control over financial reporting. Furthermore, the company's external auditors are required to attest to management's assessment. Management information systems are perhaps the most critical components of internal control systems. Thus, the ability to have an independent audit of the testing processes for new systems can be critical for future large-system development and implementation.

Dr. William Nylin, Jr.
Executive Vice Chairman and Director
Conn's, Inc.

Preface

Is your test automation strategy a losing proposition? Are you soured on the notion of automated software testing based on less than adequate past results? Are your test automation silver bullets missing their mark? Are you disappointed in your test automators? We at IDT[1] have identified a boilerplate solution, strategies, and ideas, all provided in this book, that can help increase the chances of your automated testing success.

Given the arsenal of system and application software testing strategies, techniques, and solutions, automated software testing is one of the most effective practices that if implemented correctly can help increase testing efficiencies and ultimately reduce the testing cost while contributing to increased systems and software quality in terms of faster, broader, and more efficient defect detection.

This book is a guide that can help organizations implement successful automated software testing programs and efforts. The book does not provide gimmicks or magical solutions, as none exist, but it provides experience-based discussions and recommendations. It includes a thorough dissection of automation issues, such as in Part I of the book, where we describe what automated software testing is and is not; why a business case is required for successful automation, including step-by-step instructions for developing one; why to automate and when. Then we summarize why automation often fails and the pitfalls and blunders that can be prevented; we describe the tools that are available to help implement successful automation efforts, with a focus on open-source testing tools. In Part II of the book we present six keys to successfully implementing automated software testing. These are

- Key 1: Know Your Requirements
- Key 2: Develop the Automated Test Strategy

---

1. www.idtus.com.

- Key 3: Test the Automated Software Test Framework (ASTF)
- Key 4: Continuously Track Progress—and Adjust Accordingly
- Key 5: Implement AST Processes
- Key 6: Put the Right People on the Project—Know the Skill Sets Required

IDT conducted two separate surveys related to automated software testing with approximately 700 total responses from test professionals all over the world, across organizations that were diverse in size and in what they do. The survey showed two very consistent themes:

- About 70% of survey respondents said they believe automation is high-payoff, but they are generally not sure why to automate and how automation applies to their project.
- Half of the survey respondents also said they felt they lacked the experience, time, or budgets to implement automation.

Most seem to agree: Automated software testing is useful, and an increasing need for it exists. However, the lack of experience seems to be the reason why automation is not implemented more often with a higher success rate. Finding people with the skills for the project is therefore important; a summary of skills required is provided in Chapter 10. For more details on the outcome of this survey, see Chapter 4.

Material Coverage and Book Organization

Part I: What Is Automated Software Testing and Why Should We Automate?

Chapter 1, What Is Effective Automated Software Testing (AST)?, describes what automated software testing is. The definition of *automated software testing* we use throughout this book is the "application and implementation of software technology throughout the entire software testing lifecycle (STL) with the goal to improve STL efficiencies and effectiveness."

In Chapter 2, Why Automate?, we address this question that is asked so often. Here we discuss the challenges of software testing today and how the time and cost of software testing can be reduced. Reasons for why to automate, laying the foundation to help build the business case discussed step by step in Chapter 3, are presented here.

In Chapter 3, The Business Case, we define a step-by-step approach to defining the business case, which will cover the business need, the reasons for an automated software testing project, the business benefits (tangible and intangible), an analysis of the expected costs and timescales, an investment appraisal, and return on investment (ROI).

Chapter 4, Why Automated Software Testing Fails and Pitfalls to Avoid, clarifies some of the myths and realities surrounding automated software testing. The goal is for companies and organizations to review the lessons described here and not to repeat them during their automated software testing implementations.

Part II: How to Automate: Top Six Keys for Automation Payoff

Once management has been convinced by the business case that was laid out in Part I of this book and understands the pitfalls to avoid and the realities of automated testing, the next step is to determine how to automate. Part II of the book addresses how to successfully implement the various automated software testing tasks. We have determined that successful automated software testing can be achieved by implementing six top keys, described next.

Chapter 5, Key 1: Know Your Requirements, covers the importance of understanding the requirements before developing an automated testing strategy. Here we discuss approaches to determining the problem we are trying to solve along with how to gather information when requirements are not available.

Chapter 6, Key 2: Develop the Automated Test Strategy, discusses developing an automated testing approach in detailed steps, including test environment considerations, configuration management for automated test scripts, and related artifacts, among others. Here we also discuss what to consider when deciding what to automate and the importance of choosing the right tool, whether open-source, vendor-provided, or in-house-developed.

Chapter 7, Key 3: Test the Automated Software Test Framework (ASTF), covers the importance of understanding testing techniques and documenting test cases as part of automated testing. Automators often forget that documentation is still a vital part of the automated test program. The test case documentation serves as the blueprint for the automated software testing efforts. This chapter describes the importance of tracing test cases back to requirements; the content of the test cases, such as needing to include inputs and expected results;

and how documented test cases become the basis for developing and implementing the automated tests.

Chapter 8, Key 4: Continuously Track Progress—and Adjust Accordingly, addresses the importance of tracking the goal that was set at the outset of the automation program. For example, during the discussion of business case development in Chapter 3 we explain the need for defining goals; in this chapter we discuss how peer reviews, inspections, and various automation and testing metrics can help measure and track progress against those goals.

Chapter 9, Key 5: Implement AST Processes, points out the need for a lightweight process. Some automated testing scripts can be implemented successfully without much process in place, but in order to effectively implement a large automated testing program a lightweight adaptable process should be in place. This chapter discusses a summary of this process, linking back to the details in various chapters.

Chapter 10, Key 6: Put the Right People on the Project—Know the Skill Sets Required, clarifies the skill sets needed for developing automated software testing, for instance, a skill set similar to that of the software development team, which includes requirements analysis, design, software development, and testing. Key 6 points out that although knowledge of testing techniques and analytical skills is important, effective automated software testing implementation requires software development skills. The skills described here parallel the automated testing process described in Chapter 9.

Audience

The target audience of this book is software test professionals such as test managers, leads, and practitioners. It is also geared toward all quality assurance professionals, QA leads, and practitioners. Project managers and software developers looking to improve the effectiveness and quality of their software delivery will also benefit from this book.

Acknowledgments

Thanks to all of the software professionals who have helped support the development of this book. Special thanks go to IDT employees Scott Bindas, Marcus Borch, and Vinny Vallarine, who are contributing authors to this book and whose bios are listed in the back of the book. Their valuable contributions to this effort as a whole have greatly added to the content, presentation, and overall quality of the material. Additional thanks go to IDT employees Pete Bria and Burt LeJune for their editorial contributions to sections of this book.

Additional thanks go to our reviewers who added to the quality and content of this book. They are Joe Strazzere and Jake Brake, both long-time and experienced moderators on the popular software quality assurance site www.sqaforums.com, Jim Hazen, Rob Sabourin, Professor Jeff Offutt, Dr. Satyam Priyadarshy, and Jeff Rashka, PMP, co-author of *Automated Software Testing*, and *Quality Web Systems*. Their edits and contributions were invaluable.

Also we much appreciate the inputs and efforts of our foreword writers, Admiral Edmund P. Giambastiani, Jr., USN (retired), and Dr. William Nylin, Jr.

We also would like to thank the staff at Addison-Wesley, especially Peter Gordon and Kim Boedigheimer, for all their effective ideas and useful input; also Elizabeth Ryan, John Fuller, and Stephane Nakib for their efforts; and finally our copy editor, Barbara Wood, for her valuable suggestions to help make this book a quality product.

About the Authors

Elfriede Dustin, Thom Garrett, and **Bernie Gauf** work together at Innovative Defense Technologies (www.idtus.com), which specializes in the design, development, and implementation of automated software testing solutions.

Elfriede Dustin has authored multiple software testing books and articles based on her many years of actual hands-on automated software testing experience. Elfriede leads IDT's efforts in automated software testing research programs.

Thom Garrett has experience in planning, testing, and deployment of complex systems for DoD and commercial applications for companies such as Public Broadcasting Service (PBS), Digital System Resources (DSR), Inc., and America Online (AOL). Thom received a master's degree from the University of San Francisco.

Bernie Gauf is the president of IDT. Bernie has been invited to participate in numerous DoD panels associated with the use of new technology, testing conferences, and as a guest speaker to share his insights on automated software testing.

Part I

What Is Automated Software Testing and Why Should We Automate?

What Is Effective Automated Software Testing (AST)?

Realities of automated software testing

The term *automated software testing* (AST) invokes many different meanings from members of the software development and testing community. To some the term may mean test-driven development and/or unit testing; to others it may mean using a capture/record/playback tool to automate software testing. Or the term might mean custom-developing test scripts using a scripting language such as Perl, Python, or Ruby; for yet others, automated software testing might be related to performance/stress testing only, or entirely focused on functional testing and/or security testing. In the context of this book, AST refers to all of these.

Before getting into further details, it is important to define AST clearly so the term takes on a unified meaning and is understood by our audience. We define AST in the context of our work and experience, as well as its true meaning. Additionally, in this chapter we will discuss what is involved in a successful AST effort and provide AST recipes. Here we will talk about ideas for how to streamline some automated testing efforts and discuss applying AST throughout the software testing lifecycle.

1.1 Automated Software Testing Definition

The definition of *automated software testing* as it is used throughout this book encompasses all types of testing phases, including cross-platform compatibility, and is process-independent. Generally, all tests that are currently run as part of a manual testing program—functional, performance, concurrency, stress, and more—can be automated. Often the question is asked, "How is manual software testing different from AST?" The answer is that AST

- Enhances manual testing efforts by focusing on automating tests that manual testing can hardly accomplish.
- Is software development.
- Does not replace the need for manual testers' analytical skills, test strategy know-how, and understanding of testing techniques. This manual tester expertise serves as the blueprint for AST.
- Can't be clearly separated from manual testing; instead, both AST and manual testing are intertwined and complement each other.

It is possible to develop software that converts any type of manual software test existing today into an automated test, yet our experience shows that most manual tests have to be modified in order to accommodate automation. Manual testing techniques, practices, and knowledge are intertwined with AST and therefore are discussed throughout this book as they support AST. Whether the automation will yield the necessary return on investment (ROI) is another question that requires evaluation, and experience has shown that even though it is possible to automate all tests, not all tests are worth automating. Various criteria need to be considered when making the decision of whether to automate; how to determine what to automate is further discussed in Chapter 6. Keeping ROI in mind, our high-level definition of AST is

> The application and implementation of software technology throughout the entire software testing lifecycle (STL) with the goal of improving STL efficiencies and effectiveness

AST refers to automation efforts across the entire STL, with a focus on automating the integration and system testing efforts. The overall objective of AST is to design, develop, and deliver an automated test and retest capability that increases testing efficiencies; if implemented successfully, it can result in a substantial reduction in the cost, time, and resources associated with traditional test and evaluation methods and processes for software-intensive systems.

1.2 Automated Software Testing Recipes

AST, when effectively implemented, is not exclusively GUI capture/playback (as so many understand it to be), it is not limited to a specific phase of testing, it is not specific to any particular vendor's product, and it can accommodate a particular architecture or language used by the application under test (AUT).[1]

AST implementation as described in this book is process-, technology-, and environment-independent. Following the implementation suggestions described within this book will allow you to implement AST whether you are using the waterfall model, a test-driven development model, Scrum, or any other type of software development model, and it can be implemented whether you are testing a Web application or a service-oriented architecture (SOA) solution; or whether your applications run on Linux, Mac, or Windows, independent of environment, OS, and platform.

AST, if implemented effectively, should support applications that

- Run on multiple computers
- Are developed in different programming languages
- Run on different types of OSs or platforms
- Either have or do not have graphical user interfaces (GUIs) (for example, message interface testing without a GUI)
- Run any type of network protocol such as TCP/IP, DDS, and so on

Here are some recipes to keep in mind when developing an automated testing framework. It should

- Support integration of multiple commercial testing tools, whether open-source, in-house-developed, or from different vendors (as new or better products emerge in the market they can be used)
- Support testing without having to install the framework on the same computer as the SUT
- Support both new applications under development and existing applications

- Support the entire testing lifecycle (but AST does not need to be applied to the entire testing lifecycle in order to be used)
- Support distributed testing across multiple computers and various systems engineering environments
- Support reuse of the AST framework and components among programs, as applicable

Implementation of AST requires a mini development lifecycle, including test requirements, automation framework design and construction, automated test implementation/verification, and execution. If done correctly, AST should yield reusable and expandable frameworks and components. Best practices for software development apply and should be adhered to.

Although some programs and AUTs will have similar test automation needs and many commonalities, other programs require unique individual AST implementations and tailoring. An effectively implemented automated test framework needs to be able to accommodate these unique requirements.

Figure 1-1 displays an example that has been implemented using our described automation framework recipe. Here we show cross-platform compatibility by running the tests on a Linux and Windows platform. Additionally, we show how various tools can be integrated as part of the automation framework;

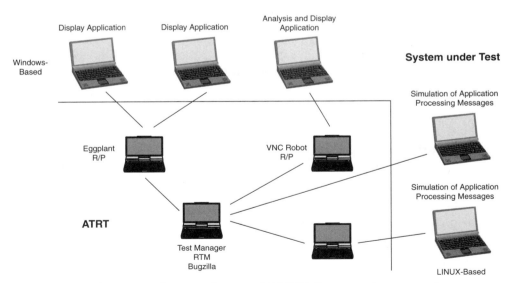

Figure 1-1   Automated test and retest (ATRT) framework—example

in this example we use Testplant's Eggplant[2] and VNCRobot[3] as the tools. We also use the software test automation framework/STA engine (STAF/STAX) framework, an AST framework that we have integrated successfully into our automated testing framework.[4] STAF/STAX is an open-source, multiplatform, multilanguage framework designed around the idea of reusable components, called *services* (such as process invocation, resource management, logging, and monitoring). STAF removes the tedium of building an automation infrastructure from scratch. The STAF framework provides the foundation upon which to build higher-level solutions and provides a pluggable approach supported across a wide variety of platforms and languages. STAF/STAX has been proven very useful, and we have successfully integrated it into our automation framework.

An AST implementation generally needs to be adaptable to specific AUT needs, depending on various criteria, such as the following:

- **AUT's testing lifecycle phase**

  AST can take a different up-front approach to automation when involved from the beginning of a software testing lifecycle, possibly during the unit testing phase, as opposed to when it is involved only toward the end, possibly during the user acceptance testing phase. The sooner AST is involved during the STL, the better. It will allow for reuse of test artifacts in subsequent phases, and it has been proven that the earlier a defect[5] is uncovered in a system testing lifecycle, the cheaper it is to fix.

- **AUT's schedule and timelines**

  Depending on the schedule and timelines, a more or less comprehensive AST solution can be implemented; that is, the more time allowed, the higher the percentage of test coverage, the higher the test automation percentage, the more detailed the analysis can be, and so on.

- **AUT's technology**

  Effective AST adapts its implementation to the AUT technology requirements. AST tools might be employed in a Windows versus Linux or a real-time versus static environment, as applicable, and are cross-compatible.

- **AUT's complexity**

  Often the more complex an AUT is, the more elaborate the AST effort that's required. Depending on the AUT complexity, different AST approaches and strategies need to be applied.

- **AUT's mission criticality and risk**

  An AUT's mission criticality and the risk associated with it affect the AST efforts involved.

We recognize the uniqueness of each program and the need to adapt AST for specific AUT needs, but independent of those needs, effective AST framework implementation can adapt to various environments. Effective AST is applied using a set of overarching phases and milestones independent of the type of program implementation; these are described in Chapter 9.

The goal is to roll out AST to various programs without having to develop an AST framework from scratch for each, and to apply lightweight processes that can be easily adapted to any organization or program.

1.3 Advances in AST Technologies

All manual tests don't need to be automated in order for an AST effort to be considered successful. Sometimes the question of whether to automate, based on calculating the ROI, determines that some of the tests don't lend themselves to automation for various reasons; for example, the ROI metric may prove it to be not cost-effective.[6]

Although AST is most often an improvement over manual software testing efforts, software development is required to test developed software. We develop software to test software because currently no better alternative exists. Efforts are under way, such as IBM's autonomic computing[7] initiative, that could possibly provide for self-testable components in the future, but while some progress has been made, at the writing of this book only a few companies have implemented and applied the autonomic computing concepts.

Given the current AST state and the need for developing software to test software, effective automated testing includes reducing human involvement and automating as much of what is involved in the effort as possible. The effort of developing software to test software needs to be efficiently streamlined. Using automation to implement software test automation is an effective way of removing required and error-prone manual human interaction. The goal as part of the automated testing streamlining is to automate the test automation.

For example, companies often spend time developing a test framework from scratch, creating functions to allow for batch testing, distributed testing, or e-mail notification, although numerous frameworks already exist that provide such features. Taking advantage of freely available open-source components or *free/shareware*[8] that provides the required features allows for reuse and ease of additional feature integration, saving time and money. Instead of developing new testing framework features, we find, scanning the open-source community, that often much of what we need has already been developed and is ready to be downloaded. We recommend that any automation test effort consider open-source components for designing and developing test automation frameworks. When considering open-source tools, keep the validity of the open-source license in mind. Some approved open-source licenses can be found and verified at http://opensource.org/licenses.

Test automators know that automated testing requires its own development lifecycle, so let's borrow from what the software development community has already figured out: using tools that help automate all phases of the lifecycle, from requirements to design, to implementation, testing, and defect tracking. As part of your test framework, for test procedure development you could follow a model-driven design. Telelogic/IBM has the most promising vendor-provided solution, with its Automated Test Generator (ATG) and Test Conductor (TC). Together ATG and TC generate a "test harness/platform" that can be used to generate test cases and the test code needed to completely test your model on the development platform as well as the target. An alternative to a vendor-provided solution would be the open-source AndroMDA; "you can now create and use your own EMF-based metamodels and write model-to-model transformations to transform from a PIM [platform-independent model] (at the highest level of abstraction) down through a stack of intermediate PSMs [platform-specific models] (using easily understandable transformation steps) until you finally reach the lowest level PSM from which it is easy to generate code using simple model-to-text transformations."[9]

There are other ideas for automating test procedure generation; for example, if all test procedures were written in an MOF Model to Text Transformation language (see the Object Management Group [OMG] Web site, www.omg.org/cgi-bin/doc?ad/04-04-07), then automated test code could be generated from the manual test procedures.

Testers are often faced with the challenge of verifying a huge set of test data combinations and permutations, and it is tedious and error-prone to manually develop such a data set using an Excel spreadsheet. But a manual test data creation process is still common in many testing shops. Why not use one of the many test data generators that provide us with automated combinatorial-based data output?[10] For example, the National Institute for Standards and Technology

(NIST) has developed a useful tool called FireEye (or ACTS), which can be downloaded at http://csrc.nist.gov/groups/SNS/acts/download/ (contact NIST for a login ID and password), which allows for such automated test data generation. NIST compares its test data generator tool FireEye to other available tools at http://csrc.nist.gov/groups/SNS/acts/documents/comparison-report.html.

There are many more ways to automate test automation: using existing Java libraries to test a user interface, such as Jemmy, or using an interface design language (IDL) to allow for code generation, or using built-in probes (see www.ocsystems.com), or developing self-testable components. As long as we are required to use/develop software to test software, we may as well automate that process as much as possible. Some additional examples of ways to streamline test automation are automated test case code generation, which includes software interface test code and test case procedure code, and use of composite applications, further described here along with the tools used:

- Automated test case code generation
  - Software interface test code
  - A software interface could be any type of middleware, such as CORBA, DDS, or a simple Multicast layout.
  - You can then generate software interface code from various input formats, such as IDLs, C-style headers, and so forth.
  - You would then generate code that glues the interface code to the test framework.
- Test case procedure code
  - Each step in the test case procedure has associated code generated to execute its behavior.
  - A standardized test case format facilitates automated step procedure extraction.
  - XML could be used to define the extracted test step information as input into the autogeneration process.
  - StringTemplates provide for a common code set as well as project-unique sets.
- Tools to be used for this example
  - ANTLR (www.antlr.org/)
    - Works off of grammar files. Several common languages' grammar files are available for download (such as IDL and C).

- Generates a lexical analyzer and parser functionality in Java. (Other languages are supported as well.)
  - StringTemplate (www.stringtemplate.org/)
    - Uses ANTLR. Developed by the same team.
    - Provides pluggable templates. Code can be generated in multiple languages without having to modify the autogen code.
  - JAXB (https://jaxb.dev.java.net/)
    - XML to Java object binding based on XML schema.
    - Generates Java classes used to interpret XML data.

See Appendix D for a case study discussion of how we used some of these automated testing technologies to implement our own framework, using mostly open-source tools. Also, see our presentation at the Google Test Automation Conference (GTAC 2008) for more details on how to implement the automated code generation.[11]

Additionally, innovative developers are turning to composite applications for the agility needed to get ahead of rapidly changing business conditions. The concept of checking out software components within a library setting in order to support software component reuse is notable. Being able to assemble existing components into custom-built components allows for a new look and feel, and new user interfaces and transactions; and behind-the-scenes composition of resources into new patterns of applications allows for quicker turnaround of a new release. We support this "library" and "software reuse" concept, because existing automated software tests can be reused on the various components. For example, an AST process will support the required efficiencies of the "library" software component checkout and reuse because the equivalent or applicable "automation component" can also be reused. This in turn will help streamline automated testing efforts.

1.4 Automating Various Software Testing Types

Various types of software testing are performed on any given system ranging from functional/verification of requirements testing to security or performance testing. These testing types basically fall into one or two main categories: black-box testing and white-box testing, with gray-box testing in between.

- **White-box testing** involves testing the internals of the system's software; unit testing and code coverage testing are examples. Some working knowledge of the code and design must be known at test time. Regardless of the types of tests that get executed, their intent is to verify that the system successfully satisfies its functional requirements overall.

- **Black-box testing** exercises most parts of the system by invoking various system calls through user interface interaction. Black-box testing involves testing the system as a "black box" while the inner workings of the system are not, and need not be, known.

  For example, if the user adds a record to the application's database by entering data into the user interface, various layers, such as the database layer, the user interface layer, and business logic layers, are executed. The black-box tester validates the correct behavior only by viewing the output of the user interface.

  Since user interface, or black-box, testing will not discover all defects, gray-box testing must also be applied, in order to increase the testing effectiveness.[12]

- **Gray-box testing:** Various definitions of gray-box testing exist, but for the purposes of this book, we'll explain and define it as follows: With black-box testing, in some cases, errors may not be reported to the user interface due to defects in the error-reporting mechanism of the software. For example, the application fails to insert a record in the database but does not report an error to the user interface—the user interface receives a "false positive" from the underlying code and continues without displaying an error to the user. Gray-box testing requires tests to be designed that require knowledge of the underlying components that make up the system. An understanding of the architecture and underlying components of an application allows the test engineer to pinpoint test outcomes to various areas of the application. It allows the tester to conduct gray-box testing, which can complement the black-box testing approach. During gray-box testing, the tester can be specific in narrowing down the parts of the application that are failing. The test engineer, for example, will be able to probe areas of the system that are more prone to failure due to a high degree of complexity, or simply due to instability resulting from "fresh" code.

Following are some examples of how a deeper understanding of the system architecture can assist a test engineer:

- **Improved ability to perform investigative testing**

  Once a test has failed, the tester will usually have to perform some "focused" testing by modifying the original test scenario, if necessary, to determine the application's "breaking point," or the factors that cause or do not cause the system to break. During this exercise, architectural knowledge of the SUT can be of great help to the tester. It will enable the test engineer to perform more useful and specific investigative testing, and perhaps allow him or her to skip additional superfluous and unrelated testing altogether, since knowledge of the underlying components allows him or her to determine additional information about the problem. For example, if the application encounters a connection problem with the database, then it is not necessary to attempt the operation with different data values. Instead, before testing can continue, the focus will be on resolving the connection issues.

- **Enhanced defect reporting**

  As discussed in the previous section, if the ability to conduct investigative testing improves, by default better defect reports can be written, because more detail can be provided. For the most part, test procedures are based on requirements and therefore have a somewhat fixed path through the system. When an error occurs in this path, the ability of the tester to include information relevant to the system architecture in the defect report is of great benefit to the system's development staff. For example, if a certain dialog box fails to display, the tester's investigation could determine that it was caused by a problem retrieving information from the database, or perhaps the application failed to make a connection to another server.

- **Increased testing precision**

  Gray-box testing attempts to exercise the application though the user interface, or directly against the underlying components, while monitoring internal component behavior to determine the success or failure of the test. Gray-box testing naturally produces information relevant to the cause of the defect, since monitoring the behavior of specific components is part of the test strategy. In general, there are four types of problems that can be encountered during testing:

- A component encounters a failure of some kind, causing the operation to be aborted. The user interface will typically indicate that an error has occurred.

- The test execution produces incorrect results, meaning that test results are different from the expected outcome. Somewhere in the system, a component has processed data incorrectly, causing an error in the results.

- A component fails during execution but does not notify the user interface that an error has occurred, which is known as a "false positive." For example, data is entered but is not stored in the database, yet no error is reported to the user.

- The system reports an error, but it actually processes everything correctly—the test produces a "false negative." An incorrect error message is displayed.

In the first case, it is important to have useful and descriptive error messages, which is often not the case. For example, if a database error occurs during an operation, the typical user interface error message is "Failed to complete operation," without any further details as to why. A much more useful error message would give more details, such as "Failed to complete operation due to a database error." Internally, the application could also have an error log with more information. Knowledge of the system components allows the tester to use all available tools, including log files and other monitoring mechanisms, to more precisely test the system, rather than depending entirely on user interface messages.

Some parts of testing still require human interaction, for example, usability testing, where only small portions lend themselves to automation, such as Section 508 adherence. Tools such as Bobby allow verification of adherence to Web site accessibility requirements.[13] Other parts of usability testing involve testing how well a system serves its intended purpose. A perfect candidate for this type of testing is Web page usability, where a panel of prospective users is employed to use the Web page as they would normally do to test its inherent "user-friendliness."

This type of testing is performed to make sure users can understand how to navigate through the page to get the information they want, or to execute the desired transaction. Usability testing research is an entire area in itself, and many companies dedicate themselves to this area of expertise.[14]

Other types of tests are better suited to automation. Appendix B provides a list of various testing types. The purpose there is to highlight tests that can hardly be accomplished in a manual fashion.[15]

Security testing, soak testing, concurrency testing, code coverage testing, memory leak detection, and so forth are testing types that lend themselves to automation and are very difficult to test manually. Manual tests for these types of tests are often error-prone, inconsistent inputs are common, and overall test time can become costly, arduous, and time-consuming.

Automated testing provides important benefits, such as repeatability, in addition to lower-level bottom-up testing, in the case of unit testing, for example, or static or dynamic code analysis in the case of security testing. The typical testing types that lend themselves to automation include

- Unit testing, i.e., validating the individual units in an application's source code

- Regression testing, i.e., verifying that previously working functionality is still working

- Functional testing, i.e., verifying the system meets the functional requirements

- Security testing, i.e., verifying the system meets the security requirements

- Performance testing, i.e., verifying the system meets the performance requirements

- Stress testing, i.e., verifying the system behaves "gracefully" under stress and doesn't simply crash

- Concurrency testing, i.e., verifying the system can handle concurrent threads and users

- Code coverage verification, i.e., measuring the percentage of a system's code that is being exercised by a test suite

1.5   Providing AST-Based Production Support

In addition to supporting programs in the software development phase, AST can be applicable to and beneficial for programs being prepared for the production phase or during the actual "live" phase. For example, the use of AST to automate all or a portion of the acceptance tests that are repeated for each production cycle would be high-payoff in reducing test time and cost for some programs. The technologies and processes previously described can also be used to support programs already in production.

AST can support a quick turnaround for testing production fixes and patches by implementing automated functions that can support troubleshooting production issues; help pinpoint the specific program areas a correction has affected to help reduce the regression test suite required, thus reducing testing timeframes; verify the quality of the program correction; and support the production system trouble report (STR) triage. These efforts are further described in the next section.

Support Troubleshooting the Production Issue, As Needed

Production support can make use of existing AST artifacts, for example, by running an automated test case that can verify the production issue. AST allows for ease of repeatability of test cases, whereas during manual test efforts an issue can often be difficult to reproduce. Effective AST can include a recording or videotaping of the production issue, and a compressed version can be sent to the developer. Various recording and compression tools exist that allow for this, such as the built-in movie recorder in Eggplant or Camtasia, to name just a couple. Once the production issue has been reproduced, AST efforts can support the troubleshooting of the issue, as needed, as described next.

Support Identifying the Specific Program Components Affected by the Correction

Once the program correction has taken place, AST efforts can help pinpoint and identify the areas/components affected by the fix. Often an entire regression test suite is run repeatedly without much analysis, because the testers are not aware of which specific areas of a program a fix has affected. The reasoning is often to be "better safe than sorry" and retest everything. However, this approach can be unnecessarily time-consuming. When best practices and software programming standards that allow for modular development, for example, are followed, program corrections and fixes can be localized to a specific module. For example, AST efforts can programmatically help analyze program areas affected by a correction, by evaluating the outcome of the automated regression test suite run. Based on the outcome of this analysis, the regression testing efforts can then be focused on the identified affected areas only, or additional automated test cases can be added, if it's determined that one doesn't exist (see the triage section for more detail). Helping to narrow down the set of regression tests needed to verify the fix allows for improved "surgical" and specific testing. This is another way AST can help reduce the time frame of the production fix/test cycle.

Verify the Accuracy and Quality of the Program Correction

AST efforts support the verification of the program correction. For example, even though a fix may be accurate and solve the production issue, it could have caused problems in other areas. AST efforts can help verify a fix by implementing automated regression tests that assure the following:

1. The patch actually fixes the production issue.
2. Previously working functionality is still working and the necessary fix didn't negatively affect the production program; that is, no new or tangential issues or possibly new unapproved features were introduced.

Support the Production STR Triage

AST efforts can support any production defect triage or root cause analysis that takes place, including an evaluation of what caused the production issue, how it slipped into production, and how it could have been prevented.

Additionally, this type of AST triage support can include

*   Evaluating the current set of regression test procedures (i.e., additionally support an automated requirement to test procedure traceability—requirements traceability matrix [RTM]—to assure consistent test coverage)
*   Automating test procedures for the STR issue that was uncovered and adding them to the automated regression test suite, as needed

- If a test procedure exists that if executed correctly could have uncovered the issue before it slipped into production, conduct a root cause analysis. For example, evaluate the test completion report, identify why the test didn't uncover the defect if it was run—possibly the test is not thorough enough and needs additional tweaking to cover the problem area—or if it wasn't run, determine why (i.e., time constraints, resource constraints, oversight, etc.).

- Automating the testing of the high-risk area that affected production

- Automating the testing of other areas, as needed

The goal of AST is to prevent defects from slipping into production. Once a production issue has been uncovered, AST efforts can help reproduce it, and once the STR is fixed, AST efforts can then be put in place to support a quick fix/retest turnaround and then help implement preventive and regression/defect detection measures. Additionally, AST efforts could include an evaluation of the current production program's quality index, as described in Chapter 2 in Section 2.3, "Impacting Software Quality."

1.6   Automating Standards Assessments

Much time is spent assessing various standards adherence as part of testing and assessment efforts, which is another area that lends itself to automation. Throughout the DoD and among commercial industry developers, projects and companies are required by contract to adhere to specific standards. Using an automated approach to standards assessment and verification could save a large percentage of the billions of dollars spent on testing/standards assessment efforts. Increasing standards adherence is dictated throughout organizations such as IEEE, OMG, and ISO. For example, the OWASP's Web Application Security Standards (WASS) project aims to create a proposed set of minimum requirements that a Web application must exhibit if it processes credit card information. Other existing security standards, for example, include the Cardholder Information Security Program (CISP) and the Health Insurance Portability and Accountability Act of 1996 (HIPAA) privacy and security regulations. An extensible automation framework for standards assessment can allow for automated standards assessment and results reporting.

Through automation we can provide a systematic, repeatable, and extensible solution that will allow various standards assessment groups to verify standards adherence. An automated solution will accelerate and streamline any standards assessment process and will quickly highlight any risks associated with nonadherence to a specific standard.

The ideal automated standards solution will guide users through a step-by-step process, automating their assessment activities. It will centralize the assessment activity and the breadth and depth of questions, and will enhance any manual assessment effort.

There are a number of initiatives currently under way, such as the Eclipse TPTP, to provide frameworks for the integration of tooling for specific problem domains such as standards verification; IBM is a major contributor to the Eclipse framework, making it one of the most reliable and secure open-source solutions available.

The DoD and commercial markets for standards assessment tools and efforts are extremely large, with billions of dollars being spent both on testing/assessment by the government and on standards compliance testing and quality assessment tools by corporations. By automating many of the currently tedious, error-prone, and time-consuming manual assessment activities, allowing for repeatability and extensibility, we could save money. For example, using a moderate estimate of 10% cost savings of the billion dollars spent on these types of standards assessment activities, our proposed automated solution can help save millions of dollars.

Figure 1-2 shows a proposed extensible automated solution that can be expanded and applied to other standardization efforts. It uses an extensible plugin framework based on Eclipse that allows the potential for extending capabilities to support integration of standards requirements and assessment across various DoD and commercial and business domains, including SOA, Web-based, embedded, and real-time systems; commercial and non-DoD interoperable communication systems; sophisticated transportation systems; and increasingly complex consumer handheld devices.

This type of automated standards assessment can be invaluable for determining levels of *development standards* compliance. Consider that you might require developers to use ANSI-compliant (American National Standards Institute) source code for a given language. AST, by taking advantage of the customizable rules-based features of some of the existing static code analysis tools, can easily "crunch" on source code to show levels of compliance and/or deviations from ANSI and other defined coding standards. In an indirect way, this can

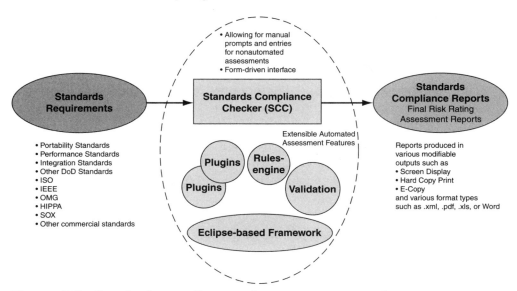

• Allowing for automation of various standards (DoD and commercial) compliance checking
• Plus manual entry for nonautomated areas
• Providing for a central repository of all assessment activities and outcomes
• Extensible solution depending on standards assessment needs

Figure 1-2 Standards compliance and assessment automation

expedite the code review process by eliminating one of the focal points generally found in code reviews or inspections. Such automation can be made available to entire development teams in order that they can assess their own source code.

Summary

This chapter presented our definition of automated software testing (AST) to establish the foundation upon which the remaining chapters will be based. The overall objective of AST is to design, develop, and deliver a technology capability that enables a substantial reduction in the cost, time, and resources associated with traditional test and evaluation methods and processes for software-intensive systems.

Effective AST aims for reusability of its processes, automation framework, and artifacts across programs along with addressing the uniqueness of any specific AUT need, without having to throw away the original AST effort or process and/or nearly develop from scratch. Developing a generic, adaptable AST framework is the goal.

AST efforts can support all facets of the testing lifecycle, to include the various software testing phases, production support, and software standards assessment and verification. To allow for streamlining of AST efforts, it is advisable to implement an automation framework as described in the section on AST recipes and AST streamlining.

No matter what the testing effort, if implemented correctly, AST can help expedite and streamline the effort.

Notes

1. We use *application under test* (AUT) and *system under test* (SUT) interchangeably throughout the book.
2. www.testplant.com.
3. www.vncrobot.com.
4. http://staf.sourceforge.net/index.php.
5. Defect and/or software/system trouble report (STR) are used interchangably throughout this book.
6. ROI is discussed in Chapter 3.
7. www.research.ibm.com/autonomic/.
8. Many code fragments of various source languages are freely available online. Along with other companies and individuals, the Microsoft Developer Network provides many code fragments.
9. See www.andromda.org/.
10. For more details on orthogonal arrays, read, for example, "Orthogonally Speaking" by Elfriede Dustin at www.scribd.com/doc/2175340/Orthogonally.
11. www.youtube.com/watch?v=HEpSdSyU03I.
12. Keep in mind that black-box and gray-box testing combined will still not produce a quality product. Testing processes, procedures, inspections, walk-throughs, and unit and integration testing are all parts of an effective testing process. Black-box and gray-box testing alone, by themselves, cannot find all the defects.
13. See www.cast.org/products/Bobby/index.html, or for a listing of Web accessibility tools see www.w3.org/WAI/ER/tools/complete.html.
14. See Elfriede Dustin, Jeff Rashka, and John Paul, *Quality Web Systems* (Addison-Wesley, 2001), and Elfriede Dustin, Jeff Rashka, and Doug McDiarmid, *Automated Software Testing* (Addison-Wesley, 1999), for more details on usability testing.
15. Dustin et al., *Automated Software Testing*.

Why Automate?

Automated software testing return on investment explained

Many of the unsuccessful AST attempts and myths related to AST implementations, plus lack of sufficient AST knowledge, lead to the question "Why should I automate?" Chapter 4 exposes and clarifies some of the myths surrounding AST and the pitfalls to avoid, but here we will first focus on answering the question "Why automate?"

We accomplish that by describing some of the key practices in software testing and the many areas that lend themselves to AST. The purpose of our discussion here is to educate the reader about software testing key practices in the context of "why AST."

AST is a key technique that addresses some of the challenges software testers face today. Our experience has shown that if implemented correctly, AST

1. Reduces the time and cost of software testing

2. Improves software quality

3. Enhances manual testing efforts via increased testing coverage and replaces the manually mundane and labor-intensive tasks

4. Does what manual testing can hardly accomplish, such as memory leak detection under specific conditions, concurrency testing and performance testing, and more

Cost, schedule, and quality are parameters that are critical to the success of any software development and product. We will discuss how AST can contribute to each.

2.1 The Challenges of Testing Software Today

The primary challenge today of testing software is that customers want more software functionality to be delivered faster and cheaper, while at the same time they expect the quality of the software to at least meet if not exceed their expectations.

The implications for the software test team are enormous. More functionality means each software baseline to be tested will be larger and more complex, which means more test cases must be run for each delivery. In other programs, faster deliveries mean less time to test each delivery, and more deliveries will be made each year, perhaps three or four product releases instead of one or two. More deliveries also mean more regression testing cycles. Reducing costs means the testing needs to be completed with fewer labor hours. Simply stated, there is more software to test, more often, with fewer people.

A report published by the NIST begins:

> Reducing the cost of software development and improving software quality are important objectives of the U.S. software industry. However, the complexity of the underlying software needed to support the U.S.'s computerized economy is increasing at an alarming rate. The size of software products is no longer measured in terms of thousands of lines of code, but millions of lines of code. This increasing complexity along with a decreasing average market life expectancy for many software products has heightened concerns over software quality.[1]

This same report estimates that software errors cost the U.S. economy an estimated $59.5 billion annually, of which they estimate one-third could be eliminated by improved testing.

Commercial hardware and software technologies have made many significant advances throughout the past several decades in development practices, methodologies, and tools which have been enablers in fielding phenomenal new, innovative, affordable, and timely information-processing capabilities. In addition, through the use of standard interfaces and common architecture frameworks, libraries of common functionality are becoming available for reuse which will further reduce development time and cost.

With a focus on reducing development time and creating reusable capabilities, efficient and thorough testing of the software will be more critical than ever. Developer software tests will no longer be used only during initial development and then not again. With incremental software builds and highly reusable software capabilities, software tests will need to be executed and reused many times before a product is even delivered. Furthermore, complex processing systems historically have been dominated by hardware costs and, as a result, the testing methodologies that have evolved are traditionally focused around the hardware. The majority of the systems being developed today, however, are largely based on affordable commodity hardware with the principal schedule and cost drivers squarely centered on the development and testing of the software.

Systems today are largely software-based, growing in complexity, and becoming more and more dependent on the successful reuse of software developed from other programs. Despite the advances in development practices and tools, the goals of accelerating the rate at which systems can be delivered and reducing their costs cannot be met by simply writing software faster without comparable improvement in the practices and tools for testing it.

New factors impacting the cost, schedule, and manpower needed for testing programs include

- Redundant testing between development teams, test teams, verification and validation (V&V) teams, contractors, and even users, i.e., during user acceptance testing

- Significantly increased levels of regression testing driven by technology insertion and new functionality

- Increasing complexity of computer software testing

- Interoperability, cross-platform, and certification testing requirements for each product release

In an article published by the Colorado State University Computer Science Department entitled "Automatic Test Software"[2] it was reported:

Much of testing (software) is still being done manually, and the process is intuitively guided. In this respect, software development lags behind hardware design and test, where use of tools is now regarded as mandatory . . . In the near future, reliability expectations in the market will particularly dictate all developers greatly rely on automation in testing. Today, no hardware engineer would think of doing a design without SPICE or VHDL level simulation. No one today thinks of doing manual test generation for hardware. The same will be true for software in only a few years.

The Colorado State University report is consistent with the findings of the IDC Software Research Group, which show that the market for automating software quality tools is growing substantially. The IDC[3] Software Research Group published a report entitled "Worldwide Distributed Automated Software Quality Tools 2006–2010 Forecast and Vendor Shares," which begins by stating that the "automated software quality tools market was once again the growth leader across application life-cycle markets." This report goes on to state, "The criticality of software to business, the increasing complexity of software applications and systems, and the relentless business pressures for quality, productivity, and faster time to market have all been positive drivers (resulting in growth in the market) and will continue to be in the foreseeable future."[4]

In its most recent market research report, IDC states that it expects the market for automated software quality tools to almost double in the five years from 2005 ($947.6 million) to 2010 ($1,842.1 million), citing increasing software complexity and the increased attention to corporate compliance as two of the key market drivers.

Organizations large and small are faced with increasingly large and sophisticated software projects while at the same time they are interested in delivering new and better products faster to market at the lowest possible cost. Unfortunately, most software development projects today are delivered late, are over budget, have less functionality, and have not been completely tested. When testing has become the bottleneck, AST can be a response to these challenges. How to approach AST and whether it can pay off are discussed throughout this book.

2.2 Reducing the Time and Cost of Software Testing

Although much attention is generally paid to the cost of software development, and much excitement is generated from technologies that offer development productivity improvement, the cost and productivity of software testing are often ignored or just accepted as "that is what it costs and how long it takes." This is ironic in that the cost and time of software testing are often comparable to the time and cost of developing the software.

Boris Beizer[5] reported that "half the labor expended to develop a working program is typically spent on testing activities."

IDT conducted its own survey regarding software testing, described in more detail in Chapter 4, which included over 700 responses. One of the questions we asked was what percentage of the overall program schedule was spent on testing. Forty-six percent of the responses said 30% to 50% was spent on testing, and another 19% of the responses said 50% to 75% was spent on testing.

The cost and time associated with software testing represent a significant portion of a project's overall cost and schedule, and therefore improvements made to increase testing productivity and reduce labor hours can have a measurable impact. The key considerations in assessing the impact are

1. What areas and how much of the test program can be automated?
2. What is the expected reduction in test time and schedule?
3. What is the expected increase in test coverage and impact on quality
4. Are there other mitigating factors to consider

How much of the test program can be automated? Not all the tests for a project can or should be automated. The best candidates for AST are those that are repeated the most often and are the most labor-intensive. Tests that are run only one time or infrequently will not be high-payoff tests to automate, unless the given context warrants for automation, for example, if the test is difficult or cost-time-prohibitive to run manually. Further, test cases that change with each delivery are also not likely to be high-payoff to automate if the AST needs to change each time. Chapter 6 discusses "whether and what to automate" in more detail.

Our experience has been that 40% to 60% of the tests for most projects can and should be automated. An initial top-level assessment should be developed for each project. An approach for this is further detailed in Chapter 6. As you gain experience in implementing AST for more projects, you will continue to refine your ability to accurately gauge the degree to which you can apply AST to the test program, based on your own historical data.

What is the expected reduction in test time and schedule? Before any test is automated, an ROI calculation should take place. Details of calculating ROI are discussed in detail in Chapter 3. Additionally, the need for automation of the best candidates in these test areas should be considered: automated test planning and development; test data generation; test execution and results analysis; error status and monitoring; and report creation, as discussed in the next sections. Our experience has shown that AST can have a big impact on reducing a project's schedule during the test execution phase. Activities during this phase would typically include test execution, test result analysis, error correction, and test reporting. If those activities are automated, our experience has shown that much time can be saved.

Our experience also has shown that during initial test automation implementation—that is, during the test automation development phase—there will be an initial time increase.[6]

Automated Test Planning and Development—Initial Test Effort Increase

Automated testing initially adds a level of complexity to the testing effort. Before the decision is made to introduce an automated test tool, many peculiarities need to be considered, which are discussed throughout this book. For example, a review of the planned AUT or SUT needs to be conducted to determine whether it is compatible with the test tool. Sometimes no tool exists on the market that meets the automation needs, and test software and frameworks have to be developed in-house. Additionally, the availability of sample data to support automated tests needs to be reviewed. The kinds and variations of data that will be required need to be outlined, and a plan developed for acquiring and/or developing sample data needs to be constructed; this is discussed in the next section. Consideration needs to be given to the modularity and reuse of test scripts. Automated testing represents its own kind of development effort, complete with its own mini development lifecycle. The planning required to support a test development lifecycle, operating in parallel with an application development effort, has the effect of adding to the test planning effort.

In the past, the development of test procedures was a slow, expensive, and labor-intensive process. When a software requirement or a software module changed, a test engineer often had to redevelop existing test procedures and create new test procedures from scratch. Using test management and automated testing tool capability for generating or modifying test procedures (as discussed in Chapter 1) takes a fraction of the time of manual-intensive processes.

Test Data Generation—Test Effort/Schedule Decrease

The use of test data generation tools also contributes to the reduction of the test effort. An effective test strategy requires careful acquisition and preparation of test data. Functional testing can suffer if test data is poor, and, conversely, good data can help improve functional testing. Good test data can be structured to improve understanding and testability. The content of the data, correctly chosen, can reduce maintenance efforts and allow flexibility. Preparation of the data can help to focus the business where requirements are vague.

When available, a data dictionary and detailed design documentation can be useful in identifying sample data. In addition to providing data element names, the data dictionary may provide data structures, cardinality, usage rules, and other useful information. Design documentation, particularly database schemas, can also help identify how the application interacts with data, as well as what relationships there are between data elements.

Due to the sheer number of possibilities, it is usually not possible to test 100% of the combinations and variations of all inputs and outputs to verify that the application's functional and nonfunctional requirements have been met. However, automated testing can help, and various test design techniques are available to help narrow down the large set of data input and output combinations and variations. One such test technique is "data flow coverage," which seeks to incorporate the flow of data into the selection of test procedure steps. Using this technique will help identify the selection of the test path that will satisfy some characteristic of data flows for all paths applicable. Other techniques such as the boundary condition testing technique are covered in Chapter 6.

Test data is required that helps ensure that each system-level requirement is tested and verified. A review of test data requirements should address several data concerns, including those listed below,[7] and is infeasible to implement in a manual fashion. Here is where automated test data generation pays off.

- **Depth**

    The test team must consider the volume or size of the database records needed to support tests. They need to identify whether ten records within a database or particular table are sufficient or 10,000 records are necessary. Early lifecycle tests, such as unit or build verification tests, should use small, handcrafted databases, which offer maximum control and minimal disturbances. As the test effort progresses through the different phases and types of tests, the size of the database should increase to a size that is appropriate for the particular tests. For example, performance and volume tests are not meaningful when the production environment database contains 1,000,000 records, but the tests are performed against a database containing only 100 records.[8]

- **Breadth**

    Test engineers need to investigate the variation of the data values (e.g., 10,000 different accounts and a number of different types of accounts).

A well-designed test will incorporate variations of test data, and tests for which all the data is similar will produce limited results. For example, tests may need to consider that some accounts may have negative balances, and some have balances in the low range ($100s), moderate range ($1,000s), high range ($100,000s), and very high range ($10,000,000s). Tests must also reflect data that represents an average range. In the case of accounts at a bank, customer accounts might be classified in several ways, including savings, checking, loans, student, joint, and business. All data categories need to be considered.

- **Scope**

  The test team needs to investigate the relevance of the data values. The scope of test data is pertinent to the accuracy, relevance, and completeness of the data. For example, when testing the queries used to identify the various kinds of bank accounts that have a balance due of greater than $100, not only should there be numerous accounts meeting this criterion, but the tests need to reflect additional data, such as reason codes, contact histories, and account owner demographic data. The inclusion of the complete set of test data enables the test procedure to fully validate and exercise the system and support the evaluation of results. The test engineer would also need to verify that the inclusion of a record returned as a result of this query is valid for the specific purpose (e.g., over 90 days past due) and not the result of a missing or inappropriate value. Another key here is that simulation of various paths of business logic and/or end-user rights and privileges requires different classes of data.

- **Test execution data integrity**

  Another test data consideration for the test team involves the need to maintain data integrity while performing tests. The test team needs to be able to segregate data, modify selected data, and return the database to its initial state throughout test operations. The test team needs to make sure that when several test engineers are performing tests at the same time, one test won't adversely affect the data required for the other test. For example, if one test team member is modifying data values while another is running a query, the result of the query may not be as expected since the records are being changed by the other tester. In order to avoid having one tester's test execution affecting another tester's test outcomes, assign separate testing tasks, asking each tester to focus on a specific area of the functionality that does not overlap with other testers. Using automated testing scripts will allow for streamlines and automated data integrity.

- **Conditions**

    Data sets should be created that reflect specific "conditions" in the domain of the application, meaning a certain pattern of data that can be arrived at only by performing one or many operations on the data over time. For example, financial systems commonly perform a year-end closeout. Storing data in the year-end condition enables the test team to test the system in a year-end closeout state without having to enter the data for the entire year. Having this data already created and ready to use for testing simplifies test activities, since it is simply a matter of loading this test data, rather than performing many operations to get the data into the year-end closeout state. Automated testing tools can help here, also.

As part of the process for identifying test data requirements, it is beneficial to develop a matrix containing a list of the test procedures in one column and a list of test data requirements in another column. As mentioned, while a small data subset is good enough for functional testing, a production-size database is required for performance testing. It can take a long time to acquire production-size data, sometimes as long as several months if done manually. Automated testing can allow for quickly populating test databases.

Once test data requirements are outlined, the test team also needs to plan the means of obtaining, generating, or developing the test data and of refreshing the test database to an original state, to enable all testing activities, including regression testing. An automated approach is needed.

Data usually needs to be prepared prior to being used for testing. Data preparation may involve the processing of raw data or text files, consistency checks, and an in-depth analysis of data elements, which includes defining data to test case mapping criteria, clarifying data element definitions, confirming primary keys, and defining data-acceptable parameters. The test team needs to obtain and modify any test databases necessary to exercise software applications and develop environment setup scripts and testbed scripts. Ideally, already existing customer or system data is available that includes realistic combinations and variations of data scenarios (it is assumed that the data has been cleaned to remove any proprietary or personal information). Customer data can also include some combinations or usage patterns that the test team did not consider, so having real customer data available during testing can be a useful reality check for the application.

Generating test data is tedious, time-consuming, and error-prone if done manually.

Test Execution—Test Effort/Schedule Decrease

Before test execution takes place, entrance criteria must be met.[9] For various reasons, entrance criteria verification should be automated. The entrance criteria describe when a testing team is ready to start testing a specific build. For example, in order to accept a software build during system testing, various criteria should be met, most of which should be automated.

- All unit and integration tests must be executed successfully.

- The software must build without any issues.

- The build must pass a smoke test that verifies previously working functionality is still working.

- The build must have accompanying documentation ("release notes") that describes what is new in the build and what has been changed.

- Defects must be updated to "retest" status for the new build.

- The source code must be stored in a version control system.

Once the entrance criteria have been verified, test execution can take place. Manual performance of test execution is labor-intensive and error-prone. A test tool or in-house-developed automation framework allows test scripts to be played back at execution time with minimal manual interference. With the proper setup and in the ideal world, the test engineer needs only to kick off the script, and the tool executes unattended. The tests will compare expected results to actual results and report respective outcomes. The tests can be executed as many times as necessary and can be set up to start at a specified time. This ease of use and flexibility allow the test engineer to focus on other priority tasks.

Today's automated test tools allow for the selection and execution of a specific test procedure with the click of an icon. With modern automated test procedure (case) generators, test procedure creation and revision times are greatly reduced in comparison to manual test methods, sometimes taking only a matter of seconds. See Appendix D for an example of test procedure generation.

Test Results Analysis—Test Effort/Schedule Decrease

Automated test tools generally have some kind of test result report mechanism and are capable of maintaining test log information. Some tools produce color-coded results, where green output might indicate that the test passed and red output indicates that the test failed. This kind of test log output improves the ease of test analysis. Most tools also allow for comparison of the failed data to the original data, pointing out the differences automatically, again supporting the ease of test output analysis. In-house-developed test tools can differentiate a pass versus fail in various ways.

To be most productive, verification of exit criteria, like verification of entrance criteria, also should be automated. Exit criteria describe conditions that show the software has been adequately tested. Testing resources are finite, the test budget and number of test engineers allocated to the test program are limited, deadlines approach quickly, and therefore the scope of the test effort must have its limits as well. The test plan must indicate when testing is complete. However, when exit criteria are stated in ambiguous or poorly defined terms, the test team will not be able to determine the point at which the test effort is complete. Testing can go on forever.

The test completion criteria might include a statement that all defined test procedures, which are based on requirements, must be executed successfully without any significant problems, meaning all high-priority defects must have been fixed by development and verified through regression testing by a member of the test team. This, in addition to all of the other suggested practices discussed throughout this book, will provide a high level of confidence that the system meets all requirements without major flaws.

As a simplified example, the exit criteria for an application might include one or more of the following statements.

- Test procedures have been executed in order to determine that the system meets the specified functional and nonfunctional requirements.

- The system is acceptable, provided that all levels 1, 2, and 3 (showstoppers, urgent, and high-priority) software problem reports, documented as a result of testing, have been resolved.

  or

- The system is acceptable, provided that all levels 1 and 2 (showstoppers, urgent) software problem reports have been resolved.

or

- The system is acceptable, provided that all levels 1 and 2 (showstoppers, urgent) software problem reports, documented as a result of testing, have been resolved, and that 90% of level 3 problem reports have been resolved.

Developers also need to be aware of the system acceptance criteria. The test team needs to communicate the list of entrance and exit criteria to the development staff early on, prior to submitting the test plan for approval. Testing entrance and exit criteria for the organization should be standardized, where possible, and based upon criteria that have been proven on several projects.

It may be determined that the system can ship with some defects that will be addressed in a later release or a patch. Before going into production, test results analysis can help to identify the defects that need to be fixed versus those whose correction can be deferred. For example, some defects may be reclassified as enhancements, and then addressed as part of a later software release. The project or software development manager, together with the other change control board members, will likely determine whether to fix a defect or risk shipping a software product with the defect.

Additional metrics have to be evaluated as part of the exit criteria (for additional discussions of test metrics, see Chapter 8). For example:

- What is the rate of defects discovered in previously working functionality during regression tests, meaning defect fixes are breaking previously working functionality?
- How often do defect corrections, meaning defects thought to be fixed, fail the retest?
- What is the newly opened defect rate (on average)? The defect open rate should decline as the testing phase goes on. If this is not the case, it is an indication of bigger problems that need to be analyzed.

Testing can be considered complete when the application/product is acceptable enough to ship or to go live in its current state, meeting the exit criteria, even though there are most likely more defects than those that have been discovered.

Another way to determine software quality and whether exit criteria have been met is reliability modeling, discussed in Section 2.3.

Once the official software build has met exit criteria, the software will only be as successful as it is useful to the customers. Therefore, it is important that user acceptance testing be factored into the testing plan.

It is important that the test team establish quality guidelines for the completion and release of software. Automating this effort will pay off.

Error Status/Correction Monitoring—Test Effort/Schedule Decrease

There are automated tools on the market that allow for automatic documentation of defects with minimal manual intervention after a test script has discovered a defect. The information that is documented by the tool can include the identification of the script that produced the defect/error, identification of the test cycle that was being run, a description of the defect/error, and the date and time when the error occurred.

The defect-tracking lifecycle is a critical aspect of error status/correction monitoring as part of the test execution program. It is important that an adequate defect-tracking tool be selected and evaluated for your system environment. Once the tool has been acquired or developed in-house, it is just as important that a defect-tracking lifecycle be instituted, documented, and communicated. All stakeholders need to understand the flow of a defect from the time it has been identified until it has been resolved. Suppose you would retest a defect only if it is in "retest" status, but the development manager doesn't comply with this process or is not aware of it. How would you know which defects to retest? This is a perfect example of a process that would benefit from automation.

Test engineers need to document the details of a defect and the steps necessary to re-create it, or simply reference a test procedure, if those steps were followed, in order to assist the development team's defect correction activities. Defects are commonly classified based on priority, and higher-priority defects get resolved first. Test engineers need to participate in defect walkthrough, if applicable, to review and discuss outstanding defect reports. Once the identified defects have been corrected and the corrections have been released in a new software build, test engineers are informed of this in the defect-tracking tool, where the defect status is set to "retest," for example. Testers can then focus on retesting defects identified as such. Ideally the fixed defect also contains a description of the fix and what other areas of the system could have been affected by it. Testers can then also focus on retesting those potentially affected areas.

Each test team needs to perform defect reporting by following a defined process.

1. **Analysis**

   The process should describe how to evaluate unexpected system behavior. Sometimes a test can produce a false negative, where the system behaves correctly but the test is wrong. Or the test (especially when a testing tool is used) can produce a false positive, where the test is passed but the system has a problem. The tester needs to be equipped with specific diagnostic capabilities to determine the correctness of the output. See the discussion of gray-box testing in Chapter 1 for additional ideas on how to approach this.

2. **Defect entry**

   Assuming the tester's diagnosis determines that the unexpected system behavior is a defect (not a false positive, false negative, duplicate, etc.), typically, a software problem report, or defect, is entered into the defect-tracking tool by a member of the testing team or a member of another team that is tasked to report defects.

3. **Recurrence**

   The automated process should also define how to handle a recurring issue—an issue that has been identified before, was fixed, but now has reappeared. Should the "old" defect be reopened, or should a new defect be entered? We usually suggest that the old defect be reviewed for the implemented fix, but a new defect be reopened with reference to the "closed, but related" defect. This reference will give an indication of how often defects are reintroduced after they have been fixed, and this may point to a configuration problem or an issue on the development side.

4. **Closure**

   Once the defect has been corrected, or deemed to be a duplicate, or not a defect, it can be closed. Don't allow anyone but the test manager to close defects. This ensures that all defects and their history are properly tracked and not inadvertently, or intentionally, closed by another staff member.

Note: Defects should not be deleted, but kept for historical purposes. There are ways around this problem via a database reset, but generally deletion of a defect through the interface can destroy the continuity of your numbering system. If people have made hard copies, they won't be able to find that defect; you want to keep those records. Instead, it is much better to simply mark the defect as "close—works as expected" or "close—duplicate."

It may be useful to have a rule regarding partially corrected defects: If a defect is only partially fixed, it cannot be closed as fixed. Usually this should not be the case; defect reports should be as detailed as possible, and only one issue should be documented at a time. If multiple problems are encountered, multiple defects should be entered, regardless of how similar the problems may be.

Once the defect has been corrected and unit-tested to the satisfaction of the software development team, the corrected software code should be checked in using the software configuration management tool. At some point an acceptable number of defects will have been corrected, or in some cases a single critical defect, and a new software build is created and given to the testing team.

When using a defect-tracking tool, the test team needs to define and document the defect lifecycle model, also called the *defect workflow* (see Chapter 9 for an example). In some organizations the configuration management group or process engineering group is responsible for the defect workflow; in other organizations it is the test team's responsibility. Regardless of responsibility, automating this process will save time and increase efficiency.

Report Creation—Test Effort/Schedule Decrease

Many automated test tools have built-in report writers, which allow users to create and customize reports tailored to their specific needs. Even those test tools that don't have built-in report writers might allow for import or export of relevant data in a desired format, making it simple to integrate the test tool output data with databases that allow report creation.

Other Mitigating Factors to Consider

Our experience in implementing automated testing for customers has been a significant payoff and reduction in test time when using AST with applications that are consistently undergoing regression testing as part of each delivery. We find projects often have a standard set of test procedures to repeat with each delivery, and in addition, these same tests need to be run across multiple configurations. As an example, a set of test procedures that required three days to execute and was run monthly was able to be automated and then run in less an hour. The project now benefits from this reduced test time each time the tests are rerun.

A likely challenge you will find is locating accurate data on exactly how long it took to manually run tests, how many people were really needed, and how often the tests were actually run. Some programs undoubtedly have kept records where this information is either easily obtainable or derived, but most programs do not. The best alternative we have found is to meet with the test team and reconstruct the information as best as possible. Teams generally have a pretty good understanding of how many people were part of the testing effort for a given delivery and how many calendar days were required for testing. Given these parameters, you can develop estimates for time and effort associated with manual testing.

Tracking the actual reduction in test hours versus what was previously required when the tests were run manually is another good measure on which to develop historical data for your organization and programs. This type of historical data will be invaluable to you when estimating the impact of AST on future projects.

Projects may have unique requirements or test procedures that may not result in AST delivering the theoretical reduction in schedule. Organizations that have new test programs, less mature test processes, and/or are completely new to AST also may not experience the theoretical reduction in schedule. Each project team should assess any mitigating factors that need to be considered. A comparison of what was achieved regarding reduction in hours versus estimated hours and the mitigating factors that resulted in the deviation is another helpful metric to track and then apply to future AST projects.

For a preliminary estimate, using the methodology of reviewing how much of the test program AST is applicable to, what kind of savings could be realized after deducting the AST development or AST tool cost and other tangential factors, plus accounting for any mitigating circumstances, is a sound approach to developing a preliminary estimate of projected time and cost savings or quality increase when AST is applied to a particular test program. This is a simplified ROI summary—a detailed discussion of projecting the ROI from AST is provided in Chapter 3—but having an approach to estimating the savings from AST early on is generally necessary to plan the project and will help answer the question "Why automate?"

2.3 Impacting Software Quality

Here we want to describe what we mean by software quality within the context of how AST impacts it.

Think of quality first based on the following two definitions and then apply them to the context of software.

ISO definition of quality: "The totality of features and characteristics of a product or service that bear on its ability to satisfy stated or implied needs."[10]

Another definition of quality: The nature of a system that performs as expected (meeting all requirements), making available the required system features in a consistent fashion, demonstrating high availability under any type of constraint, such as stress, concurrency, security breach, and so on, thus consistently meeting the user's expectations and satisfying the system's user needs (a user can be a person or another system).

In both definitions, the essence of software quality is how well it meets expected functionality and performance.

There are also many metrics associated with quantifying software quality. Examples include

- Software defect density (number of defects per source lines of code or function points or any other source code metric used on the program)
- Mean time to failure (MTTF)
- Mean time to critical failure (MTTCF)
- Number of high-priority defects that have not been found and removed
- Reliability (probability that no failure will occur in the next n time intervals)

One method for projecting software quality is the use of software reliability models. Software reliability models predict the results from continued testing and overall defect statistics associated with a software baseline under test. Therefore, one can use software reliability models to forecast the impact of additional testing on software quality.

Typical software reliability model results project the number of undiscovered software defects over time. One expects that as the test program continues, more testing will result in fewer defects yet undiscovered. A conceptual software model projection is shown in Figure 2-1. The slope of the curve is uniquely projected for each project, based on defects discovered to date combined with the size and complexity of the SUT.

The use of AST enables more testing to be completed. In particular, AST offers these benefits:

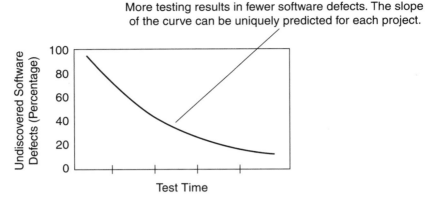

Figure 2-1   Improved quality with increased test time

- A full set of regression tests can be run every time without the testers having to worry about which portions of the system should be retested (even though ideally an analysis takes place to identify the areas affected by a change; see the related discussion in Chapter 1).

- There is increased test coverage; AST tests can cover more combinations (more data variations and test scenarios) and more paths and branches than manual testing can, given the same amount of time.

- AST increases the amount of effective test time, because

  - It can be run during off-shifts (lunch, nights, weekends).

  - During automated test runs, testers can focus on more complex and new issues/areas.

  - For some systems, AST may be able to run faster than clock-time rates (be careful when applying this; sometimes there are system dependencies that need to be considered).

- Automated tests don't get tired or inattentive.

- Automated tests are easier to replicate (avoiding nonreproducible defects).

- Some tests, such as performance tests, memory leak detection tests, concurrency, and so on, are nearly impossible to run manually.

- AST allows for distributed testing—spreading the workload across multiple machines, simulating the "live" or production environment. This is another very efficient way of using automation.

The impact of more effective test time on software quality can be illustrated as shown in Figure 2-2, using the software reliability model results from before. The more testing that can be completed, the greater will be the direct impact on reducing the number of software defects still undiscovered. The size of the impact is a function of the state of the software baseline relative to undiscovered defects (i.e., where you are on the curve).

Ultimately, the question everyone has to answer is "How do we know when we are done testing?" Software reliability models provide a projection of how many defects are still undiscovered and can serve as a basis for answering the question of knowing when enough testing has been done. The reality is that often testing stops when the product needs to be shipped or when it was promised to a customer. The test team conducts as much testing as possible in the allotted time. AST provides a means of conducting more tests in ideally less time, but conducting even more tests in the same amount of time provides efficiencies that can have a direct impact on software quality. Software reliability models can be used as tools to estimate the impact.

Even without using software models, you can use results from past deliveries to start to analyze where problems were found after the product was delivered to see the impact AST could have on software quality. In assessing the results from previous releases or deliveries, were any problems reported regarding functionality that previously worked, but that the test team did not have time to fully regression-test? How many problems were identified as a result of sequence-of-operator actions not exercised because there was not enough time to test, or a combination of values that was never tried? Were there any problems

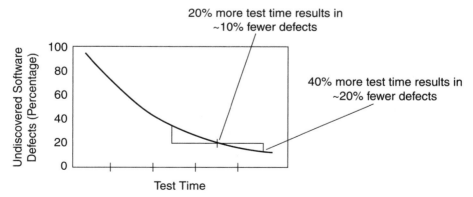

Figure 2-2   Improved quality with increased test time (additional detail)

due to boundary condition values that were not tested? How many issues were there with incompatibility with all configurations or after the application ran for a certain period of time? Were issues identified because there was not enough time to even test the functionality? Reviewing results from past deliveries can provide insight into the impact additional testing and AST would make on software quality.

2.4 Improvements to Your Software Test Program

Using automated test tools can increase the depth and breadth of testing. Additional benefits are the following:[11]

- Improved build verification testing (smoke testing)
- Improved regression testing
- Multiplatform compatibility and configuration testing
- Improved execution of mundane tests
- Improved focus on advanced test issues
- Testing what manual testing can't accomplish, such as security or memory leak testing
- Ability to reproduce software defects
- Enhancement of system expertise
- After-hours "lights-out" testing
- Improved requirements definition
- Improved performance testing
- Improved stress and endurance testing
- Quality measurements and test optimization
- Improved system development lifecycle
- Improved documentation and traceability
- Distributed workload and concurrency testing

Improved Build Verification Testing (Smoke Test)

The smoke test (build verification test) focuses on test automation of the system components that make up the most important functionality. Instead of having to repeatedly retest everything manually whenever a new software build is received, a test engineer plays back the smoke test, verifying that the major functionality of the system still exists. An automated test tool allows the test engineer to record the manual test steps that would usually be taken in support of software build/version verification. With an automated test tool, tests can be performed that verify that all major functionality is still present, before any unnecessary manual tests are performed. As an example, when delivering the systems for one of our largest customers, it was critical that every delivery to every platform be smoke-tested. The smoke test involved overnight runs that were semiautomated and checked after a period of time, and then reports were generated based on the outcome. The goals (numbers of platforms) for delivering verified software to platforms were big and also necessary in order to bring needed capability and functionality to the customer. The point is that streamlining smoke testing through automation is a huge benefit and value to many of our customers. It is also a time and cost control, so you don't test a system in depth that is not basically stable. This reduces rework and is another great cost-containment strategy.

Improved Regression Testing

A regression test is a test or set of tests executed on a baselined system or product (baselined in a configuration management system), when a part of the total system product environment has been modified. The test objective is to verify that the functions provided by the modified system or products are as specified and there has been no unintended change in operational functions.

An automated test tool provides for simplified regression testing. Automated regression testing can verify that no new bugs were introduced into a new build. Experience shows that modifying an existing program is a more error-prone process (in terms of errors per statement written) than writing a new program.[12]

Regression testing should occur after each release of a previously tested application. The smoke test described previously is a mini and rapid regression test of major functionality. Regression testing expands on the smoke test and involves testing all existing functionality that has already been proven viable. The regression test suite is the subset of all the test procedures which exercises the basic functionality of the application. It may also include test procedures that have the highest probability of detecting the most errors. Regression testing should be done through an automated tool since it is usually lengthy and tedious and thus prone to human error.

Multiplatform and Configuration Compatibility Testing

Another example of the savings attributable to automated testing is the reuse of test scripts to support testing from one platform (hardware configuration) to another. Prior to the use of automated testing, a test engineer would have had to repeat each manual test required for a Windows 2003 environment step by step when testing in a new Windows environment. Now when test engineers create the test scripts for an AUT on platform x or configuration x, they can just play back the same scripts on platform y or configuration y, when using multiplatform-compatible tools. As a result, the test has been performed for the AUT on all platforms or configurations.

Improved Execution of Mundane Tests

An automated test tool will eliminate the monotony of repetitious testing. Mundane repetitive tests are the source of many errors. A test engineer may get tired of testing the same monotonous steps over and over again. We call that *tester fatigue* or *immunity to defects*. Habituation is when you become used to the way the system works and don't see the problems—it has become a habit to see the working solution without considering the negative, possibly nonworking, paths. A test script will run those monotonous steps over and over again and can automatically validate the results.

Improved Focus on Advanced Test Issues

Automated testing allows for simple repeatability of tests. A significant amount of testing is conducted on the basic user interface operations of an application as well as on analyzing outputs and comparing expected to actual results.

Automated testing presents the opportunity to move on more quickly and to perform a more comprehensive overall test within the schedule allowed. Automatic creation of user interface operability tests or automated test result output comparison gets these tests out of the way, allowing test teams to turn their creativity and effort to more advanced test problems and concerns.

Testing What Manual Testing Can't Accomplish

Software systems and products are becoming more complex, and sometimes manual testing is not capable of supporting all desired tests. There are some types of testing analysis that simply can't be performed manually anymore, such as code coverage analysis, memory leak detection, and cyclomatic complexity testing. It would require many man-hours to produce the cyclomatic complexity of the code for any large application. And manual test methods employed to perform memory leakage tests would be nearly impossible.

Security testing of an application is almost impossible using manual testing techniques. Today, there are also tools on the market that allow automated security testing. Consider, for example, tests to determine whether the application's Web links are up and running in a matter of seconds. Performing these tests manually would require hours or days, or would be almost impossible.

Ability to Reproduce Software Defects

Test engineers often encounter the problem of having detected a defect, only to find later that the defect is not reproducible. With an automated test tool the application developer can simply play back the automated test script, without having to worry about whether all exact steps performed to detect the defect were properly documented, or whether all the exact steps can be re-created.

Enhancement of System Expertise

Many test managers have probably experienced a situation where the one resident functional expert on the test team is gone from the project for a week during a critical time of testing. The use of existing automated test scripts allows the test team to verify that the original functionality still behaves in the correct manner even without the expert. At the same time, the tester can learn more about the functionality of the AUT by watching the script execute the exact sequence of steps required to exercise the functionality.

After-Hours "Lights-Out" Testing

Automated testing allows for simple repeatability of tests. Since most automated test tools allow for scripts to be set up to kick off at any specified time, automated testing allows for after-hours testing without any user interaction. The test engineer can set up a test script program in the morning, for example, to be kicked off automatically by the automated test tool at, say, 11 that night, while the test team is at home sound asleep. The next day, when the test team returns to work, the team can review the test script output and conduct an analysis. Another convenient time for kicking off a script is when the test engineer goes to lunch, attends a meeting, or is about to depart for home at the end of the workday. Initiating tests at these times makes maximum use of the test lab and time.

During these times automated testing can also take advantage of distributed testing after hours, as described later on. After the engineers have gone home, multiple machines in the lab can be used for concurrency and distributed testing.

Improved Requirements Definition

If requirements management is automated as part of the STL, various benefits can be gained, such as being able to keep historical records of any changes or updates—i.e., an audit trail—and producing an automated RTM—i.e., linking requirements to all artifacts of the software development effort, including test procedure pass/fail and defects. Automated maintenance of the RTM is another major benefit.

Improved Performance Testing

Performance information or transaction timing data is no longer gathered with stopwatches. Even very recently, in one Fortune 100 company performance testing was conducted while one test engineer sat with a stopwatch, timing the functionality that another test engineer was executing manually. This method of capturing performance measures is labor-intensive and highly error-prone, and it does not allow for automatic repeatability. Today, many performance- or *load-testing* tools are available open-source or vendor-provided, which allow the test engineer to perform tests of the system/application response times automatically, producing timing numbers and graphs, pinpointing the bottlenecks and thresholds of the system. This genre of tool has the added benefit of traversing application functionality as part of gathering transaction timings. In other words, this type of test automation represents an end-to-end test. A test engineer no longer needs to sit there with a stopwatch. Instead, the test engineer initiates a test script to capture the performance statistics automatically. The test engineer is now free to do more creative and intellectually challenging testing work. Performance testing is described in more detail in Appendix B.

Improved Stress and Endurance Testing

It is expensive, difficult, inaccurate, and time-consuming to stress-test an application adequately using purely manual methods. This is because of the inability to reproduce a test when a large number of users and workstations are required for it. It is costly to dedicate sufficient resources to these tests, and it is difficult to orchestrate the necessary number of users and machines. A growing number of test tools provide an alternative to manual stress testing. These tools can simulate a large number of users interacting with the system from a limited number of client workstations. Generally, the process begins by capturing user interactions with the application and the database server within a number of test scripts. Then the testing software runs multiple instances of test scripts to simulate large numbers of users.

A test tool that supports performance testing also supports stress testing. Stress testing is the process of running client machines and/or batch processes in high-volume scenarios, subjecting the system to extreme and maximum loads to find out whether and where the system breaks and identify what breaks first. It is important to identify the weak points of the system. System requirements should define thresholds and describe how a system should respond when subjected to an overload. Stress testing is useful for operating a system at its maximum design load to make sure it works. Stress testing is also useful to make sure the system behaves as specified when subjected to an overload.

Many automated test tools come with a load simulator, which is a facility that lets the test engineer simulate hundreds or thousands of virtual users simultaneously working on the AUT. Nobody has to be present to kick off the tests or monitor them; a time can be set when the script will kick off and the test scripts can run unattended. Most tools produce a test log output listing the results of the stress test. The automated test tool can record any unexpected active window, such as an error dialog box, and test personnel can review the message contained in the unexpected window, such as an error message. Stress endurance, also called soak testing, is described in more detail in Appendix B.

Quality Measurements and Test Optimization

Automated testing produces quality metrics and allows for test optimization; test results can be measured and analyzed. The automated testing process can be measured and repeated. Without automation it is difficult to repeat a test. Without repetition it is difficult to get any kind of measurements. With a manual testing process, the chances are good that the steps taken during the first iteration of a test will not be the exact steps taken during the second iteration. As a result, it is difficult to produce any kind of compatible quality measurements. With automated testing the testing steps are repeatable and measurable.

Test engineer analysis of quality measurements support efforts to optimize tests, only when tests are repeatable. Automation allows for repeatability of tests. A test engineer can optimize a regression test suite by performing the following steps:

1. Run the regression test set.

2. If cases are discovered for which the regression test set ran OK, but errors surface later, include the test procedures that uncovered those bugs in the regression test set.

3. Keep repeating these steps as the regression test set is being optimized, by using quality measurements.

4. Evaluate regression tests for validity.

Improved System Development Lifecycle

AST can support each phase of the system development lifecycle, and various vendor-provided automated test tools are available to do just that. For example, there are tools for the requirements definition phase, which help produce test-ready requirements in order to minimize the test effort and cost of testing. Likewise, there are tools supporting the design phase, such as modeling tools, which can record the requirements within use cases. Use cases represent user scenarios that exercise various combinations of system-level (operational-oriented) requirements. Use cases have a defined starting point, a defined user (a person or an external system), a set of discrete steps, and defined exit criteria.

There are also tools for the programming phase, such as code checkers, static and dynamic analyzers, metrics reporters, code instrumentors, product-based test procedure generators, and many more. If requirements definition, software design, and test procedures have been prepared properly, application development may just be the easiest activity of the bunch. Test execution will surely run more smoothly given these conditions.

Improved Documentation and Traceability

Test programs using AST will also benefit from improved documentation and traceability. The automated test scripts along with the inputs and expected results provide an excellent documentation baseline for each test. In addition, AST can provide exact records of when tests were run, the actual results, the configuration used, and the baseline that was tested. AST is a dramatic improvement over the scenario where the product from the test program is half-completed notebooks of handwritten test results and a few online logs of when tests were conducted.

Some of the benefits AST can provide to a test program include expanded test coverage, enabling tests to be run that cannot practically be run manually; repeatability; improved documentation and traceability; and freeing the test team to focus on advanced issues.

Distributed Workload and Concurrency Testing

It is almost impossible to conduct a distributed workload or concurrency test that provides useful results without some form of AST. This is one of the types of testing that benefits most from AST. Since hardware can be expensive and replicating a production environment is often costly, using virtual machine (VM) ware along with an AST framework allows for the most effective implementation of this type of test. Concurrency testing is described in more detail in Appendix B.

Summary

This chapter provides many reasons for AST in the context of software testing practices. "Why AST?" begs the question "Why not AST?" Inherently, many software testing activities lend themselves to automation, because they are often too tedious to implement using manual methods.

The market demands that software products continue to be delivered faster and cheaper with increasing reliability and usability. Testing is a big part of the time, cost, and quality equation, and without changes in how testing is done, software projects will not be able keep up. In fact, there is much evidence that this is already the case. AST can play a big part in addressing these needs. More specifically, AST provides an opportunity to reduce the time and cost of software testing, improve software quality, and improve software test programs in measurable and significant ways.

Notes

1. NIST, "Economic Impact of Inadequate Infrastructure for Software Testing," May 2002. See www.nist.gov/director/prog-ofc/report02-3.pdf.

2. Y. K. Malaiya, "Automatic Test Software," Computer Science Department, Colorado State University. See www.cs.colostate.edu/~malaiya/tools2.pdf.

3. IDC Market Analysis, "Worldwide Distributed Automated Software Quality Tools 2006–2010 Forecast and Vendor Shares," December 2006.

4. S. D. Hendrick, K. E. Hendrick, and M. Webster, "Worldwide Distributed Automated Software Quality Tools 2005–2009 Forecast and 2004 Vendor Shares," IDC Software Research Group, July 2005.

5. Boris Beizer, *Software Testing Techniques* (Thompson Computer Press, 1990).

6. Our findings are consistent with studies described in Dustin et al., *Automated Software Testing*.

7. Adapted from SQA Suite Process. The SQA tool and related SQA Suite Processes have been acquired by Rational/IBM. See www.ibm.com.

8. For more details on performance testing, see www.perftestplus.com/.

9. Elfriede Dustin, *Effective Software Testing* (Addison-Wesley, 2003).

10. ISO Standard 8402: 1986, 3.1.

11. Dustin et al., *Automated Software Testing*.

12. Glenford J. Myers, *The Art of Software Testing* (John Wiley & Sons, Inc., 2004), 20.

Chapter 3

The Business Case

Getting off to the right start

As discussed throughout this book and highlighted in Chapter 2, there are many benefits to implementing AST. If applied correctly, those benefits can include reducing the time and cost of software testing, improving software quality, and many other factors that will positively impact your software test program. Understanding these potential benefits and being able to explain them are important when introducing the idea of AST to your management and test programs. Additionally, it is important to have buy-in from upper management and the various stakeholders affected, in order to secure the funding required for AST, for example. It is important to be able to articulate for your particular project the specific business needs that will be met, the expected ROI, and any other considerations beyond ROI. This chapter is focused on strategies and techniques for developing the business case for AST for your project, so that you can gain the buy-in and support required.

3.1   Definition of the Business Case

Various definitions of *business case* exist, much has been written about how to write a business case, and various related templates are available. A quick search on Google for the term brings up thousands of references. The purpose of this chapter is not to redefine what a business case is, but to use existing definitions to develop a business case for AST. Our definition is a combination of the existing ones. To summarize, the purposes of a business case are to

- Identify the business need—provide the reasoning for initiating a project or task, in this case AST
- Justify the business need in terms of costs and benefits—calculate the ROI
- Include the expected risks

An example of a summarized business need for AST could be that an AST program will support the timeline decrease of the *software testing lifecycle* (STL), facilitate defect identification, and thus help improve quality. Naturally, improved quality through minimal defects leads to improved customer satisfaction.

In our experience, large-scale AST projects are much more successful when the team has thought through the specific areas and reasons for implementing AST, is able to describe the expected benefits and costs, and has also taken into account what is needed to be successful in terms of time, skills, and processes. Additionally, it is important that upper management and other stakeholders buy in to the business case associated with the AST effort.

On the other hand, too often we see projects that start out with the purchase of an automation tool without any proper automation skill acquisitions or real analysis of what the tool can reasonably be expected to accomplish, other than speeding up testing. No thought has been given to how this "speeding up" is to be accomplished. The automation tool is provided to a team that has no experience or training with the tool, with an expectation that some automated tests will soon be running. The team then identifies the tests that look like the easiest to automate so they can run some with the new automation tool, and through hard work and perseverance they get some tests automated. Then the questions come: "Now that we have these tests automated, how much will this save us in the future? How much better testing did we do?" The answers are disappointing because the tests that were automated were selected because they were easy, not because they have a big impact on the test program, or they result in minimal savings because they are not even run very often because they cover low-risk areas. The consensus becomes "We tried AST once but it didn't really make much of a difference for our project." The team blocks existing or future automation because of a bad experience based upon the wrong ingredients and false starts.

We have found that spending the time up front to identify how AST can support a project's goals and what the expected benefits are to be an important step that is often left out. The process of developing the business case is a discipline we highly encourage when introducing AST to your project.

3.2 Identifying the Business Needs

As you identify the business need and justify it in terms of cost and benefits, you should ask yourself a few questions, to narrow down your specific needs. For example:

- Do we want to reduce the lifecycle cost of a software product?
- Do we want to deliver software products with fewer defects, and have extremely high confidence that certain functionality or capability is working as expected; for example, are some tests nearly impossible to run manually, requiring AST?
- Do we want to remove the mundaneness for members of the testing team, whose skills are best applied to more complex areas of the AUT than rerunning manual tests over and over?

Most often the answer to these questions is "All of the above!" You want to deliver faster, at a lower cost, with fewer defects and higher confidence, and at the same type increase test team efficiency. In this scenario, then, the consideration of how to best apply AST to a project should take into account all areas that contribute to each of these factors, such as

- The need for speeding up the testing effort and increasing the testing efficiency
- The need for decreasing the testing cost
- The need for applying test team member skills most effectively

Need for Speeding Up the Testing Effort and Increasing Efficiency

How much would speeding up the testing really impact the product delivery timeline? If a particular test activity is not really in the critical path, automating it will probably not impact delivery time much. On the other hand, if a test or set of test program activities can be identified that is truly on the critical path, automating it can improve software delivery time. For example, a test setup activity—restoring a test baseline and setting up the required preconditions for a test—is very time-consuming, but automating these activities would reduce the effort by 60%. Using these types of "potential time savings" metrics allows for an assessment of the potential impact on schedule of reducing the execution time and can be used for developing the business case.

Generally you can speed up the testing effort and decrease cost if you increase the testing efficiency. When assessing the testing efficiency, various questions should be asked: What category of software defects is most important to minimize? Which set of test activities, tests, and test techniques have proven to be the most important in discovering these types of software defects? Which are the tests that are critical to be able to consistently repeat and also likely to be the ones you will want to run most often, because they cover a complex, high-risk, or problematic area and have the tendency to uncover the most defects? Also consider the tests that manual testing cannot perform because they are so complex, such as memory leak detection, concurrency, performance, and so forth, where automation is needed. Consider what the impact on software quality would be if they were run more often as overnight regression tests. Are the right skills on board to allow for testing efficiency? Are defects found early enough or too late in the testing cycles? Are schedules adequate? The most efficient testing team can't be successful if there isn't enough time to implement and execute the test program's best-laid plans.

Test program activities should be tailored to your business needs and your specific project. Then, once you complete an inventory of the test activities and assess them against your business needs, you can provide an objective recommendation of the benefits of automation areas, which phases of the STL to automate, which specific tests to automate, why you selected those areas and tests, and an expectation of the impact. In most cases, the test activities that contribute to multiple business needs are the ones that are most beneficial to automate.

Need for Decreasing the Testing Cost

If testing is sped up and efficiencies are increased, one of the resulting benefits can be a decrease in testing cost. For calculating the business benefit, you want to determine how much testing currently costs. If you break down the cost of testing into the various phases such as unit testing, component testing, system testing, and other testing phases and types discussed in Appendix B, which phase costs the most? Which tests add most value, i.e., cover the highest-risk areas, and absolutely have to be run? In other words, are the tests that cost the most to execute adding the most value? Of these tests, which ones are repeated the most often? How much time and effort are required to run these tests? What would be the impact on confidence in the software delivery if these tests could be run more often because they are now automated and the test coverage from these tests could be expanded? Testing cost can be decreased if the test activities are analyzed carefully and AST is applied to the appropriate areas.

Need for Applying Test Team Member Skills Most Effectively

Chapter 10 talks about putting the right people on the project and describes the skills required of members of an effective test program. Manual testing can be tedious, cumbersome, error-prone, and very mundane. It can be exciting when a new software release of the AUT is received for the first time and testers start testing it to find defects. This might still be interesting to do when receiving the second and third releases, but running the same mundane manual tests over and over on the fourth and *n*th AUT release can become boring very fast. During the fifth or later releases, testers often decide that they ran a test previously and certainly it will still work the same, and so they don't repeat the test again on the *n*th release. The decision to not rerun a test can be detrimental to the quality of a product, and that's how defects often slip into production. AST takes away the guesswork as to whether to rerun a test and is ideal for this type of mundane, cumbersome, and tedious testing. Test team member skills are best applied in the more complex areas, while the automated tests play back behind the scenes. AST can help improve tester morale, because not only can they learn new AST skills, but they can also focus on new or more interesting activities than rerunning a manual test for the *n*th time.

3.3 Justifying Automation in Terms of Cost and Benefits

Estimating ROI

As discussed in the previous section on assessing business needs, estimating the potential cost savings is a critical part of evaluating and articulating the impact of implementing AST. This section describes how to calculate the potential cost savings or ROI when implementing AST in comparison to performing the same tests manually. ROI accounts for not only the time savings from automation but also the investment it will take to implement AST to give you a complete picture.

AST ROI can also be intangible; i.e., automation pays off for areas of the test program that are difficult to describe in metrics and numbers, but are simply more beneficial to automate. Some of these areas are described later.

For the tangible areas, we have developed an ROI "calculator" that allows for entering all the factors needed to determine AST time and cost savings. As presented in this section, the ROI calculator is broken down into a set of worksheets focusing on each of the major activities associated with testing: test setup, test development, test execution, and test evaluation.

The following example demonstrates using the ROI calculator for a project in which the tests are yet to be developed in order to estimate a comparison to manual testing if implemented using AST. For the example project it is assumed that 1,000 tests are planned, the tests will be rerun a total of ten times over the testing lifecycle of the project, and the hourly labor rate is $100.

The purpose of this example is to help you develop a plan for roughly estimating the ROI of AST for your project and to provide you with a framework for starting your assessment. Estimates of how much faster automation can execute and evaluate manual tests should be based on your best engineering judgment for your particular project.

The primary points in determining the ROI for automation are the following:

- Developing automated tests requires more effort up front than manually documenting a test.

- Maintenance of these tests needs to be considered, but while that is true for automated and manual tests, more time can be spent on maintenance for either of the testing types.

- The payoff really comes from tests that are rerun on a regular basis, increased test coverage, or tests that manual testing can hardly accomplish.

- The automation of the test results evaluation can realize time savings as big as or even bigger than those of the actual test execution—it doesn't do any good to pump thousands more test cases through a system in an automated fashion if the results have to be analyzed manually.

Overall Test Automation Savings

The *Overall Test Automation Savings* worksheet (Figure 3-1) calculates the overall ROI totals based on the sum of the following worksheets: Test Environment Setup Time Savings, Test Development Time Savings, Test Execution Time Savings, and Test Evaluation/Diagnostics Time Savings. Each of the worksheet totals is derived from various test activity details, such as the example in Table 3-1.

In addition, there is an entry for other automation costs to account for items such as the purchase of automated testing software and training or potential new hiring requirements. As part of the costs we also have to incorporate the recurring costs, such as the annual maintenance cost of a testing tool, and any one-time costs.

Overall Test Automation Savings Worksheet			
Tasks	**Automated Testing Time Savings (hours)**	**Tasks**	**Automated Testing Cost Savings ($)**
Test setup time savings	xxx	Test setup time savings	xxx
Test development time savings	−250	Test development cost savings	−$25,000
Test execution time savings	1,583.33	Test execution cost savings	$158,333
Test evaluation/ diagnostics time savings	2,250	Test evaluation/ diagnostics cost savings	$225,000
		Other automation costs	−$25,000
Hours	**3,583.33**	Dollars	**$333,333**
Days (8-hour days)	447.9		
Months (20-day months)	**22.4**		

Figure 3-1 The Overall Test Automation Savings worksheet—example

Test Environment Setup Time Savings

The *Test Environment Setup Time Savings* worksheet (Figure 3-2) calculates the time estimates for manual versus automated test environment setup.

Table 3-1   Detailed Breakdown of Activities for Test Development Savings—
Example

Traditional Testing Activities	Time (in minutes)	Automated Testing Activities	Time (in minutes)
Requirements analysis		Requirements analysis	
Test analysis		Test analysis	
		Automation analysis (what to automate?)	
		Evaluate reuse of existing scripts	
Test design		Test design	
		Automated test design	
Test scenarios		Test scenarios	
Simulation scenarios			
Preconditions		Preconditions	
Input data		Input data	
Expected outcomes		Expected outcomes	
Data conversion/input		Data conversion/input	
Traditional test procedure		Automated testing procedure	
Detailed procedures			
		Develop test tool	
		Test tool training	
		Test driver	
		Test harness	
		Design dynamic comparison	
Debug tests		Debug tests	
Post-test analysis		Post-test analysis	
Verify testing effectiveness		Verify testing effectiveness	

Testing Phase	Test Environment Setup Time Savings Worksheet			
	Manual Test Setup		Automated Test Setup	
Regression testing	Test setup time (in minutes)		Test setup time (in minutes)	
	Other	N/A	Other	N/A
	Number of iterations	10	Number of iterations	10
	Total test setup time (in hours)	0.00	Total test setup time (in hours)	0.00
	Test setup time savings (in hours)			

Figure 3-2 The Test Environment Setup Time Savings worksheet—example

As part of an AST effort, the test setup activity can be automated, thus allowing for time savings. Test setup can include various preparation activities, such as

- Test environment setup
- Component installation
- Re-baselining a test environment
- Test data population
- Configuration verification

Test Development Time Savings

The *Test Development Time Savings* worksheet (Figure 3-3) calculates the time estimates for manual versus automated test development.

The Test Development Time Savings worksheet is broken down into the following categories:

Number of tests planned: If the actual number of tests planned is not available, an estimate can be developed based on a variety of metrics. One way to estimate the number of tests planned is based on the requirements. For example, when testing boundaries, a ratio of three test cases to one requirement[1] (and

Test Development Time Savings Worksheet			
Manual Test Development		**Automated Test Development**	
Number of tests planned	1,000	Number of tests planned	1,000
Time to develop one test (in minutes)	15	Time to develop 1 test (in minutes)	30
Total test development time (in hours)	250	Total test development time (in hours)	500
Test development time savings	**−250**		

Figure 3-3 The Test Development Time Savings worksheet—example

other ratios can be considered) is necessary, depending on the complexity and granularity of the requirements. Also, depending on the requirement risk, a higher test-case-to-requirements ratio can be used.

Estimated time to develop one test: The estimated time to develop each test is the estimated average time it takes to develop each test in minutes. We suggest using estimates based on actual historical numbers for manual testing. For the purpose of estimating time to develop automated tests, a 50% increase over the time to develop the test manually would be a conservative estimate to begin with. As you develop experience with automating your tests, you should update this factor with the actual ratio you measure.

Total test development time is then approximately

Number of tests planned * Estimated time to develop one test

Total test development time for automated testing is expected to be larger than that for manual testing.

The test development cost savings are derived by multiplying the test development time savings by the labor rate. A negative number means the cost of automation is greater than the cost of completing the task manually.

When calculating each category of savings, such as test development time savings, the details in Table 3-1 need to be evaluated in order to come up with the numbers in the Test Development Time Savings worksheet (see Figure 3-3).

Test Execution Time Savings

The *Test Execution Time Savings* worksheet (Figure 3-4) calculates the time estimates for manual versus automated test execution.

The Test Execution Time Savings worksheet is broken down into the following categories:

Number of tests planned: This is the same as in the Test Development Time Savings worksheet, Figure 3-3.

Estimated time to execute each test (in minutes): This is the estimated time it takes to run each test in minutes. We suggest using estimates based on actual historical numbers for manual testing. For the purpose of estimating time to execute the automated tests, a reduction in test time of 20 relative to the time to execute the test manually would be a conservative estimate to start with. As you develop experience with automating your tests, you should update this factor with the actual ratio you measure.

Estimated number of test iterations: This is the estimated number of times the tests will be rerun. It includes estimates of how many builds are expected or how many cycles it will take to complete the testing phase. *Note*: If the same test has to be run using various configurations, this number of iterations can reflect those additional configuration cycles.

Total test execution time is then

Number of tests planned *
Estimated time to execute one test *
Number of test iterations

Test Execution Time Savings Worksheet			
Manual Test Execution		**Automated Test Execution**	
Number of tests planned	1,000	Number of tests planned	1,000
Estimated time to execute each test (in minutes)	10	Estimated time to execute each test (in minutes; manual/20)	.5
Estimated number of test iterations	10	Estimated number of test iterations	10
Total time estimate to execute manual test (in hours)	1,666.66	Total time estimate to execute automated tests (in hours)	83.33
Total time savings (in hours)	**1,583.33**		

Figure 3-4 Test Execution Time Savings worksheet—example

The test execution cost savings are derived by simply multiplying the test execution time savings total by the labor rate.

Test Evaluation/Diagnostics Time Savings

Much time can be spent on test evaluation and understanding how the results compare to the expected results. It is therefore beneficial to automate the test output evaluation and diagnostics.

The *Test Evaluation/Diagnostics Time Savings* worksheet (Figure 3-5) calculates time savings for manual test evaluation/diagnostics versus automated test evaluation/diagnostics.

The *number of test outputs to diagnose* is an estimate of the total number of results from the planned tests that need to be evaluated.

Estimated time to evaluate each test output is the estimated average time it takes to evaluate each test in minutes. We suggest using estimates based on actual historical numbers for manual testing. For the purpose of estimating time to evaluate the test results, a reduction in test time of 10 relative to the time to evaluate the test manually would be a conservative estimate to start with. As you develop experience with automating your tests, you should update this factor with the actual ratio you measure.

Test Evaluation/Diagnostics Time Savings Worksheet			
Manual Test Evaluation/Diagnostics		**Automated Test Evaluation/Diagnostics**	
Number of test outputs to diagnose	3,000	Number of test outputs to diagnose	3,000
Estimated time to evaluate/compare/diagnose test output (in minutes)	5	Estimated time to evaluate/compare/diagnose test output (in minutes; manual/10)	.5
Estimated number of test iterations	10	Estimated number of test iterations	10
Total test evaluation time (in hours)	2,500	Total test evaluation time (in hours)	250
Test evaluation/diagnostics time savings (in hours)	**2,250**		

Figure 3-5 The Test Evaluation/Diagnostics Time Savings worksheet—example

Estimated test iterations is the same as before.
Total test evaluation time is then

> Number of test outputs to evaluate *
> Estimated time to evaluate each output *
> Number of test iterations

The test evaluation diagnostics cost savings is derived by multiplying the test evaluation/diagnostics time savings by the labor rate.

In summary, the ROI calculation is not a trivial activity and various criteria need to be considered.

Other ROI Considerations
Personnel Requirements

When calculating the AST cost savings, keep in mind that different skills are required to implement an effective automated testing program from those required for manual testing. The cost of possibly training existing personnel or the cost of hiring qualified AST engineers (aka software developers) needs to be considered and included in the ROI considerations. Chapter 10 discusses the skill set required for implementing an effective automated testing program.

During this ROI consideration also compare the number of people required for manual versus automated testing efforts. Although you might have to hire software developers to implement the AST tasks, it may be possible to retrain the testers who run the various labor-intensive manual regression tests over numerous days to do some of the AST activities. Additionally, those test personnel can focus on additional testing tasks or projects, which is an additional ROI, but often too difficult to put into an actual metric that shows the gains.

Lab Equipment Requirements

Also, as part of AST ROI calculations, you should factor in any additional equipment required, considering the most efficient way to support AST, such as evaluating the feasibility of implementing the test lab using VMWare or other OS image software. Test environment is further discussed in Chapter 6.

Test Case Maintenance

So far we've discussed original test case setup, but test case maintenance should also be included as part of the ROI considerations. When evaluating AST ROI, it is also important to compare test case maintenance for manual versus automated testing efforts.

Intangible Automation Savings (ROI)

Some intangible or difficult-to-measure automated ROI can be achieved. For instance, it is difficult to measure the impact on an automated testing effort when test coverage is increased via automated test data generation and increased test scenario coverage that only automation can achieve. It is difficult to measure the impact of increased test coverage if using different data but, for example, using the same data paths, resulting in different scenarios. Here you need to evaluate whether running additional test data scenarios really will benefit the testing effort or if you are just duplicating the same test path without adding any value—ignoring the rules of equivalence partitioning, for example. Note: Wikipedia has a good definition of equivalence partitioning:[2]

> "Equivalence partitioning is a *software testing* technique in which test cases are designed to execute representatives from each equivalence partition, i.e. a partition of input values undergoing similar treatment."

In principle, test cases are designed to cover each partition at least once. This has the goals of

- Reducing the number of test cases to a necessary minimum
- Selecting the right test cases to cover all possible scenarios

How many data combinations to run through the same data paths is a strategic decision, depending on complexity and implementation criteria. An additional difficult intangible benefit is to measure automated test success that manual testing couldn't achieve, i.e., tests that were previously not run because they would have been too cost-prohibitive or almost impossible to execute, such as memory leak detection, stress testing, performance testing, concurrency testing, and so forth. ROI needs to be added for a high-priority defect found using AST that a manual test could not have uncovered because one didn't exist. Additionally, some of our customers tell us that currently they don't run a regression test as often as they would like to, because it's labor-intensive and a lot of setup is involved. However, once the regression test has been automated, they want to run the test more often. How do we measure "peace of mind"?

More ROI Metrics

Once automated testing has been implemented, another useful ROI metric to consider is the cost savings calculations for defects detected via automation versus defects detected via manual testing. This, however, is another challenging metric to calculate, because most often defects are uncovered during the automated test creation—one could argue that the test uncovered a defect as part of manual testing (tests were still being set up), not as part of an automated test run. However, as mentioned previously, if automated testing adds test cases that manual testing didn't cover before, and these uncover additional defects, this could be a valuable ROI metric to track.

Generally it is difficult to compare defects found in manual versus automated testing, because we have to be sure to compare apples to apples. To calculate an accurate comparison, we would have to compare the same software component in the same software testing stage with automated and manual tests running in parallel to determine the difference automation would make. Only this parallel effort could truly show the defects the manual effort uncovers versus the ones the automated tests uncover.

Additionally, it is a good practice to track the savings produced by detecting defects during automated testing, especially if defects are uncovered early in the testing lifecycle, as opposed to the savings over discovering the same defect later or even in production. Different weights can be assigned when developing this type of metric; i.e., a high-severity defect uncovered by automation gets a greater weight than a low-severity defect.

3.4 Risks

Automated test program *assumptions, prerequisites,* and *risks* need to be understood and presented as part of the business case. These include any events, actions, or circumstances that will prevent the automated test program from being implemented or executed successfully, such as lack of skills, late budget approvals, the delayed arrival of test equipment, fluid and constantly changing requirements and software, or late availability of the software application.

The risk description needs to incorporate ways that help minimize it and prevent failure. Failure is defined in terms of cost overruns, schedule slippage, undetected critical software errors, rework required, and so on, despite the automated testing effort.

Most risk is caused by a few factors.

- **Short time-to-market**

  Risks include a short time-to-market schedule for the software product. As mentioned previously, testing budgets and schedules are often determined at the onset of a project, during proposal efforts, without any "real" or "actual" estimates or inputs from testing personnel, based on past experiences or other effective estimation techniques. However, a test manager can quickly see when the short time-to-market schedule does not allow for adequate testing. As part of the business case, this high-risk issue needs to be pointed out. Either schedules should be adjusted, or risk mitigation strategies should be developed.

- **Lack of adequate skills**

  Other risks may exist because new skills are required to implement the automated testing effort and currently adequate skills are not available in-house. The limited availability of engineering resources for the project would be considered another potential risk to AST success. For more on the skills required for implementing AST programs, see Chapter 10.

- **New technology**

  If new technology is implemented, the risk can be high that no automated testing tool exists and the tool needs to be developed in-house.

- **Difficult-to-automate requirements or features**

  Some system features exist that are not documented, are complex, and most often are the biggest problem area. Learning curves of the functionality, subject matter expert (SME) support, and documentation requirements need to be considered, before claiming a requirement or feature can successfully be tested in an automated fashion. Functional or nonfunctional requirements that are difficult to be tested because of complexity and lack of documentation will also pose a high risk to an AST effort. Some nonfunctional requiements are discussed in Appendix A.

As risks are identified, they need to be assessed for impact and then mitigated with a strategy for overcoming them should they be realized as part of the business case. Carefully examine potential risks in order to try to prevent them from being realized; hiring people with the right skills for the job, reassessing the deadline, and listing all the requirements needed to support a successful AST effort are ways to mitigate those listed risks. However, if risks are realized even though all precautions have been taken, a mitigation strategy needs to be in place.

3.5   Other Considerations

In earlier sections we described the benefits that AST can offer, ideas for how to evaluate business needs and assess AST against those needs, and estimating ROI. This section lists other ways to approach the topic and other questions to consider in relation to AST.

AST may be the solution if you don't have an answer to some of the following questions:

- How will your test team keep up with testing the ever increasing complexity of new technologies implemented?

- How will your test team's productivity keep up with the rate of productivity improvement expected from the development team?

- What is your testing strategy to support the increasing level of software and component reuse that is planned?

- What artifacts can you provide to demonstrate the software was tested to meet specified standards? How quickly can those be produced and reproduced for each test run?

- How do you capture and reuse the knowledge of the subject matter experts your test program currently depends on?

- What is your plan for being able to document and re-create problems found during testing for a development team that is geographically distributed?

- When the software product can be installed remotely, what is your approach to providing verification or diagnostic tests that can be executed remotely?

- How will you run tests that manual testing can hardly accomplish, such as memory leak detection, stress testing, performance testing, and concurrency testing?

- Will you need to justify having testers work night shifts, weekends, and overtime when an automated tool can just be kicked off at day's end and the results viewed the next morning?

Other such questions can be added, and in considering these questions and the future of your test program, AST should be evaluated as part of the potential solution.

So far we've discussed the importance of a business case and addressed how to identify the business need, how to justify AST in terms of cost and benefits, and how to identify risks. The strategic approach to implementing AST and measuring the key success indicators also needs to be defined as part of the business case. Strategy is discussed in Chapter 6, and the keys to success and metrics are discussed throughout this book.

Summary

In order to get buy-in from upper management and all stakeholders involved, the business case for AST needs to be made. Our experience has shown that if buy-in exists (i.e., all stakeholders have bought into the automated testing effort), all parties feel responsible for the success of that effort. If all contribute, chances for success are much higher. It is therefore an important goal to develop the business case and get approval. The market demands that software products continue to be delivered faster and cheaper with increasing reliability. Testing is a big part of the time, cost, and quality equation, and without changes in how testing is done, software projects will not be able to keep up. In fact, there is much evidence that this is already the case. AST can play a big part in addressing these needs. More specifically, AST provides an opportunity to reduce the time and cost of software testing, improve software quality, identify defects earlier in the development lifecycle, and improve your software test program in measurable and significant ways.

In order to implement AST successfully, an approved business case can set the right tone. You are now off to a good start.

Notes

1. Considering boundaries—testing "minus one," "plus one," and "on the boundary."
2. http://en.wikipedia.org/wiki/Equivalence_partitioning. For additional reference, see Chapter 6.

Why Automated Software Testing Fails and Pitfalls to Avoid

Approaching AST in a realistic manner

Even though most companies believe that AST is useful, few companies can claim actual success. Various user group postings and a comprehensive survey conducted by IDT over the course of one year in 2007 support this finding.

In this chapter we will analyze the issue of why so many AST efforts fail and how to avoid some of the pitfalls, and we will clarify some of the misperceptions surrounding AST. Chapter 9 further explains why our proposed lightweight process based on the automated test lifecycle methodology (ATLM) already described in *Automated Software Testing*[1] will help solve many of the current AST woes.

A year-long IDT automated software testing survey was conducted; it was posted on commercial QA user group sites, sent to tens of thousands of test engineers, posted on government tech sites such as Government Computer News and Defense Systems, and announced during a webinar[2] we conducted called "Automated Testing Selected Best Practices." We received over 700 responses, worldwide. Here is a breakdown of the respondents' demographics:

- Over 73% of the respondents were from the United States, and the rest were from India, Pakistan, China, Europe, and other locations throughout the world.

- Nearly 70% identified their organization type as commercial, 10% claimed government direct employment, and the rest "other," such as governmental contractors, educational, or independent.

- For 40% the size of the organization was less than or equal to 300 employees; 60% claimed an organization size of more than 300 employees.

The outcome of the survey showed that the value of AST is generally understood, but often automation is not used or it fails. In the survey we asked respondents why in their experience automation is not used, and the largest percentage responded that AST does not get implemented because of lack of resources—time, budget, skills.

Closely related to these questions, we also received feedback as to why automation fails. The highest percentage responded that many AST efforts fail and the tools end up as shelfware for reasons similar to those for why it's not used in the first place The reasons given for failure of AST were

- Lack of time: 37%
- Lack of budget: 17%
- Tool incompatibility: 11%
- Lack of expertise: 20%
- Other (mix of the above, etc.): 15%

In summary, although 72% stated that automation is useful and management agrees, they either had not implemented it at all or had had only limited success. Here are various quotes providing reasons for limited AST success or failure:

- "We have begun implementing, but aren't allowed significant time to do so."

- "Have implemented some efforts but lack of time, budget, and resources prohibit us to fully perform this function."

- "The company has previously implemented automated testing successfully, but this was years ago and we currently don't have the time or budget to reimplement."

- "I'm the only one automating (so have some automation), but spend too much time on new feature release, need more people."

- "Accuracy of automated processes [is] the largest issue we have encountered."

Our survey results match what our experience has shown over the years: Many agree that AST is the best way to approach testing in general, but there is often a lack of budget, time, or experience available to execute it successfully.

Additional reasons why AST fails include the following:

- R&D does not generally focus on testing (manual or automated).

- Myths and misperceptions about AST persist.

- There is a lack of AST processes.

- There is a lack of software development considerations for AST.

- There is a lack of AST standards.

Each of these issues is further discussed in the next sections.

4.1 R&D Does Not Generally Focus on Automated or Manual Testing Efforts

R&D and its resulting technologies have been fueling high-tech product innovation over the last 20 to 30 years. Yet our ability to test these technologies has not kept pace with our ability to create them. In our experience, most reports on technology advances cover only R&D, and not related test technologies. For example, *Business Week* reported on "The World's Most Innovative Companies" in an April 17, 2008, article.[3] As so often happens, the article focuses on R&D only, but no attention is paid to research and development and test (R&D&T), i.e., how should this great technology be tested? Innovation does not seem to consider related required testing technologies; testing, however, has become more important than ever.

We have spent much time researching the latest testing technologies, and based on our research we have come up with the "Automatically Automate Your Automation" (AAA) concept,[4] described in Chapter 1 but also here—see "GUI Testing Recommendations" for additional examples of this concept—and throughout this book. We are currently further refining the concept of AAA, but we also have determined some interesting trends that need to be dealt with, which include the following:

- **Software development and testing are driving the business.**

  Business needs almost exclusively used to drive software testing technologies, but the trend is shifting in both directions: Software testing is now also driving the business. Business executives can have the best business ideas, but if the software and testing efforts lag behind and/or the system or product is delivered late and/or with low quality, the competition is only a few clicks away. First to market with high quality is key.

- **Attention should be paid to "perceived" versus "actual" quality.**

  The best-quality processes and standards cannot solve the perception issue. For example, ten defects that occur very frequently and impact critical functionality would be *perceived* by any customer as poor quality, even if the defect density was very low. On the other hand, 100 defects that occur very infrequently and have almost no impact on operations would usually be *perceived* by an end user as good quality, even if the defect density was high. Not much research goes into "usage-based testing," which exploits the concept of perceived quality, yielding higher perceived quality, and thus happier customers. One such example of great perceived quality and usability is Amazon.com versus all other online booksellers—in our experience, Amazon.com is just more user-friendly; they are, as *Business Week* refers to them, an "e-tail maverick."[5]

  The goal needs to be improving perceived quality. This can be accomplished by focusing testing on the usability of the most often used functionality (which absolutely has to work without defects), and on reliability (the probability that no failure will occur in the next n time intervals. (See Section 2.3 in Chapter 2 for more detail on MTTF.)

- **Testing invariably gets some of the blame, if not all.**

  Deadlines are looming and the testing cycle in multiple environments can be numerous and seemingly endless. Testing often gets blamed for missed deadlines, projects that are over budget, uncovered production defects, and lack of innovation. But often the real culprits are inefficient systems engineering processes, such as the black-box approach where millions of software lines of code (SLOC) are developed, including vast amounts of functionality, only to be handed over to a test team so they can test and peel back the layers of code, painstakingly finding one defect after another, sometimes not uncovering a major showstopper until another defect is fixed. In summary, some of the real culprits of testing being late are

– Poor development practices, resulting in buggy code, requiring long and repetitive fixing cycles; these include

  ▪ Lack of unit testing. Statistics show (and our experience backs them up) that the more effective the unit testing efforts are, the smoother and shorter the system testing efforts will be.

  ▪ Inefficient build practices. Build and release processes should be automated. If they are not, building software can be time-consuming and error-prone.

  ▪ Inefficient integration or system tests by the development teams (see "Developers don't system-test" below).

– Unrealistic deadlines. Often deadlines are set in stone without much consideration for how long it will actually take to develop or test particular software. Poor estimating practices do not typically include or give credence to test team estimates, or development estimates are not acceptable to those who have overpromised the product. Setting unrealistic deadlines is a sure way of setting up deliverables for failure.

– Also see Section 3.4, Risks, for other culprits.

• **Developers don't system-test.**

Although many developers conduct unit testing, and proponents of test-driven software development generally do a good job of testing their software modules, there is still a lack of developer integration or system testing. Some might suggest shifting away from the testing focus and instead focusing on improving development processes. This is not a bad idea, but even with the best processes and the most brilliant developers in-house, software development is an art—integration and system testing will always be required. Human factors influence why developers don't system-test: They generally don't have time; or they don't specialize in testing and testing techniques; and often they are busy churning out new code and functionality. Developers are strapped cranking out new features while trying to meet unreasonable deadlines. First to market, again, is the key.

In summary, technology research groups often focus only on R&D, but the focus should rather be on R&D&T, i.e., how to test these latest and greatest inventions.

4.2   AST Myths and Realities

When we originally wrote the book *Automated Software Testing,* we tried to clarify many of the misperceptions and myths about AST. The book was published in 1999. Now, ten years later, unfortunately, our experience has shown and our survey backs up the fact that many of these same myths still exist.[6]

Let's say that while you're at a new project kickoff meeting, the project manager introduces you as the test lead. The project manager mentions that the project will use an automated test tool and adds that because of this the test effort is not expected to be significant. The project manager concludes by requesting that you submit within the next week a recommendation of the specific test tool required, together with a cost estimate for the procurement of the tool. You are caught by surprise by the project manager's remarks and wonder about the manager's expectations with regard to automated testing. Any false automated testing expectations need to be cleared up immediately. Along with the idea of automated testing come high expectations. A lot is demanded from technology and automation. Some people have the notion that an automated test tool should be able to accomplish everything from test planning to test execution, without much manual intervention. Although it would be great if such a tool existed, there is no such capability on the market today. Others believe that it takes only one test tool to support all test requirements, regardless of environmental parameters such as the operating system or programming language used.

Some may incorrectly assume that an automated test tool will immediately reduce the test effort and the test schedule. It has been proven successfully that automated testing is valuable and can produce a return on investment, but there isn't always an immediate payback on investment. This section addresses some of the misconceptions that persist in the software industry and provides guidelines for how to manage some of the automated testing misconceptions.

Automatic Test Plan Generation

Currently, there is no commercially available tool that can create a comprehensive test plan while also supporting test design and execution.

Throughout a software test career, the test engineer can expect to witness test tool demonstrations and review an abundant amount of test tool literature. Often the test engineer will be asked to stand before a senior manager or a small number of managers to give a test tool functionality overview. As always, the presenter must bear in mind the audience. In this case, the audience may consist of individuals with just enough technical knowledge to make them enthusiastic about automated testing, but they may be unaware of the complexity involved with an automated test effort. Specifically, the managers may have obtained information about automated test tools third-hand and may have misinterpreted the actual capability of automated test tools.

What the audience at the management presentation may be waiting to hear is that the tool that you are proposing automatically develops the test plan, designs and creates the test procedures, executes all the test procedures, and analyzes the results for you. You meanwhile start out the presentation by informing the group that automated test tools should be viewed as enhancements to manual testing, and that automated test tools will not automatically develop the test plan, design and create the test procedures, and execute the test procedures. AST does not replace the analytical thought required to develop a test strategy or the test techniques needed to develop the most effective tests.

Not far into the presentation, and after several management questions, it becomes apparent just how much of a divide exists between the reality of the test tool's capabilities and the perceptions of the individuals in the audience. The term *automated test tool* seems to bring with it a great deal of wishful thinking that is not closely aligned with reality. An automated test tool will not replace the human factor necessary for testing a product. The proficiencies of test engineers and other quality assurance experts are still needed to keep the testing machinery running. AST can be viewed as an additional part of the machinery that supports the release of a good product, and only after careful consideration and effective implementation will it yield success.

Test Tool Fits All

Currently not one single test tool exists that can be used to support all operating system environments.

Generally, a single test tool will not fulfill all the testing requirements of an organization. Consider the experience of one test engineer encountering such a situation. The test engineer was asked by a manager to find a test tool that could be used to automate all real-time embedded system tests. The department was using VxWorks and Integrity, plus Linux and Windows XP, programming languages such as Java and C++, and various servers and Web technologies.

Expectations have to be managed, and it has to be made clear that currently there is no one single tool on the market that is compatible with all operating systems and programming languages. Often more than one tool and AST technique are required to test the various AUT technologies and features (GUI, database, messages, etc.).

Immediate Test Effort Reduction

Introduction of automated test tools will not immediately reduce the test effort.
A primary impetus for introducing an automated test tool into a project is to reduce the test effort. Experience has shown that a learning curve is associated with the attempts to apply automated testing to a new project and the effective use of automated testing. Test effort savings do not necessarily come immediately. Still, test or project managers have read the test tool literature and are anxious to realize the potential of the automated tools.

Surprising as it may seem, our experience has shown that the test effort actually increases initially when an automated test effort is first introduced into an organization. When introducing automated testing efforts, whether they include a vendor-provided test tool or an open-source, freeware, or in-house-developed solution, a whole new level of complexity and a new way of doing testing are being added to the test program. And although there may be a learning curve for the test engineers to become smart and efficient in the use of the tool, there are still manual tests to be performed on the project. Additionally, new skills might be required, if, for example, the goal is to develop an automated test framework from scratch or to expand on an existing open-source offering. The reasons why an entire test effort generally cannot be automated are outlined later in this chapter.

Initial introduction of automated testing also requires careful analysis of the AUT in order to determine which sections of the application can be automated (see "Universal Application of AST" for further discussion). Test automation also requires careful attention to automated test procedure design and development. The automated test effort can be viewed as a mini development lifecycle, complete with the planning and coordination issues that come along with a development effort. Introducing an automated test tool requires that the test team perform the additional activities as part of the process outlined in Chapter 9.

Immediate Reduction in Schedule

An automated test tool will not immediately minimize the testing schedule.
Another automated test misconception is the expectation that the introduction of automated tests in a new project will immediately minimize the test schedule. Since the testing effort actually increases when an automated testing effort is initially introduced, as previously described, the testing schedule will not experience the anticipated decrease at first. This is because in order to effectively implement AST, a modified testing process has to be considered, developed, and implemented. The entire test team and possibly the development team need to be familiar with this modified effort, including the automated testing process, and need to follow it. Once an automated testing process has been established and effectively implemented, the project can expect to experience gains in productivity and turnaround time that have a positive effect on schedule and cost.

Tool Ease of Use

An automated tool requires new skills; therefore, additional training is required. Plan for training and a learning curve!
Many tool vendors try to sell their tools by exaggerating the *ease of use* of the tool and deny any learning curve associated with it. The vendors are quick to point out that the tool can simply capture (record) a test engineer's keystrokes and (like magic) create a script in the background, which then can simply be reused for playback. Efficient automation is not that simple. The test scripts that the tool automatically generates during recording need to be *programmatically* modified manually, requiring tool scripting and programming knowledge, in order to make the scripts robust and reusable (see "Equating Capture/Playback to AST" for additional detail). Scripts also need to be modified in order for them to become maintainable. A test engineer needs to be trained on the tool and the tool's built-in scripting language to be able to modify the scripts, or a developer needs to be hired in order to use the tool effectively. New training or hiring requirements and/or a learning curve can be expected with the use of any new tool. See Chapter 10 on skills required for AST.

Universal Application of AST

Not all tests can be automated.
As discussed previously, automated testing is an enhancement to manual testing. Therefore, and along with other reasons already articulated in this book, it is

unreasonable to expect that 100% of the tests on a project can be automated. For example, when an automated GUI test tool is first introduced, it is beneficial to conduct some compatibility tests on the AUT in order to see whether the tool will be able to recognize all objects and third-party controls.

The performance of compatibility tests is especially important for GUI test tools, because such tools have difficulty recognizing some custom controls features within the application. These include the little calendars or spin controls that are incorporated into many applications, especially Web or Windows applications. These controls or widgets are often written by third parties, and most test tool manufacturers can't keep up with the hundreds of clever controls churned out by various companies. The grid objects and embedded objects within the various controls are very popular and much used by developers; however, they can be challenging for test automators, as the tool they are using might not be compatible with control *x*.

It may be that the test tool is compatible with all releases of C++ and Java, for example, but if an incompatible third-party custom control is introduced into the application, the tool may not recognize the object on the screen. It may be that most of the application uses a third-party grid that the test tool does not recognize. The test engineer will have to decide whether to automate this part of the application, for example, by defining a custom object within the automation tool; find another work-around solution; or testing the control manually.

Other tests are impossible to automate completely, such as verifying a print-out. The test engineer can automatically send a document to the printer but then has to verify the results by physically walking over to the printer to make sure the document really printed. The printer could be off-line or out of paper. Certainly an error message could be displayed by the system—"Printer off-line" or "Printer out of paper"—but if the test needs to verify that the messages are accurate, some physical intervention is required. This is another example of why not every test can be automated.

Often associated with the idea that an automated test tool will immediately reduce the testing effort is the fallacy that a test tool will be able to automate 100% of the test requirements of any given test effort. Given an endless number of permutations and combinations of system and user actions possible with *n*-tier (client/middle layer/server) architecture and GUI-based applications, a test engineer or team does not have enough time to test every possibility, manually or automated (see "100% Test Coverage," next).

Needless to say, the test team will not have enough time or resources to support 100% test automation of an entire application. It is not possible to test all inputs or all combinations and permutations of all inputs. It is impossible to test exhaustively all paths of even a moderate system. As a result, it is not feasible to approach the test effort for the entire AUT with the goal of testing 100% of the software application. (See 100% Test Coverage, below.)

Another limiting factor is cost. Some tests can be more expensive to automate than to execute manually. A test that is executed only once is often not worth automating. For example, an end-of-year report of a health claim system might be run only once, because of all the setup activity involved to generate the report. Since this report is executed rarely, automating it may not pay off. When deciding which test procedures to automate, a test engineer needs to evaluate the value or payoff of investing time in developing an automated script.

The test team should perform a careful analysis of the application when selecting the test requirements that warrant automation and those that should be executed manually. When performing this analysis, the test engineer will also need to weed out redundant tests. The goal for test procedure coverage, using automated testing, is for each test to exercise multiple items, while avoiding duplication of tests. For each test, an evaluation should be performed to ascertain the value of automating it. This is covered in Chapter 6.

100% Test Coverage

Even with automation, not everything can be tested.

One of the major reasons why testing has the potential to be an infinite task is that in order to know that there are no problems with a function, it must be tested with all possible data, valid and invalid. Automated testing may increase the breadth and depth of test coverage, yet with automated testing there still isn't enough time or resources to perform a 100% exhaustive test.

It is impossible to perform a 100% test of all the possible simple inputs to a system. The sheer volume of permutations and combinations is simply too staggering. Take, for example, the test of a function that handles the verification of a user password. Each user on a computer system has a password, which is generally six to eight characters long, where each character is an uppercase letter or a digit. Each password must contain at least one digit. How many possible character combinations do you think there are in this example? According to Kenneth H. Rosen in *Discrete Mathematics and Its Applications*[7], there are 2,684,483,063,360 possible variations of passwords. Even if it were possible to create a test procedure each minute, or 60 test procedures per hour, equaling 480 test procedures per day, it would still take 155 years to prepare and execute a complete test. Therefore, not all possible inputs can be exercised during a test. With this rapid expansion it would be nearly impossible to exercise all inputs, and in fact it has been proven to be impossible in general.

It is also impossible to exhaustively test every combination and path of a system. Let's take, for example, a test of the telephone system in North America. The format of telephone numbers in North America is specified by a numbering plan. A telephone number consists of ten digits, which are split into a three-digit area code, a three-digit office code, and a four-digit station code. Because of signaling considerations, there are certain restrictions on some of these digits. A quick calculation shows that in this example 6,400,000,000 different numbers are available—and this is only the valid numbers; we haven't even touched on the invalid numbers that could be applied. This is another example that shows how it is impractical, based upon development costs versus ROI, to test all combinations of input data for a system and that various testing techniques need to be applied to narrow down the test data set.[8]

The preceding paragraphs outlined why testing is potentially an infinite task. In view of this, code reviews of critical modules are often done. It is also necessary to rely on the testing process to discover defects early. Such test activities, which include requirement, design, and code walk-throughs, support the process of defect prevention. Both defect prevention and detection technologies are discussed further throughout this book. Given the potential magnitude of any test, the test team needs to rely on test procedure design techniques, such as equivalence testing, where only representative data samples are used. See Chapter 6 and throughout this book for references to this technique.

Equating Capture/Playback to AST

Hitting a Record button doesn't produce an effective automated script.
Many companies and automated testers still equate AST with simply using capture/playback tools. Capture/playback in itself is inefficient AST at best, creating nonreusable scripts at worst.

Capture/playback tools record the test engineer's keystrokes in some type of scripting language and allow for script playback for baseline verification. Automated test tools mimic the actions of the test engineer. During testing, the engineer uses the keyboard and mouse to perform some type of test or action. The testing tool captures all keystrokes and subsequent results, which are recorded and baselined in an automated test script. During test playback, scripts compare the latest outputs with the baseline. Testing tools often provide built-in, reusable test functions, which can be very useful, and most test tools provide for nonintrusive testing; i.e., they interact with the AUT as if the test tool were not involved and won't modify/profile code used in the AUT.

Yet capture/playback-generated scripts provide many challenges. For example, the capture/playback records hard-coded values; i.e., if you record a data input called "First Name," that "First Name" will be hard-coded, rendering test scripts usable only for that "First Name." If you wanted to read in more than one "First Name," you would have to add the capability of reading data from a file or database, and include conditional statements and looping constructs. Variables and various functions have to be added and scripts need to be modified—i.e., software development best practices have to be applied—to make them effective, modular, and repeatable.

Additionally, capture/playback doesn't implement software development best practices right out of the box; scripts need to be modified to be maintainable and modular. Also, vendor-provided capture/playback tools don't necessarily provide all testing features required; code enhancements are often necessary to meet testing needs. Finally, vendor-provided tools are not necessarily compatible with the systems engineering environment, and software testing scripts need to be developed in-house.

AST Is a Manual Tester Activity

Capture/playback tool use and script recording do not an automated tester make.

Although AST does not replace the manual testing and analytical skills required for effective and efficient test case development, the AST skills required are different from manual software testing skills. Often, however, companies buy into the vendor and marketing hype that AST is simply hitting a Record button to automate a script. However, capture/playback tool use does not an automated tester make.

It is important to distinguish the skills required for manual software testing from those required for automated software testing: Mainly, an automated software tester needs software development skills. What is required from a good automated software tester is covered in detail in Chapter 10. The important point to note here is that different skills are required, and a manual tester without any training or background in software development will have a difficult time implementing successful automated testing programs.

Losing Sight of the Testing Goal: Finding Defects

The AST goal is to help improve quality, not to duplicate development efforts.

Often during AST activities the focus is on creating the best automation framework and the best automation software, and we lose sight of the testing goal, i.e., to find defects. As mentioned, it's important that testing techniques, such as boundary value testing, risk-based testing, and equivalence partitioning, are being used to derive the best suitable test cases.

You may have employed the latest and greatest automated software development techniques and used the best developers to implement your automation framework. It performs fast with tens of thousand of test case results, efficient automated analysis, and great reporting features. It is getting rave reviews. But no matter how sophisticated your automated testing framework is, if defects slip into production and the automated testing scripts didn't catch the defects it was supposed to, your automated testing effort will be considered a failure.

It's therefore important to conduct a metrics assessment similar to the one discussed in the ROI section of Chapter 3 that will allow you to determine whether the automated testing effort is finding the defects it should.

Focusing on System Test Automation and Not Automating Unit Tests

Automating unit tests can contribute to the success of all later test activities.

Our experience has shown that if unit testing is automated, along with automated integration test and build processes, subsequent system testing activities uncover fewer defects, and the system testing lifecycle can be reduced. Another benefit of automated unit testing is that the sooner in the STL a defect is uncovered, the cheaper it is to fix; i.e., much less effort is involved in fixing a unit test defect affecting one unit or even fixing an integration test defect affecting some components than in finding and fixing a defect during system testing, when it could affect various system components, making analysis cumbersome, or even affect other parts of the STL effort, in the worst case pointing back to an incorrectly implemented requirement.

Additionally, software evolution and reuse are very important reasons for automating tests. For example, ideally, automated unit, component, and integration tests can be reused during system testing. Automating a test is costly and may not be justified if the test is going to be run only once or a few times. But if tests are run dozens of times, or hundreds of times, in nightly builds, and rerun during different testing phases and various configuration installs, the small cost of automation is amortized over all those executions.[9]

4.3 Lack of Software Development Considerations for AST

AST efforts can fail when software development doesn't take into account the automated testing technologies or framework in place. Software developers can contribute to the success of automated testing efforts if they consider the impacts on them when making code or technology changes. Additionally, if developers consider some of the selected best practices described here, AST efforts can reap the benefits. The selected best practices include the following:

- Build testability into the application.
- Facilitate automation tool recognition of objects: Uniquely name all objects, considering various platforms—client/server, Web, etc.—and GUI/interface testing considerations, such as in the case of Windows development, for example, within the Windows architecture. Additionally, don't change the object names without AST considerations; see also "GUI Object Naming Standards" later in this chapter.
- Follow standard development practices; for example, maintain a consistent tab sequence.
- Follow best practices, such as the library concept of code reuse, i.e., reusing existing already tested components, as applicable (discussed in Chapter 1).
- Adhere to documentation standards to include standard ways of documenting test cases and using the OMG[10] IDL, for example, which would allow for automated test case code generation (further defined in "Use of OMG's IDL" later in this chapter).
- Adhere to the various standards discussed later on in this chapter, such as Open Architecture standards, coding standards, and so forth.

Each of these recommendations is discussed in more detail in the following sections.

Build Testability into the Application

Software developers can support the automated testing effort by building testability into their applications, which can be supported in various ways. One of the most common ways to increase the testability of an application is to provide a logging, or tracing, mechanism that provides information about what components are doing, including the data they are operating on, and any information about application state or errors that are encountered while the application is running. Test engineers can use this information to determine where errors are occurring in the system, or to track the processing flow during the execution of a test procedure.

As the application is executing, all components will write log entries detailing what methods, also known as functions, they are currently executing and the major objects they are dealing with. The entries are written typically to a disk file or database, properly formatted for analysis or debugging, which will occur at some point in the future, after the execution of one or more test procedures. In a complex client-server or Web system, log files may be written on several machines, so it is important that the log include enough information to determine the path of execution between machines.

It is important to place enough information into the log that it will be useful for analysis and debugging, but not so much information that the overwhelming volume will make it difficult to isolate important entries. A log entry is simply a formatted message that contains key information that can be used during analysis. A well-formed log entry includes the following pieces of information:

- **Class name and method name:** This can also simply be a function name if the function is not a member of any class. This is important for determining a path of execution through several components.

- **Host name and process ID:** This will allow log entries to be compared and tracked if they happen on different machines or in different processes on the same machine.

- **Timestamp of the entry (to the millisecond at least):** An accurate timestamp on all entries will allow the events to be lined up if they occur in parallel or on different machines.

- **Messages:** One of the most important pieces of the entry is the message. It is a description, written by the developer, of what is currently happening in the application. A message can also be an error encountered during execution, or a result code from an operation. Gray-box testing will greatly benefit from the logging of persistent entity IDs or keys of major domain objects. This will allow objects to be tracked through the system during execution of a test procedure. See also gray box testing, described in Chapter 1.

Having these items written to the log file by every method, or function, of every component in the system can realize the following benefits:

- The execution of a test procedure can be traced through the system and lined up with the data in the database that it is operating on.

- In the case of a serious failure, the log records will indicate the responsible component.

- In the case of a computational error, the log file will contain all of the components that participated in the execution of the test procedure and the IDs or keys of all entities used.

- Along with the entity data from the database, this should be enough information for the test team to pass on to the development personnel who can isolate the error in the source code.

Following is an example of a log file from an application that is retrieving a customer object from a database:

```
Function:   main (main.cpp, line 100)
Machine:    testsrvr (PID=2201)
Timestamp:  3/10/2009 20:26:54.721
Message:    connecting to database [dbserver1,
            customer_db]

Function:   main (main.cpp, line 125)
Machine:    testsrvr (PID=2201)
Timestamp:  3/10/2009 20:26:56.153
Message:    successfully connected to database [dbserver1,
            customer_db]

Function:   retrieveCustomer (customer.cpp line 20)
Machine:    testsrvr (PID=2201)
Timestamp:  3/10/2009 20:26:56.568
Message:    attempting to retrieve customer record for
            customer ID [A1000723]
```

```
Function:     retrieveCustomer (customer.cpp line 25)
Machine:      testsrvr (PID=2201)
Timestamp:    3/10/2009 20:26:57.12
Message:      ERROR: failed to retrieve customer record,
              message [customer record for ID A1000723 not
              found]
```

This log file excerpt demonstrates a few of the major points of application logging that can be used for effective testing.

- In each entry, the function name is indicated, along with the filename and line number in the code where the entry was written. The host and process ID are also recorded, as well as the time that the entry was written.

- Each message contains some useful information about the activity being performed; for example, the database server is dbserver1, the database is customer_db, and the customer ID is A1000723.

- From this log it is evident that the application was not able to successfully retrieve the specified customer record.

In this situation, a tester could examine the database on dbserver1, using SQL tools, and query the customer_db database for the customer record with ID A1000723 to verify its presence. This information adds a substantial amount of defect diagnosis capability to the testing effort, since the tester can now pass this information along to the development staff as part of the defect information. The tester is now not only reporting a "symptom," but along with the symptom can also document the internal application behavior that pinpoints the cause of the problem.

Adhere to Open Architecture Standards

Open Architecture (OA) principles, described in the Open Architecture Computing Environment Design Guidance and in the Open Architecture Computing Environment Technologies and Standards documents,[11] were developed by the U.S. Navy and emphasize the use of widely adopted industry standards and component-based technologies. The open standards approach has been demonstrated to reduce cost and improve rapid insertion of new software capability into an existing system.

By implementing and following the OA standards, developers can expect various benefits, including assured technical performance, reduced lifecycle cost, affordable technology refresh, and reduced upgrade cycle time. Additional expected benefits include

- Scalable, load-invariant performance
- Enhanced information access and interoperability
- Enhanced system flexibility for accomplishment of mission and operational objectives
- Enhanced survivability and availability
- Reduced lifecycle cost and affordable technology refresh
- Reduced cycle time for changes and upgrades

The Defense Advanced Research Projects Agency (DARPA), academia, and industry's R&D efforts have focused on certain architectural concepts intended to foster lifecycle cost benefits, as well as technical performance benefits. Developing software using OA will result in additional benefits, such as

- Open architectures
- Distributed processing
- Portability
- Scalability
- Modularity
- Fault tolerance
- Shared resource management
- Self-instrumentation

For additional details and best development practices specific to automated testing tool development, see Table 8-5, "Test Development Guidelines," in the book *Automated Software Testing*.[12]

Adhere to Standard Documentation Format

Software testing efforts often include sifting through documentation to verify that all information is provided. Documentation assessment efforts can also be automated, but we would like to offer the following recommendation for software developers or documentation teams in order to support their successful automation: Currently almost all software providers and vendors use various documentation formats to produce documentation deliverables; no one specific format is being followed. We recommend that a standard documentation format be used, i.e., templates that offer multiple-choice offerings, standard notations, and naming conventions.

Adherence to standard templates, using a finite set of allowable keywords, will make the automation of documentation assessment a straightforward exercise. We recommend developing documentation templates that follow OMG documentation standards, for example, or any other type of standard that the customer would like its developers to adhere to (ISO, IEEE, and so forth).

Document Test Cases in a Standard Way

Much time is spent on test case documentation. While some sort of test case documentation is always desired, this process can be automated partially, if automated test case generation from use cases or models, for example, is allowed. Much research has gone into various technologies that allow test case generation from models, etc., and a standard way of documenting test cases is the goal. Various efforts are under way to develop standards, such as the MOF to Text standard (the Web site is www.omg.org/cgi-bin/doc?formal/08-01-16.pdf) and IBM/Telelogic's Rhapsody, which provides an automated test case generator (ATG) to produce unit test cases.

ATG is developed using a formal methodology to decompose requirements written in a natural language in order to produce a set of unambiguous rules, object relationships, states, and so on that define the rules/behavior described by the requirements document(s). The rules and relationships are captured using a formal language.

The "formal" language description then becomes the blueprint to generate and identify rule dependencies (actions/reactions), which form "threads" of potential sequences. These dependency threads are the basis for test case development (to develop required data sets, system configuration, and event triggers/and system stimulation). ATG has a test driver component that is used to stimulate system sensor and communication interfaces in a controlled or ad hoc environment and monitor responses.

The concept of ATG can be applied to virtually any rule set. Our work has focused on developing test cases and test capability to assess tactical data link standards, as these standards use a lot of automated processes that can be readily verified using automated test case documentation and test case generation.

We have developed a to-be-patented technology that allows for test case generation using GUI stimulation. This is another way to automate the development of standard test case documentation. A case study of this is provided in Appendix D.

Adhere to Coding Standards

Software generally needs to be cross-platform-compatible and developed in a standardized fashion, in order to allow for maintainability and portability and to be most efficient. For best AST support, it is important that customer developers adhere to coding standards such as those defined in the OMG C++ Language Mapping Specification, version 1.1, June 2003, or the OMG C Language Mapping Specification, June 1999 and other standards, such as ISO/ANSI C++, and so forth.

Use of OMG's IDL

Another example of using standardized documentation is to use the OMG IDL[13] to help define the interfaces. The OMG IDL is also an ISO International Standard, number 14750. The use of IDL allows for automatic code generation, turning a time-consuming and error-prone manual task into an efficient automated task, saving valuable time. This is another concept as part of our recommended AAA practice.

GUI Testing Recommendations

Numerous user interface standards and guidelines exist for developers to adhere to when developing their AUT's GUI. However, their usability is limited because they are numerous—i.e., there are different guidelines depending on technology—conflicts within and among standards documents, redundancy between documents, and a lack of specific guidance. Many GUI builders are available, such as NetBeans, the Eclipse GUI builder, and so forth, each allowing the developer various opportunities to create a GUI but none really providing specific standards to allow for ease of AST.

A great idea for effective GUI generation that can support AST efforts is provided by IBM's Reflexive User Interface Builder (RIB), which builds Java

GUIs simply and quickly with new technology from alphaWorks.[14] It provides the following features:

- RIB specifies a flexible and easy-to-use XML markup language for describing Java GUIs and provides an engine for creating them. You can define color scheme, font, icon usage, menu/functionality placement, etc.

- You can use RIB to test and evaluate basic GUI layout and functionality, or to create and render GUIs for an application. This concept for AST of a GUI application is ideal.

The RIB concept allows for GUIs to be generated in a standard way, which contributes to effective AST.

Some tools use virtual network computing (VNC) technology for AST. As mentioned, capture/playback tools record the test engineer's keystrokes in some type of scripting language and allow for script playback for baseline verification. Often a requirement exists that the capture/playback tool cannot reside on the AUT, and remote technology is required to access it; in this case VNC technology is applied. In the case of the automated tool using VNC technology, the following recommendations should be considered, because these types of capture/playback tools are sensitive to such changes:[15]

- Control "font smoothing" and other text characteristics should not be changed.

- Don't change the color depth of the AUT.

- Display settings need to stay the same (resolution, etc.).

- If possible, keep the default settings in the OS; use standard visual settings.

Many more practices can be applied to support standard GUI generation and to make GUI testing more effective. For example, when a tester clicks on a GUI control, customized code modules get generated that allow for quick and consistent code generation, eliminating manual code entry/development (this is another concept that is part of our AAA practice).

Additionally, we recommend GUI object naming standards, which are discussed next.

GUI Object Naming Standards

Many automation tools key on the names of objects. Not only does this facilitate development of automation test programs, but it also encourages good software development practices. Microsoft, for example, promotes naming standards at http://support.microsoft.com/kb/110264.

Failure of application developers to name objects and then not name them uniquely is certain to delay test automation programming.

Library Concept of Code Reuse

Software consisting of various components that can be checked out, integrated, and reused, as with the library concept of code reuse described in Chapter 1, lends itself to effective AST. The goal here is to apply AST to various code baselines; and when code components are reused, the corresponding automated tests are applied. This code and automated test reuse will allow for automated testing of each component in a shortened time frame, thus improving AST efficiencies.

4.4   The Forest for the Trees—Not Knowing Which Tool to Pick

When scanning online testing user group postings (such as www.sqaforums.com), many times throughout the week, you may see this query: "Which is the best tool for *xyz*?" where *xyz* equals any testing category/tool, such as automated software testing, performance testing, defect tracking, configuration management, security testing, and other tools used to improve the STL. No matter which testing category or tool this specific query is related to, the answer to the question is often surprising to newcomers but generally will be "It depends." There is no one best tool on the market that will fit every organization's needs.

Finding the best tool for an organization requires a detailed understanding of the problem to be solved and depends on the specific needs and requirements of the task at hand. Once the problem is clear, it is possible to start evaluating tools. You can choose from commercial and open-source solutions—or you can decide to build your own.

Commercial solutions certainly have their advantages, including published feature road maps, institutionalized support, and stability (whether real or perceived). But buying from a software vendor also has its downsides, such as vendor lock-in, lack of interoperability with other products, lack of control over improvements, and licensing costs and restrictions. Those downsides might be applied to some open-source projects, but the advantages of leveraging the open-source community and its efforts are holding sway with more and more companies. Advantages of open-source include

- No licensing fees, maintenance, or restrictions
- Free and efficient support (though varied)
- Portability across platforms
- Modifiable and adaptable to suit your needs
- Comparatively lightweight
- Not tied to a single vendor

Given the large open-source code base that now exists, there is no need to reinvent the wheel and re-create a code base that already exists and has been tested in the field.

How to Evaluate and Choose a Tool

When tasked with selecting the "best" tool for our needs or for a specific client, we generally approach any type of tool evaluation strategically, as follows:

1. Identify the problem we are trying to solve.
2. Narrow down the tool requirements and criteria.
3. Identify a list of tools that meet the criteria.
4. Assign a weight to each tool criterion based on importance or priority.
5. Evaluate each tool candidate and assign a score.
6. Multiply the weight by each tool candidate score to get the tool's overall score for comparison.

Based on the tool evaluation criteria, we assign a weight based on feature importance to each tool criterion—i.e., the more important a tool criterion is for the client, the higher the weight (from 1 to 5)—then rank the various tools. The rank ranges from 1 to 5 and is based on how closely each tool criterion is met by the tool. Weight and rank are then multiplied to produce a final "tool score." Features and capabilities of candidate tools are then compared based on the resulting tool score in order to determine the best fit.

There are hundreds of choices for each tool category, and it doesn't make sense to implement these steps for 100 tools. Instead, it's a good idea to narrow down the broad tool list to a select few. This can be done using criteria such as the following:

- **Requirements:** Does the tool meet the high-level requirements? For example, if you are looking for a Web-based solution, but the tool works only as client-server, it would not be considered.

- **Longevity:** Is the tool brand-new or has it been around a while? Darwin's principle of "survival of the fittest" applies specifically to the tool market. Decide on a number of years you think the tool should have been in use.

- **User base:** A large user base generally indicates a good utility. With open-source, a busy development community also means more people providing feedback and improvements.

- **Past experience:** In the past, you or your client has had a good experience with a specific defect reporting tool that meets the high-level requirements, longevity, and user base criteria described.

Using these criteria, you can generally narrow down the field from the scores of tools to a smaller subset.

Additionally, when evaluating tools, the following high-level tool quality attributes need to be considered; they are applicable to almost all tools independent of category.

- Ease of product installation
- Cleanliness of uninstall
- Adequacy and responsiveness of the support team; also, available user groups to help answer questions, etc.
- Completeness and comprehensibility of documentation
- Configurability—the ability to be adapted to each evaluation activity; refers to how easy it is to set up each new evaluation project

- Tuneability, or the ability to guide and focus the analysis toward specific desired features, flaw types, or metrics; refers to how easy it is to fine-tune or tailor different assessments of the same project

- Integratability/interoperability—the level of integration into a larger framework or process supported by the tool, if that's part of the plan

- Balance of effort—the ratio of tool analysis to human analysis in finding actual flaws; refers to how much information the tool needs from a human to complete its analysis

- Expandability—whether the tool suite works on various applications and infrastructures

- Extensibility and technology lag—all commercial tools will eventually experience a technology lag behind the architectures they are targeted to support. When new development architectures are revised to add new features for software developers, there is a good chance that test automation tools may not recognize new objects. Therefore, it is important to evaluate tool extensibility and/or flexibility when dealing with new technology, objects, or methods.

These are some areas to consider when picking a tool. Appendix C provides actual examples for picking the right tool.

4.5 Lack of Automation Standards across Tool Vendors

Numerous vendors provide AST tools, and various open-source testing tools are available, but a lack of automation standards persists.

Many different types of standards have the potential to affect AST. Improved ROI from automated testing can be realized through standards applied to the component(s) under test, the test tools and harness, and other aspects of the test environment. Key considerations in determining the types of standards of greatest interest include the degree to which standards of that type support the following characteristics:

- **Ease of automation**—reduction of the time and complexity needed for automation, resulting in a reduction of the initial investment or an increase in the degree of automation that can be achieved

- **Plug and play**—increased reuse of automated test patterns across products, allowing for reusability of various automation components given the same test scenario

- **Product availability**—increased selection of products supporting automated testing, including test tools as well as other related capabilities such as products to support monitoring and control of the application during testing

- **Product interchangeability**—reduction of vendor lock-in, enabling developers to choose different automation tools for different parts of the testing process or for different baselines, while leveraging prior automation efforts

- **Product interoperability**—ability to use multiple products within a single test set, enabling developers to leverage the capabilities provided by multiple products, resulting in a more robust and higher-quality test

- **Cross-platform compatibility**—ability of one or more tools to be cross-platform-compatible across various OSs and technologies

- **Testing capability**—improved robustness and thoroughness of automated testing, resulting in higher-quality tests

Sample Automated Test Tool Standards

Automated test tools provide many opportunities for standardization. Currently, most automated test standards address hardware testing. However, significant benefits could be gained by standardizing various aspects of software test tools.

- **Scripting language:** Automated test tools use a scripting language to control the events of the tests. Each test tool comes with its own scripting language. Although some of these languages conform to open standards, others are proprietary. A standard for a common scripting language would improve product interchangeability. A set of scripts that work with one automated testing tool could potentially be used with others. For example, currently, even if tool A uses the same scripting language as tool B, the scripts are not interchangeable, because tool A and tool B have different recording mechanisms.[16]

- **Capture feature:** Many automated testing tools come with a capture feature, where the testers' keystrokes are recorded as they execute a test.

All automated testing tools have different and unique recording features. None of the features are standardized, thus producing different script outputs for the same testing steps.

- **Test data:** Many automated testing tools provide a way to generate test data. Some provide a test data database, others provide a flat file, but rarely provide both. A standardized way of generating test data would be useful.

- **Modularity:** Currently the various automated testing tools provide different features to allow for test script componentizing and modularity; i.e., a subscript can be called from a superscript. Providing a modularity feature that's standardized across tools would allow for reusability of modular and componentized scripts.

- **APIs:** Many automated tests require a test harness; i.e., the test harness receives inputs from the test tool via an application program interface (API) that is specific to the tool. It converts the inputs into API calls that are specific to the application being tested, effectively serving as a bridge between the test tool and the AUT. The harness is also responsible for collecting the results and providing them back to the test tool. The API between the test tool and the test harness is not currently standardized. Standardization of this API would be another significant step toward enabling interchangeability of automated test tools. The consistency provided by common scripting languages and APIs would also provide greater ease of use and would reduce the learning curve associated with each new test tool.

- **Test tool output and reporting:** Many automated testing tools currently use various methods to produce test results output and reporting. No standard way of test-run output and reporting exists.

- **Integration with other testing support tools:** Many automated testing tools provide APIs that allow imports and/or exports to other test support tools, such as requirements management, configuration management, and defect tracking tools. However, not all tools provide this standard capability.

In addition to the standards described here, other areas can benefit from standardization to support the automation cause, such as systems engineering standards to be applied during software development in support of AST. Currently an effort is under way at OMG, which IDT helped initiate, to standardize some of the AST efforts, called automated test and retest (ATRT).

4.6 Lack of Business Case

In Chapter 3 we discussed the need for a business case. Our experience, described there, revealed that if the business case has been developed, is approved, and buy-in exists from all stakeholders regarding the automated testing effort, then everyone will feel responsible for its success. If all contribute to the success of the automated testing program, chances for success are much higher. It is therefore an important goal to develop the business case and get approval. See Chapter 3 for how to develop a business case.

Summary

Even though most agree that AST is an efficient tool or practice in the testing toolbox, AST efforts still fail for various reasons. R&D needs to consider not only research and development but associated testing concepts, since testing can have a big impact on the success of technology implementation and/or failure of a company's perceived quality.

Many AST myths still persist, and the realities of AST have been described here. It is necessary to manage expectations accordingly.

If software developers follow selected best practices, such as the Open Architecture standards described here, or use our proposed concept of AAA, use standard documentation, and abide by some of the GUI/interface recommendations listed here, as well as follow selected best practices such as the library concept of component reuse and coding standards adherence, AST efforts stand to succeed and can be seamlessly integrated into an already effective process. Vendors could work on automated tool standards across tools, which additionally could contribute to the success of AST efforts.

Notes

1. Dustin et al., *Automated Software Testing*.

2. http://video.google.com/videoplay?docid=8774618466715423597&hl=en.

3. www.businessweek.com/magazine/content/08_17/b4081061866744.htm?chan=magazine+channel_special+report.

4. Described at www.sdtimes.com/content/article.aspx?ArticleID=32098.

5. www.businessweek.com/magazine/content/08_17/b4081061866744.htm?chan=magazine+channel_special+report.

6. Dustin et al., *Automated Software Testing*.

7. Kenneth H. Rosen, *Discrete Mathematics and Its Applications* (McGraw-Hill, 1991).

8. Ibid.

9. Contributed by J. Offutt. See also P. Ammann and J. Offutt, *Introduction to Software Testing* (Cambridge University Press, 2008).

10. www.omg.com/.

11. www.nswc.navy.mil/wwwDL/B/OACE/.

12. Dustin et al., *Automated Software Testing*.

13. www.omg.org/gettingstarted/omg_idl.htm.

14. www.ibm.com/developerworks/java/library/j-rib/.

15. Recommendations from the makers of Eggplant; see www.testplant.com.

16. We verified this by comparing two major vendor-provided testing tools using the same scripting languages. Too much proprietary information is included in each script to make it transferable.

Part II

How to Automate: Top Six Keys for Automation Payoff

Key 1: Know Your Requirements

Requirements serve as the blueprints to your automated testing effort.

In the previous chapters we discussed the whats and whys of AST (with some hows sprinkled in to better illustrate a point). The next six chapters discuss six key points related to how to successfully implement AST, broken down as follows:

Key 1: Know Your Requirements

Key 2: Develop the Automated Test Strategy

Key 3: Test the Automated Software Test Framework (ASTF)

Key 4: Continuously Track Progress—and Adjust Accordingly

Key 5: Implement AST Processes

Key 6: Put the Right People on the Project—Know the Skill Sets Required

Thoroughly knowing and understanding your SUT, test, and subsequent automation requirements is one of the most important factors that will impact the success of your AST implementation. Requirements will be used as the baseline to build, implement, and measure the AST program.

This chapter covers the importance of understanding the requirements that will feed into the automated testing strategy, which is discussed in detail in Chapter 6 as Key 2. Chapter 7 then discusses how to test the AST design and implementation to include test cases. In Chapter 8 we describe the importance of continually tracking progress, and implementing high-level processes is discussed in Chapter 9. Chapter 10 discusses having the right people on board for the respective tasks. It is important to note that even though the six keys are described in separate chapters, all the keys are intertwined, feed into each other, and at times include parallel activities.

Much research has been conducted into how to successfully develop requirements. This chapter will not convey the outcome of all of this research, but instead will focus on a high-level approach to requirements information gathering in support of AST efforts.

Here we will guide you through determining the requirements information that is available and suggest what to do when that important information is missing. Determining which test requirements to automate is an additional analysis that needs to take place and is covered in detail in Chapter 6. Finally, we will also discuss the importance of documenting the requirements in a central database, the development of a requirements traceability matrix, and what is required to successfully implement one.

5.1 Understand the AST Support Requirements

Various requirements need to be considered for an effective AST program, including

- AUT or SUT requirements
- Automation framework and tool requirements
- AST data requirements
- AST environment requirements
- AST process requirements

Requirements should be documented in a clear, concise manner, so they can be understood and serve as the basis for accurate AST planning. As with all information gathering, the quality and accuracy of the information collected are generally proportional to the amount of time and effort allocated to the task. It is imperative that while gathering the pertinent information you can distinguish between what is important to the AST effort, and what may be considered fluff and not important. Often that is accomplished by evaluating the requirements priority classification, if one is assigned, and understanding the high-risk functionality, i.e., functionality that is critical to the application or system. Additionally, various information-gathering techniques can be applied, such as the interviewing techniques described in Section 5.3.

AUT or SUT Requirements

SUT requirements are sometimes informal, but they can also be formal and at times are contractual obligations, reflecting what the customer wants and has approved and what the project team has agreed to deliver. *Customer* here is defined as the person or group for which the product, system, or project is being developed; a customer can be internal or external.

Ideally the test automator is involved from the beginning of the software development process for various reasons, such as gaining an early understanding of the task at hand, developing automatable and testable requirements, and in general building in quality from the beginning. But let's assume you are new to the program and effort, i.e., you have not been involved from the beginning of the program and you have to determine available information. Or you are trying to gain a clearer understanding of the business logic outside of the typical "The system shall . . ." requirements statements. Such information generally comes in many forms and from many areas. As Figure 5-1 shows, project requirements, AUT requirements, architecture and design documents, and even test procedures can serve as the ideal basis for gathering the test requirements and subsequent automation requirements information.

Armed with this information, you can drill down further to understand the task to be accomplished. Understanding the task at hand, its scope, and its associated testing goals are the top-level elements of AST planning and are accomplished in the following ways:[1]

- **Understanding the system**

   The overall system view includes an understanding of the functional and nonfunctional (such as security, performance, usability, etc.) requirements

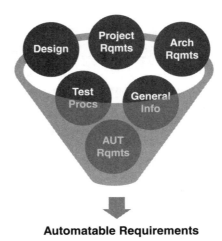

Automatable Requirements

Figure 5-1   Input to AST requirements

that the SUT must meet. Reading a fractured list of "The system shall ..." statements in a requirements specification document hardly provides this overall picture, because the scenarios and functional flow are often not apparent in these separate and isolated statements, and the business logic may not be clear. To provide the overall picture, meetings to discuss the system should be held, and other relevant and available documentation needs to be reviewed, such as proposals discussing the problem the proposed system is trying to solve, product management case studies, high-level business requirements, detailed system and design requirements, and use.

- **Understanding the scope**

  Next it is important to understand the scope of the test requirements. Automated tests that need to be performed can include functional requirements testing, network testing, server performance testing, user interface testing, performance testing, program module complexity analysis, code coverage testing, security testing, memory leak testing, and usability testing (among others).

Requirements definition is a crucial part of the automation project. Incorrect interpretation of or even missing requirements may result in schedule delays, wasted resources, and ultimately customer dissatisfaction.

Some requirements are simply not testable or automatable as written and thus need to be identified as such. For example, a requirement that "the application shall be compliant with the ANSI/C++ standard" is too broad and by itself would be very difficult to automate. The requirement needs to be broken down into its necessary details, and priorities need to be assigned to each.

AST Framework (ASTF) and Tool Requirements

Once you understand the SUT or AUT requirements and the AUT's architecture and design components, including the technologies used, and possibly have even been able to exercise parts of the actual SUT or a prototype of it, it will serve as a good baseline to start identifying your ASTF and/or AST tool requirements. Chapter 6 discusses the automated test strategy in detail, as part of understanding the overall requirements; but it is a good idea to start thinking about the ASTF requirements early: what requirements the ASTF needs to meet in order to be able to verify the SUT requirements. At times a tool can successfully be used alone as part of an AST effort independent of an entire ASTF; other times the tool is more effectively integrated as part of an ASTF. Appendix C discusses how to pick the right AST tool for the job.

Framework requirements need to be identified based on automated testing needs that are specific to each program and automation task at hand. See Appendix D for a case study of an automated testing framework and an example set of framework requirements, and adapt them to your needs. As mentioned previously, developing an ASTF and/or implementing a tool requires software development, and a mini development lifecycle needs to be implemented. Developing an ASTF can parallel the software development lifecycle, but first we have to consider and develop ASTF requirements and needs, design and implement the ASTF, and then test it, which is discussed in Chapter 7.

AST Data Requirements

A review of test data requirements should address several data concerns such as data depth, breadth, scope, test execution data integrity, and conditions, already discussed in Chapter 2.

AST can inherently exercise high volumes (depth, breadth, and amount of conditions) of test data. The section "Test Data Generation—Test Effort/ Schedule Decrease" in Chapter 2 covers test data requirements in some detail to show how AST efforts can decrease the test data generation effort. An effective AST test strategy requires careful acquisition and preparation of test data; the AST test strategy is discussed in Chapter 6, but careful consideration of test data requirements needs to take place during this requirements-gathering phase. Various criteria need to be considered in order to derive effective test data, and a review of test data requirements should address several data concerns such as data depth, breadth, scope, test execution data integrity, and conditions, such as:

- Amount/volume of test data needed (see data depth discussions in Chapter 2)

- Data to cover all business scenarios (see data breadth discussions in Chapter 2)

- Type of testing techniques applied; e.g., for boundary testing, understand all the data boundaries; for equivalence partitioning, understand the equivalence partitions, which are first referenced in Chapter 3 under "Intangible Automated Savings (ROI)"; for risk-based testing, understand the highest-risk areas

Next we have to consider how the test data will be acquired; i.e., will we use a subset of "live" or production data, if available? Sometimes live data is used for test data. On the surface this seems to be a viable and effective solution for a few good reasons:

- Live data generally is in the correct format, containing proper fields, values, etc., unless of course the application's database schema or database design has changed entirely and data fields and requirements have been modified, which needs to be confirmed.

- Live data can provide a testing condition perhaps not thought of in test data generation.

- Live data can provide load testing scenarios.

However, depending on the AUT, live data should be treated with caution and "cleaned" of any personal identity information, as mentioned in Chapter 2. An alternate solution is to write a script or have the automated testing tool generate the test data.

With both methods of gathering test data, consideration needs to be given to test data coverage, i.e., verifying that the test data provides the various scenarios and business logic coverage needed to verify the requirement.

Next we need to decide whether test data should be "modifiable" or "unmodifiable."

Modifiable test data: Modifiable test data can be changed without affecting the validity of the test. A test case can have a requirement that calls for testing the sending of a message at 1..*n* data rates, for example. Giving the user a list of data rates to choose from or allowing the user to enter a data rate will give the flexibility needed to test the requirement fully. Modifiable test data should be captured in a format that allows easy editing by the users. It gives the user of the test the flexibility to change the test inputs without any knowledge of the actual test automation software. This can be done with a user interface, as shown in Figure 5-2. There you see that the user has easy access to all test cases, only data values that are allowed to be modified are presented to the user, and current data values being used are recalled.

Unmodifiable test data: Test data that is required to verify that a specific test requirement condition is met should not be modifiable. For example, if a requirement states, "Verify that message is sent at a 10Hz rate," you cannot allow the operator to modify the data rate. Doing so would not test that specific requirement of a message being sent at that specified rate. Although you still need to extract the specific test data and account for it in your software design, your goal is to keep it static.

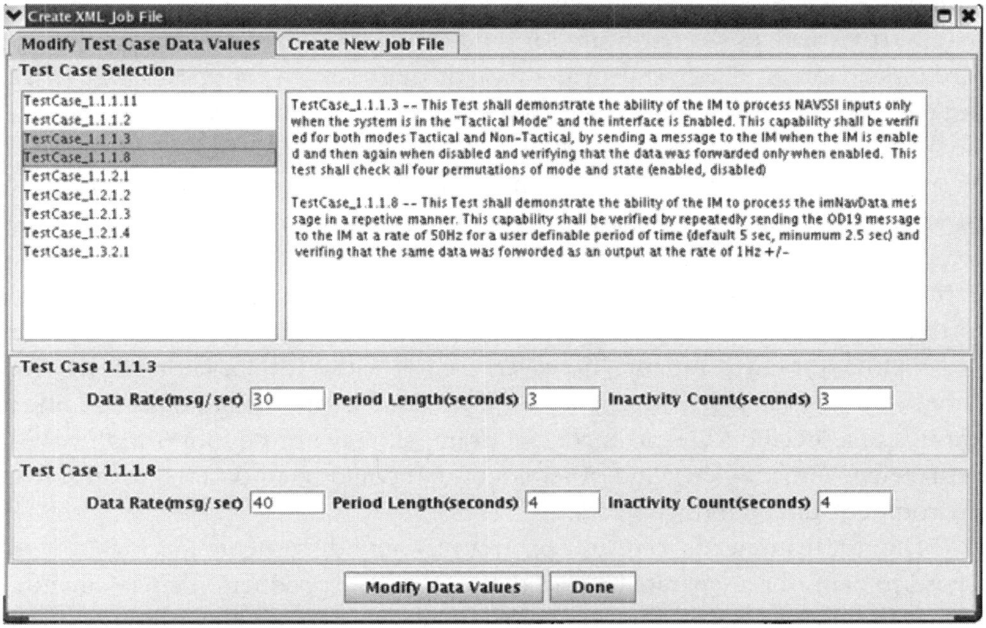

Figure 5-2   User interface screen capture example

Test Environment Requirements

The test environment is made up of all the elements that support the physical testing effort, such as test data, hardware, software, and the network and facility requirements needed to create and sustain the test environment. Test environment plans need to identify the number and types of individuals who will need to access and use the test environment and ensure that a sufficient number of computers will be available to accommodate these individuals. Consideration should be given to the number and kinds of environment setup scripts and test-bed scripts that will be required. Note that the term *production environment* is used here to refer to the environment in which the final software will be running. This could range from a single end-user computer to a network of computers connected to the Internet functioning as a complete Web site.

Sometimes, to improve cost effectiveness, you may want to consider creating virtual test environments. This can be accomplished with virtualization software products. In addition to being cost-effective, a virtual environment allows the tester to completely control the test environment. Much information is available on the Internet related to virtual environments. VMware Workstation, for example, is a software suite that allows users to run multiple instances of x86- or x86-64-compatible operating systems on a single physical PC.[2] VMware software provides a completely virtualized set of hardware to the guest operating system. It virtualizes the hardware for a video adapter, a network adapter, and hard disk adapters. The host provides pass-through drivers for guest USB, serial, and parallel devices. In this way, VMware virtual machines become highly portable between computers, because every host looks nearly identical to the guest. In practice, a systems administrator can pause operations on a virtual machine guest, move or copy that guest to another physical computer, and there resume execution exactly at the point of suspension. Alternately, for enterprise servers, a feature called VMotion allows the migration of operational guest virtual machines between similar but separate hardware hosts sharing the same storage.

Virtual test environments, however, are not without their faults, so be sure to become very familiar with the virtual environment and its limitations; some features of a specific AUT protocol, for example, may not be supported by the virtual environment (VE), and other issues that could be uncovered in an actual environment can be hidden in a VE.

The test team needs to review project planning documents specifically with regard to plans for a separate test lab that mimics the production environment. Although unit and integration-level tests are usually performed within the development environment by the development staff, system and user acceptance tests are ideally performed within a separate test lab setting, which represents an identical configuration of the production environment or, at the minimum, a scaled-down version of the production environment. The reason why the test environment configuration needs to be representative of the production environment is that the test environment must be able to replicate the baseline configuration of the production environment, to uncover any configuration-related issues that may affect the application, such as software incompatibilities, clustering, and firewall issues. However, replicating the production environment is often not feasible, because of cost and resource constraints. Use of extrapolation techniques should be evaluated.

Next, the test team needs to perform the following preparation activities to support the development of a test environment design:[3]

- Obtain a sample set of SUT production environment information, including a listing of support software, vendor-provided tools, computer hardware, and operating systems. Other information should include such items as video resolution, hard disk space, processing speed, and memory characteristics. Printer characteristics include type, capacity, and whether the printer is operating as a stand-alone or is connected to a network server.

- The test environment may also require an archive mechanism of some sort, such as a tape drive or CD-R drive, to allow the storage of large files (especially log files on client-server systems) post-test.

- Identify network characteristics of the environment, such as the use of leased lines, modems, Internet connections, and various protocols.

- In the case of a client-server or Web-based system, identify the required number of servers, server operating systems, databases, and other required components.

- Identify the number of automated test tool licenses that the test team needs.

- Identify other software that will be necessary to execute certain test procedures, such as VMware, other support tools, spreadsheets, or report writers.

- Consider test data requirements, including the size of the test databases, if applicable, when specifying test environment hardware. It is important to ensure that enough capacity is available on the machines and that a facility exists to install the data, such as a tape drive or network connection.

- For configuration testing, removable hard drives, image retrieval software, etc., may also be required.

- Evaluate the need for security certificates and budget accordingly.

Following these preparation activities, the test team develops a test environment design that consists of a graphic layout of the test environment architecture, together with a list of the components required to support it. The list of components needs to be reviewed in order to determine which components are already in place, which ones can be shifted from other locations within the organization, and which ones need to be procured. The list of components that must be procured comprises a test equipment purchase list. This list needs to include quantities required, unit price information, and maintenance and support costs. The test team may want to include in the test equipment order a few backup components in order to mitigate the risk that testing may come to a halt due to a hardware failure.[4]

The test environment should be sufficiently robust to provide the necessary infrastructure for functional testing, stress testing, performance testing, and other AST phases.

Hardware Requirements

The hardware requirements for the testing environment in support of running the automated tests must be defined. With the hardware requirements list, the project team should be able to procure the hardware necessary for the effort. At a minimum, the list should have the name of the hardware, the quantity needed of that type, and a description, like the sample shown in Table 5-1.

Table 5-1 Hardware Requirements List

Name	Quantity	Description
AUT host	2	Dual 3.46GHz Intel processors with 2GB RAM, 100GB hard drive
ASIM host	1	2 GHz Intel processor, 1 GB RAM, NDDS interface
BSIM	1	Specialized simulator from X Company, Ethernet interface (100BT)
Analysis host	1	2 GHz Intel processor, 1 GB RAM, 500GB hard drive
Network switch	2	24-port 100BT Hub, 1GB fiber uplink

With this list the project team can identify the number of hosts, specialized pieces of equipment, network configuration, etc., that are needed. Some items may take longer to order or procure than others, particularly nonstandard items. The hardware requirements list will help identify those items early so that their delivery can be scheduled appropriately.

Software Requirements

Software requirements for running the automated tests in the testing environment should also be clearly defined and documented.

The following are typical software requirements that need to be identified:

- Operating systems (versions, patch levels, etc.)
- Network communications protocols (TCP/IP, UDP, DDS, etc.)
- Languages
- Compilers
- Tools required to run AUT and to support automated testing (these will be further refined in Chapter 6 as part of the test strategy)

A typical software requirements sheet may look like Table 5-2.

Table 5-2 Software Requirements

Type	Description	Comment
Operating systems	Linux RedHat v8.0	AUT
	Windows XP Pro (SP2)	Analysis host
	LyxOS v3.1	Real-time host
	IOS v12.4	Router software
Network protocols	TCP/IP, UDP	
	DDS OCI/Tao v1.2°	
Languages	C++ v6.1, Java (J2SE v4.2.1)	
Compilers	gcc v4.2.2	
	Perl v5.10	
	Python v2.5.1	

(continues)

Table 5-2   Software Requirements *(Continued)*

Type	Description	Comment
Tools	STAF v3.1.5	
	Eclipse v3.3	
	ASIM v1.0b	Software for simulator

AST Process Requirements

Understanding AST process requirements and expectations is part of the scope
of the overall requirements understanding. A high-level AST process is defined
in Chapter 9, and we have touched on these types of process requirements
throughout this chapter. Implementing and adhering to AST processes will contribute to the success of an AST program. Understanding the corporate culture,
type of development processes applied, testing expectations, lessons learned,
level of effort, technology choices, budgets, and schedules are all part of this.

- **Testing phases**

  It is important to understand the testing expectations; i.e., what testing
  expectations does management have? What type of testing does the customer expect? For example, is a user acceptance testing phase required?
  If yes, which methodology needs to be followed, if any, and what are the
  expected milestones and deliverables? What are the expected testing phases?
  The answers to these questions will help refine the AST planning.

- **Lessons learned**

  Were there any issues or lessons learned from previous testing efforts
  similar to the one being planned? This information is important for
  gauging expectations, implementing according to them, and/or adjust-
  ing them, if necessary.

- **Level of effort**

  What is the expected level of effort to build the proposed SUT? How
  many developers will be hired? Will the ultimate compound solution be
  implemented, or a more cost-effective solution with less development
  time? This information is useful for many reasons, such as understanding
  the potential complexity of the test effort, types of testing, and resources
  required.

- **Technology choices**

  What are the selected technologies for the system's implementation and the potential issues associated with them? What kind of architecture will the system use? Is it a desktop application, a client-server application, or a Web application? This information will help determine test strategies and choose testing tools, as discussed in the section on AST frameworks and tools in Chapter 6.

- **Budget**

  What is the budget for implementing this product or system, including testing? This information will be helpful in narrowing down the type of testing that will be funded. Unfortunately, budgets are often determined without including any real amounts for testing efforts, thus requiring the test manager to adapt a testing budget to the allocated numbers.

- **Schedule**

  How much time has been allocated to developing and testing the system? What are the deadlines? Unfortunately, too often schedules are determined without taking test efforts into account, thus requiring the test manager to adapt a testing schedule to the official deadline.

- **Phased solution**

  Does the implementation consist of a phased solution, meaning will there be many releases consisting of incremental functionality or one big release? If it is a phased solution, the phases and priorities must be understood, since AST development should be geared toward the phases and implemented according to the iterations.

- **Understanding corporate culture and processes**

  Knowledge of the corporate culture and its software development and testing processes is important for AST planning. Understand who owns the processes; does the testing team? If not, does the testing team have input? Though every team member should be trying to improve the processes, in some organizations process improvement is the primary goal of QA or a process engineering group.

- **Type of testing team**

  Does the testing effort involve an independent testing team, such as independent validation and verification (IV&V)? Is the testing team independent from the development team, or are the test engineers integrated with the development team?

- **Type of development process**

  Is an extreme programming, agile, or test-driven development effort under way to which testing methods have to be adapted?

- **Roles and responsibilities**

  It is important to understand the AST team's roles and responsibilities; for example, is the team responsible for the final SUT release? Is the testing team the "final" quality gate; i.e., does the testing team give the green light regarding whether the testing criteria have been met?

In addition to understanding all AUT requirements, it is essential to understand all components that affect the STL. The earlier in the test planning cycle all the process elements are understood and the need for a test tool, additional skills, or more time is recognized, the better are the chances that the correct AST approach can be taken.

5.2   Additional Information in Support of AST Requirements

At times the requirements documentation and other related artifacts are not relevant or current, and you will need to review additional documentation or gather information from additional sources to determine AST program-related requirements. Such documentation and information can include manual and automated testing procedures as well as design documents and prototypes.

Manual Testing Procedure

Manual test procedures developed by SMEs are often an excellent source of information for understanding the AUT. Unfortunately, often they do not exist, and as the automator you are responsible for developing the test procedure. However, if such manual test procedures are available, they should prove to be helpful in analyzing the automation effort. In Chapter 7 we discuss the detailed test steps for the hyperlinked test cases illustrated in Figure 5-5 and how to verify their accuracy.

Design Documents

Design documents for the AUT can help greatly when implementing automated testing. Design documents are the descriptions of the software components to be developed and how they are architected to make up the system. They not only provide details of the product; they also provide guidance for the developers throughout the project, they can be a source of valuable information regarding the AUT, and they will support development of additional details to develop effective automated testing.

Typical design documents for technical efforts can include the following:

- **System and software design document (SDD)**

  This is a comprehensive software design model consisting of the following design activities: architectural design, interface design, data design, and procedural design.

- **Interface design document (IDD)**

  The IDD describes the interface characteristics and interface design of one or more systems, subsystems, hardware configuration items, computer software configuration items (CSCIs), manual operations, or other configuration items or critical items.

- **Database design document (DDD)**

  The DDD defines a method for the capture, storage, and dissemination of data. It describes the design of the database to be used and can also describe software used to access or manipulate the data. It is used as the basis for implementing the database and related software.

Prototypes

Prototypes serve various purposes. They allow users to "see" the expected result of a feature implementation, providing them with a preview of the actual look and feel of the application. They allow users to give feedback on what is being developed, which can be used to revise the prototype to be more acceptable to the user prior to system development.

Prototyping high-risk and complex SUT areas early allows the appropriate testing framework to be developed and the appropriate testing tool to be acquired. A prototype can help determine where the automated testing tool will run into compatibility issues. This allows time for work-arounds to be investigated and automated test designs to be adjusted prior to the actual delivery of software builds. Sometimes a prototype can actually reveal a flaw in the automated testing tool early on, allowing for enough lead time to acquire a patch from the tool vendor. Attempting to engineer a complex testing framework late in the test program cycle will typically not add much value. With a prototype in place, it is possible to begin defining the outline and approach of the test framework early on, since the prototype is one step closer to the actual application, and thus AUT technical requirements can be better understood. Prototypes can provide a level of detail that a static requirements document is not able to provide, and thus can be useful in the design of automated tests.

Some may view prototyping as "throwaway" work. At times that may be true of the actual code; however, the knowledge gained is knowledge retained. Prototyping and iterative testing were extremely valuable when we were employed on a project where we did not have access to any SMEs, original developers, or detailed requirements. We needed to develop requirements for AST and knew little about the application. The customer didn't understand the detailed architecture of the system as well, so we started with baseline assumptions and the little information we did have and prototyped our first iteration. Figure 5-3 shows the prototype process we followed to obtain automatable requirements that subsequently enabled us to build an effective ASTF.

Both increasing your knowledge base and prototyping usually require an enormous amount of time; however, if you are in a situation where little to no information is available, prototypes not only help development of the SUT, but also support the development of the ASTF.

5.3 When Information Is Not Available

Previously we described our prototyping process for a situation when we had little information about an SUT. Prototyping efforts can also be applied when no information is available; this section further elaborates on what else can be done when no information is available in support of AST efforts. Recently our team was asked to develop automated testing for an application that from our point of view was a black box. We did not have AST requirements, we did not have any test cases or test procedures, and we did not have access to the developers or SMEs for that application or system. As painstaking as it was for us to accept and continue an effort with so little information available, we knew that applying automated testing to such applications was very important to the customer.

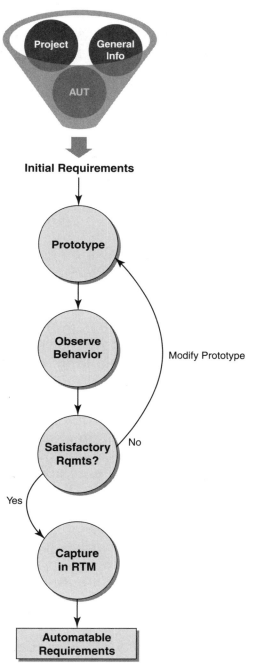

Figure 5-3   Prototyping process

Fortunately, we were able to apply a methodology to the problem and develop requirements, test cases, and a successful automated framework that produced significant results. We now have successfully applied this methodology, which involved an exploratory, developmental process of helping the customer discover what they wanted, to a variety of such efforts. The process includes conducting interviews; incrementally prototyping the ASTF along with the test cases and together with the customer verifying that we are achieving our testing goal (our prototyping approach has been described previously); and at times building AST requirements based on an existing application (the pitfalls to avoid in that scenario are discussed in the section "Developing Requirements Based on a Legacy Application or Legacy System," page 121).

Conducting Interviews

Probably the most common and most valuable method of information gathering is the interview.

Interviewing the customer in one-to-one, one-to-many, or even many-to-many sessions can produce comprehensible requirements if the interviews are conducted properly. It is important to understand the advantages and limitations of interviews and how they should be conducted. The following are a few suggestions for conducting effective requirements-gathering interviews:

1. **Plan an appropriate amount of time; do not rush the process.**

   How much information is out there to be gathered? The answer to this question is usually not known at the onset of the process. Because of this, devote ample time to finding out. Since the requirements that are to be gathered will be the blueprint for the automation strategy and development process, it is essential to start with a firm foundation. Rushing the information-gathering process may result in missing a vital piece of information; information found later in the process will ultimately take more time to integrate. Simply put, would you rather spend a few more hours in the information-gathering process or a few more days or weeks in a bug fixing/recoding effort?

2. **Define terms at the beginning of the process.**

   More than once we have discussed requirements with a customer only to find out later we were using a different definition for the same word. A way to avoid this is to agree on the meaning of terms that you and the customer will be using at the beginning. For example, not all organizations define the following terms the same way: *test plan*, *test set*, *test procedure*, *test case*, and *test steps*. Verify the use of terms and do not assume your definition is what your customer uses.

3. **Start with broad questions and work toward questions with yes or no answers, as applicable.**

   Prior to sitting down for the interview, develop a wide range of questions to ask. This is your time to gather as much information as you can, so take advantage of it. During the interview, start with broad questions, trying to get a sense of what information may be available and the scope of the automation project, then work toward questions that can be answered with yes or no, as applicable. It is a good idea to thoroughly document your interview sessions to avoid possible discrepancies in the future.

4. **Give feedback to answered questions.**

   Another sensible practice during the interview session is to give feedback to the answer received from the customer. This will help mitigate miscommunication or misunderstanding of a particular topic. Feedback can be given incrementally, with each question, or in summary, after a set of questions. For example, after several questions regarding the availability of design documents, you can summarize by asking the customer, "You stated that our automation team can access and use the following design documents: interface requirements document, interface design document, system design document. Is this correct, and are there any more that may be useful?"

Along with the suggestions given above, another very useful tactic if you feel that you are not getting a clear picture of requirements is to ask the question "Why?" It is important that "why" explorations be expressed in a way that does not sound confrontational, accusatory, or challenging.[5] Your role is to gather the information and logically sift through it to obtain the desired automatable requirements. Often you can phrase your "why" question in different, more palatable ways.

There are numerous ways to phrase the simple question "Why?" Find ways that are comfortable for you, and chances are your interviewees will be comfortable as well. Gently probing with "why" can reveal other sorts of useful information as well:[6]

- Asking "why" sometimes surfaces assumptions held by the person you are questioning.

- Asking "why" can reveal implicit requirements that no one thought to mention yet.

- Asking "why" a requirement is necessary a few times could provide additional details that solidify understanding of that requirement.

- Asking "why" or similar questions can help the analyst distinguish essential knowledge from extraneous information.

You should ask "why," in one form or another, as many times as it takes for you to fully understand what is going on. You cannot always believe what is told to you; be a skeptic and continue to probe. If you plan an appropriate amount of time and let everyone know how important this information-gathering phase is, then usually everyone is willing to participate.

Further Increasing Your Knowledge Base

In general, implementing AST does not require that you become an SME every time you take on a project, but you generally need access to one. If there is no SME around, then one option could be to increase your own knowledge of the particular subject by conducting your own study of the SUT. This obviously takes time and effort; however, it is required in order to develop an effective AST strategy. To become the SME in a particular domain requires much additional research and resources. Since your time is probably limited, you will likely not become a full "expert" in the area, but you should be able to gain enough understanding and skills to be the most knowledgeable on your team and, in essence, become the local SME. You can accomplish this by exercising the SUT and analyzing and documenting the various high-risk business scenarios. You also want to become familiar with what types of data generate what types of results and start documenting this as part of your test strategy; but proceed with caution, as described in the next section on developing requirements based on a legacy application or system.

Additionally, prototype development as described previously has also been proven successful in helping increase the knowledge base.

Developing Requirements Based on a Legacy Application or Legacy System

In many software development projects, a legacy application or system already exists, with little or no existing requirements documentation, that is the basis for an architectural redesign or platform upgrade. Most organizations in this situation will insist that the new system be developed and tested based exclusively on continual investigation of the already existing application, without taking the time to analyze or document how the application functions. On the surface, it appears that this will result in an earlier delivery date, since little or no effort is "wasted" on requirements reengineering and analyzing and documenting an application that already exists, because the existing application in itself supposedly manifests the needed requirements. Unfortunately, on all but the smallest projects, this strategy of using an existing application as the requirements baseline comes with many pitfalls and often results in few, if any, documented requirements, improper functionality, and incomplete testing.

Although some functional aspects of an application are self-explanatory, many domain-related features are difficult to reverse-engineer since it is easy to overlook business logic that may depend on the supplied data. Since it is usually not feasible to investigate the existing application with every possible data input, it is likely that some intricacy of the functionality will be missed. In some cases, the reasons why certain inputs produce certain outputs may be puzzling, and the result is that software developers provide their "best guess" as to why the application behaves the way it does. To make matters worse, once the actual business logic is determined, it is typically not documented but is instead coded directly into the new application, causing the guessing cycle to be perpetuated. Aside from business logic issues, it is also possible to misinterpret the meaning of user interface fields, or miss whole sections of user interface completely.

Many times, the existing baseline application is still live and under development, probably using a different architecture, along with an older technology, such as desktop versus Web, or it is in production and under continuous maintenance, which often includes defect fixing and feature additions for each new production release. This presents the "moving target" problem: Updates and new features are being applied to the application that is to serve as the requirements baseline for the new product, even as it is being reverse-engineered by the developers and testers for the new application. The resulting new application may become a mixture of the different states of the existing application as it moved through its own development lifecycle.

Finally, performing analysis, design, development, and test activities in this sort of environment makes it difficult to properly estimate time, budgets, and staffing required for the entire software development lifecycle. The team responsible for the new application doesn't know exactly the effort involved, and no requirements are available to clarify in detail what they are attempting to build or test. Most estimates are based on a casual understanding of the application's functionality, which may be grossly incorrect, or change suddenly if the existing application is upgraded. Estimating tasks is difficult enough even when based on excellent requirements, but it is almost impossible if based on so-called requirements embodied in a legacy and/or moving-target application.

On the surface, it may appear that one benefit of building an application based on an already existing one is that testers can compare the output of the old application that has been in production for a while to that of the newly implemented application, if the outputs are supposed to be the same. However, this assumption can be faulty, too, because now the testers are relying solely on the old application's output. What if the old application's output has been wrong for some scenarios for a while but no one has noticed it before? If the new application is behaving correctly, but the old application's output is wrong, the tester would now document an "invalid defect" and require this so-called defect to be fixed, since the already existing application is being relied upon as a requirements baseline.

Or, take the case where the testers decide that they simply can't rely on the old application for output comparison. They execute their test procedures, compare the outputs of the two applications, and find that the outputs differ. Now the testers are left with the question of which output is correct. What is a tester supposed to do in situations where the old application produces a different output from the new application? If the requirements are not documented, how can a tester know for certain which output is correct? The analysis that should have taken place during the requirements phase to determine the expected output is now in the hands of the tester.

As outlined in the preceding paragraphs, basing a new software development project on an existing application can be difficult, but there are ways to handle the situation. The first thing that must be done is to manage expectations. Discuss the issues involved when basing new development on an existing application. The following paragraphs outline several points to consider when basing new development on an existing product.

Select a Single Version of the Application

All stakeholders need to understand and agree that the new application will be based on one specific version of the already existing software. Select the version of the existing application on which the new development is to be based, and use only that version for the initial development.

In addition, working from a fixed application version makes tracking defects more straightforward, since the selected version of the existing application determines whether there is a defect in the new application, regardless of upgrades or corrections to the existing, legacy, application's code base. However, it is still necessary to verify that the existing application is indeed correct using domain expertise, as it is possible for the new application to be correct while the legacy application is defective.

Document the Existing Application

The next step is to have a domain or application expert document the existing application, writing at least a paragraph on each feature, supplying various testing scenarios and their expected output. Preferably, a full analysis would be done on the existing application, but in practice this can add considerable time and personnel to the effort, which may not be feasible and is rarely funded. A more realistic approach is to document the features in paragraph form and create detailed requirements only for more complex interactions that require more detailed documentation.

It is usually not enough to document only the user interface(s) of the current application. Generally the interface functionality doesn't show the intricacies of the underlying, functional behavior inside the application, and the interactions with the interface, so this documentation will be useless.

Standards and specifications: If no requirements exist, look for and investigate industry standards or other common specifications from which requirements may be drawn. For example, regarding a DDS application, requirements may be uncovered from the OMG DDS specification.[7]

Similar comparisons: Often applications exist that may be similar in nature to the application you are trying to document. If, for example, the AUT is a Web server or a database application, then potential requirements can be drawn from existing, documented Web servers or databases.

Experience, knowledge, skills: Sometimes there are no standards or specifications for the AUT and no similar comparisons that can be found to help with requirements gathering. In this situation, your past experience, ability to become the SME, and effectiveness at prototyping may lead to creating the best requirements.

Document Updates to the Existing Application

Updates—additional or changed requirements—to the existing legacy and baseline application from this point forward should be documented for use later when the new application is ready to be upgraded. This will allow stable analysis of the existing functionality and the creation of design and testing documents. If applicable, requirements and test procedures and other test artifacts can be used for both products.

If updates are not documented, development on the new product will become "reactive"—inconsistencies between the legacy and new products will surface piecemeal, some will be corrected and others will not, some will be known and others will be discovered during testing, or worse, during production.

Implement an Effective Development Process, Going Forward

Even though the legacy system has been developed without requirements, design or test documentation, or any type of system development processes, going forward, whenever a new feature is developed for any of the applications (legacy or new), make sure a system development process has been defined, is communicated, and is being followed and adjusted as required, so that you don't perpetuate the bad software engineering practices.

After you have followed these steps, the feature set of the application under development will be outlined and quantified, which allows for better organization, planning, tracking, and testing of each feature.

It is important to note in the situation where there are no requirements that no one method by itself will yield all the requirements. A creative strategy using the suggestions above will get you closer.

5.4   Start Implementing Your Requirements Traceability Matrix (RTM)

This section will discuss what a requirements traceability matrix (commonly referred to as RTM) is and the importance of such a document. As we have seen so far, a lot of time and effort is often invested in information gathering, including requirements. Requirements can vary in number from tens to hundreds to thousands that need to be managed for a given product. That's where having a proven, reliable, and workable requirements management process can add value to the entire project lifecycle.

Information in an RTM

The requirements deciphered so far from your information-gathering process will drive the AST strategy, the ASTF implementation, and test case development, which drives the test case automation, which then becomes the test suite to be run, which produces the automated test results that get reported back to the RTM. This cycle is depicted in Figure 5-4.

An RTM generally allows for tracing all software artifacts (i.e., requirements, design, test) to each other in order to measure coverage; in its simplest form it is a document that lists and defines test requirements and maps them to associated test cases. An RTM should categorize, prioritize, and follow the life of the requirement throughout the project lifecycle. An RTM can be a straightforward Word document, or it can be an elaborate mix of documents, hyperlinks, databases, and other specialized tools. The implementation of an RTM will vary depending on your environment. However, the goal remains the same for the AST effort: to effectively manage requirements and provide traceability and track coverage for the automated test effort. The RTM serves an additional purpose for other areas of the software development lifecycle. Those additional areas and how to automate the RTM are discussed in Chapter 6.

Example RTM

This section contains a sample AST RTM. The AUT in this example is a middleware application used in network communications called DDS.

Figure 5-5 shows the AUT requirements, including the requirement number, a categorization column, a detailed description, a column with the associated hyperlinked test case, which describes each step to accomplish the tests in detail, a pass/fail column to be filled in after the automated test is run, and a column denoting the priority of the requirement.

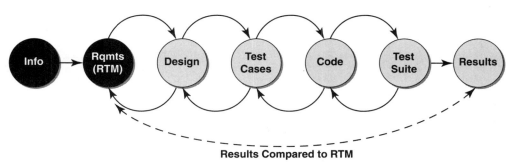

Figure 5-4 Requirements traceability activities

AUT Requirements in RTM

Req. #	High-Level Category	Detailed Requirements	Test Case (hyperlink)	Pass/Fail Status (filled in by test tool)	Priority
1.1	Basic feature	Shall demonstrate the ability of the DDS to send/receive (publish/subscribe) a message containing a data structure of mixed data types; i.e., message shall contain a combination of the basic data types: long, float (32/64 bit), integer, and text.	SubTestPlans\1.1.1 Pub-Sub MixedDataTypes.xls		1
1.3	Performance tests				
1.3.1	*Message latency data tests:*	Message latency (propagation delay of a message through the DDS service). Latency tests shall be point-to-point, i.e., one-way.			
1.3.1.1	Latency test—data stream	Shall determine the message propagation delay (latency) of a message through the DDS service. This latency information shall be obtained for a message repeatedly transmitted at a predetermined rate (1 to 10,000 messages per second) for a predetermined period (5 min to 1 hour). The message shall be of a predetermined size and data type (array of octects or array of struts {all basic types}). The sent and received timestamps shall be collected for each message send. The differences between these two time-stamps shall be recorded to a CSV file.	SubTestPlans\1.3.1.1 Latency Single Message.xls		1
1.3.1.2	Step up (stair step)	This test shall determine the message propagation delay (latency) through the DDS service. This latency information shall be obtained for a 200-byte message repeatedly transmitted at rates of 10, 100, 1,000, and 2,000 messages per second, for a predetermined specified period (5 min up to 1 hour). This test shall be repeated to collect additional latency information for messages sized (200, 300, 400, ... to 2,000 bytes). The sent and received timestamps shall be collected and analyzed for each message send. The differences between these two timestamps shall be recorded to a CSV file.	SubTestPlans\1.3.1.2 Latency Stair Step - Multiple Size Rate.xls		1

2.0	System-level tests	Publisher and subscriber and middleware are distributed on multiple computers on the same network. The number of computers used is controlled during test time to suit the requirements of a particular test session.		
2.1	Basic features tests			
2.1.1		Shall demonstrate the ability of the DDS to send/receive (publish/subscribe) a message containing a data structure of mixed data types; i.e., message shall contain a combination of the basic data types: long, float (32/64 bit), integer, and text.	SubTestPlans\2.1.1 System - Pub-SubMixedDataTypes.xls	1
2.4	Performance tests			
2.4.1	Message latency data tests:	Message latency (propagation delay of a message through the DDS service). Latency tests shall be point-to-point, i.e., one-way.		
2.4.1.1		Shall determine the message propagation delay (latency) of a message through the DDS service. This latency information shall be obtained for a message repeatedly transmitted at a predetermined rate (1 to 10,000 messages per second) for a predetermined period (5 min to 1 hour). The message shall be of a predetermined size and data type (array of octects or array of struts (all basic types)). The sent and received timestamps shall be collected for each message send. The differences between these two timestamps shall be recorded to a CSV file.	SubTestPlans\2.4.1.1 System - Latency Single Message.xls	2
2.4.2	Stress and reliability tests:			
2.4.2.1	Reliability ratio	Shall determine the DDS service's message transmission reliability ratio. This information shall be obtained by transmitting a 200-byte message at a rate of 2,000 messages per second for a predetermined specified period (5 min up to 1 hour). The ratio shall be calculated using the following formula: (# of messages sent/# of messages received). Note: The higher the number, the less reliable the transmission. The best value is 1.	SubTestPlans\2.4.2.1 System - Stress Test Reliability.xls	3

Figure 5-5 Sample AUT requirements in RTM

Summary

This chapter covered the importance of information gathering and knowing your requirements for testing, with a focus on understanding related requirements that can contribute to a successful AST effort. It discussed the information-gathering process and offered techniques that may help with that process. We emphasized the fact that various requirements greatly impact other factors in the test automation development process. Just as traditional blueprints influence the development and end result of what they describe, the requirements and related information available influence the AST results. Some of the areas impacted in that process include how the AST strategy will be approached, how test cases will be designed, the development of the test cases and ASTF, the test data definition, and ultimately the test results. The requirements traceability matrix (RTM) was introduced and discussed in this chapter as well. We presented a sample RTM; how to automate the RTM effort is described in Chapter 6.

Notes

1. Adapted from Dustin, *Effective Software Testing*.
2. http://en.wikipedia.org/wiki/VMware.
3. This should also be identified in the test environment section of any IEEE-Standard-829-compliant test plan or other test plan.
4. All this information will be documented in your test plan or test strategy document.
5. Ester Derby, "Building a Requirements Foundation through Customer Interviews," *Insights* 2, no. 1 (2004):1–4.
6. Karl E. Wiegers, *More about Software Requirements* (Microsoft Press, 2006).
7. www.omg.org/docs/formal/04-12-02.pdf.

Chapter 6

Key 2: Develop the Automated Test Strategy

A well-thought-out automated test strategy serves as the floor plan for automation success.

In Chapter 5 we discussed the importance of requirements and decided that they serve as the blueprints for the automation program. Armed with the requirements, we now can embark on Key 2: Develop the Automated Test Strategy.

Key 1: Know Your Requirements

Key 2: Develop the Automated Test Strategy

Key 3: Test the Automated Software Test Framework (ASTF)

Key 4: Continuously Track Progress—and Adjust Accordingly

Key 5: Implement AST Processes

Key 6: Put the Right People on the Project—Know the Skill Sets Required

Developing an automated test strategy is like laying out a floor plan, based on the blueprint. Within the automation strategy, we define the scope, objectives, approach, test framework, tools, test environment, schedule, and personnel requirements related to the automated testing effort.

Here we will discuss the concept of an overall automation approach: what steps to take and what considerations are needed to derive a successful automated testing strategy. The test strategy should also be documented, as it will become the floor plan for implementing automated testing. Everyone involved with the project—all the stakeholders—should be able to gain a clear understanding of what is being automated and get an overall sense of how it will be implemented by reading the test strategy document.

For example, it is common for a company's idea of AST to be a loose arrangement of automated test scripts and sparsely generated test data, often rendering the automation efforts nonreusable and throwaway. Throwaway may be good enough for some contexts; however, the cost of developing reusable automation may not always justify the benefit, whereas a tester can always quickly reuse a Perl script to automate some part of the test explorations, or a .csv file parser or other quick scripts to support a small automation task. Other times companies select an automated testing tool without much consideration of the specific problem they are trying to solve; they may be misinformed, or perhaps they simply selected the most popular tool, thinking, "This tool has the biggest market share, so it ought to work for us, right?" or "The vendor gave us an excellent demo; the tool is easy to use." In Chapter 4 we discussed the AST pitfalls to avoid, including these types of false assumptions, and Appendix C discusses how to pick the right tool for the job; here we will provide step-by-step instructions for what to consider when designing and developing automated software tests and provide a sample case study of how to build an AST framework (ASTF) in order to support our objectives.

In Chapter 1 we defined AST to mean "the application and implementation of software technology throughout the entire software testing lifecycle (STL) with the goal of improving STL efficiencies and effectiveness." Automated testing efforts can be implemented during any phase of the STL or for all phases. So your overall goal might be to improve testing efficiencies along the STL—such as automated RTM maintenance, automated test environment baseline, restore, and configuration management—along with automated testing, in order to improve quality while also reducing the time to execute the tests. For some projects, on the other hand, you may want to automate only specific tests. The scope and objectives of the AST effort need to be defined. What areas of the STL should be automated? Are there particular areas that could benefit the most from automation? Is the bandwidth available to implement automation along the STL? Section 6.1 will define the content of the strategy document, which then is further detailed in the next sections, such as Section 6.2, where we refine the "what to automate" decision making. Here we will decide whether to focus our AST efforts on specific tests or testing phases only, or on facets of the entire STL lifecycle. After deciding the scope and objectives, we then will define our AST approach, provide a sample ASTF case study, discuss the automated test environment and management along with test environment samples and configuration, point to the importance of schedule and roles and responsibilities (which are covered in Chapters 9 and 10 respectively), and finally talk about our approach to automating the RTM and defect tracking.

6.1   The AST Strategy Document

In Chapter 5 we touched on the need for initial automated test requirements planning; here we will refine this process further. Now that you have reviewed various design documents, developed prototypes when needed, gathered enough information to establish requirements, and understand the task at hand, it is time to develop an automation test strategy.

A typical test strategy is documented and may have the categories described here. Each category is further discussed in the sections listed.

1. Overview
2. Scope and automated test objectives (see Section 6.2)
3. Automated test approach (see Section 6.3)
   a. Designing and developing the test cases
4. Automated test framework architecture (see Section 6.4)
5. Automated test environment management (see Section 6.5)
6. Test environment configuration management
   a. Hardware
   b. Software
   c. Other
7. Automating the RTM (see Section 6.6)
8. Schedule (see Chapter 9)
9. Personnel, i.e., roles and responsibilities (see Chapter 10)

6.2   Scope and Automated Test Objectives

The AST project scope and automated test objectives need to be clearly defined, documented, and communicated. The test objectives do not need to include detailed information regarding how the test is to be performed. A high-level description of what the AST effort is trying to accomplish is sufficient.

For example, we might decide that we want to automate the entire STL. Figure 6-1 provides an example of what this type of automation could look like.

Figure 6-1 shows an example implementation of the entire STL automation and support. For each testing lifecycle phase/tool, AST could include import/ export from/to all ASTL tools to allow for integrated support of all STL testing phases, i.e., links from requirements management (RM) tools to test management (TM) tools to test automation (TA) tools (in order to track all automated and manual tests) and to problem trouble reporting (PTR) or defect reporting and tracking tools. The benefit of having an AST central portal is that all information is maintained in a central repository, tests can be run and monitored from a central location, outlines of PTRs can be generated for evaluation and then submitted/imported to the PTR tool; PTRs can be tracked in one place, and reporting across the testing lifecycle is provided. The RTM to summarize test requirements coverage and test pass/fail throughout the test program is automated as part of this effort. Details of RTM automation are discussed further in Section 6.6.

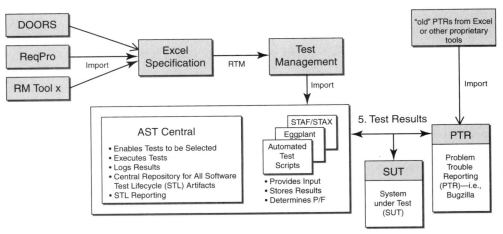

Figure 6-1   Example of AST throughout the software testing lifecycle (STL) (Note: A direct import from the RM tool to the TM tool can take place, as preferred)

This STL AST in this example is built in a modular fashion, such that tools can be added or replaced entirely if another tool is considered more suitable, as new requirements arise.

Our scope also needs to define the testing phases applicable as part of this AST effort. For example, generally we automate not only functional tests but also performance, security, concurrency, and other tests.

As part of the STL AST automation we also have to define which tests we'll automate, or our scope could be limited to automating only a subset of the STL, such as a subset of specific tests that we discuss next.

Deciding Which Tests to Automate

Our experience shows that before defining what tests to automate, it is best to conduct an analysis using a criteria checklist that allows you to determine which tests are feasible to automate. Figure 6-2 shows a sample checklist that we have used on various projects to help decide whether test automation for a specific test objective is feasible or reasonable.[1]

Test Automation Criteria	Yes	No
Is the test executed more than once?		
Is the test run on a regular basis, i.e., often reused, such as part of regression or build testing?		
Does the test cover most critical feature paths?		
Is the test impossible or prohibitively expensive to perform manually, such as concurrency, soak/endurance testing, performance, and memory leak detection testing?		
Are there timing-critical components that are a must to automate?		
Does the test cover the most complex area (often the most error-prone area)?		
Does the test require many data combinations using the same test steps (i.e., multiple data inputs for the same feature)?		
Are the expected results constant, i.e., do not change or vary with each test? Even if the results vary, is there a percentage tolerance that could be measured as expected results?		
Is the test very time-consuming, such as expected results analysis of hundreds of outputs?		
Is the test run on a stable application; i.e., the features of the application are not in constant flux?		
Does the test need to be verified on multiple software and hardware configurations?		
Does the ROI as discussed in Chapter 3 look promising and meet any organizational ROI criteria?		

Figure 6-2 Checklist for deciding what to automate

This checklist will help guide the decision making. If some or all of the answers are yes, and the schedules, budgets, and expertise required have been considered, the test seems to be a good candidate for automation. Additionally, the following guidelines for performing the automation versus manual test analysis can be considered.[2]

Don't Try to Automate Everything at Once—Take It Step by Step

Avoid trying to automate all test requirements at once. Take the example of a test team who decided to add all of their test requirements to the test management tool in support of system-level testing. The test team was eager to automate every possible test. As a result, they identified 1,900 test procedures that they planned to support by automation. When the time came to develop these test procedures, the test team discovered that the automated test tool was not as easy to use as they had thought. Expectations and objectives could not be met. As with all testing efforts, prioritization needs to take place.

It doesn't make sense to try to automate every test without considering the necessary experience with the kinds of tests and the particular test tools, frameworks, scripts, planned schedule, budget, and resources available. It is better for the test team to apply an incremental approach to increasing the depth and breadth of test automation with the support of prototyping efforts, for example. When prototyping an AST framework, you can begin with developing a preliminary set of requirements that you can use to build an initial version of an automated testing solution. After building the first version of the automated testing framework, you can evaluate further, and/or demonstrate it to the customer, who can then give you feedback and additional requirements and suggestions. This repetitive process continues for a few iterations until the solution meets the customer's expectations.

Consider Budget, Schedule, and Expertise—Not Everything Can Be Tested or Automated

The "what to automate" analysis needs to take budgets, schedules, and available expertise into account. Given limited resources (time and budget) and carved-in-stone deadlines, not all possible combinations and permutations of a program can be tested, and therefore not all possible tests can be automated. Additionally, some tests cannot be automated or it is simply cost-prohibitive to do so. For example, we illustrated in Chapter 4 how it's very difficult to automate the verification of a physical paper printout for various reasons. Technology is constantly churning, and given enough resources, almost anything can be automated, but the question remains, Does it make sense to automate? What is the ROI?

Automate Test Requirements Based on Risk

When reviewing the defined test procedures for the purpose of determining which to automate, take a look at the highest-risk functionality and its related test requirements and analyze whether those requirements warrant AST priority. The test team should also review the test procedure execution schedule when selecting test procedures to automate since the schedule sequence should be generally based on risk and dependencies, among other issues.

Risk can be based on the following factors:

- **Probability of failure of critical path functionality**

  Assess the priority of the test requirement. Is this a feature path executed by the user often, or rarely (if at all)? The best rule is to rank test requirements from the most critical functionality down to the least critical functionality. Focus on the most often executed functional feature paths, those that absolutely have to work.

- **Impact or business risk**

  What impact would a feature failure have on system operations and the end users' ability to perform their jobs? Does the failure represent a potential liability for the company?

- **Complexity**

  Analyze which functionality is complex to test manually and almost cost-prohibitive to set up and test in a manual fashion. For example, memory leak detection and performance testing are cumbersome or almost impossible to conduct as manual tests. However, a user could have a tool like BoundsChecker (a memory leak detection tool) running in the background during manual testing to catch memory leaks. Complexity of testing is an important context driver of risk.

Analyze the Automation Effort

The suggestion that the initial automation effort should be based on the highest-risk functionality has one caveat. The highest-risk functionality is often the most complex and thus the most difficult to automate. Therefore, analyze the automation effort first. One rule of thumb is the notion that if it takes as much effort (or more) to automate a test script for a specific test requirement as it did to develop the feature, reuse potential and other ROI of the automated script have to be questioned and assessed (ROI is discussed in detail in Chapter 3).

Also, whenever reviewing the effort required to automate a test, the allotted test schedule has to be considered. If only two weeks are available to support test development and execution, the schedule may be insufficient for developing elaborate automated test scripts.

Analyze the Reuse Potential of an Automated Module

Our experience has shown that when determining what test procedures to automate, it is good to keep reuse in mind. Suppose that the test team decided to automate the highest-risk functionality of the application, without contemplating the level of effort required to automate the test procedures or considering the extent to which test scripts could be reused. If an automated test that required quite some effort to implement cannot be reused, did it really pay off to implement it (i.e., was it worth the effort)? Reuse of the test scripts in a subsequent software application release needs to be considered. One of the questions to pose regarding reuse is whether and how much the baseline functionality would be expected to change. The test team should investigate whether the initial software baseline represents a one-time complex functionality that could change significantly with the next release. If so, it is not likely that automation will be cost-effective overall.

Focus Automation on Repetitive Tasks—Reduce the Manual Test Effort

It is beneficial to focus automation efforts on repetitive tasks. If these are automated, test engineers are freed up to focus on testing more complex functionality.

For example, say a test engineer is tasked with testing a requirement that states, "The system shall allow for adding 1 million account numbers via the GUI interface." This test lends itself perfectly to automation. Using a compatible capture/playback tool, the test engineer would record the activity of adding an account number once, then would work with the generated program code to replace the hard-coded values with variables and would use a program loop to increment and test the account number with each iteration up to the required number. This kind of script could be developed in less than 15 minutes, whereas it could take the test engineer weeks and many repetitive keystrokes to test this requirement manually. In actuality it probably would not be tested in that manner. There are various ways this could be tested in that manner. There are various ways this could be tested; generally, however, the test engineer will test up to 50 account additions and assume that the application can handle 1 million, which may turn out to be a false assumption. Automated testing scripts don't have to rely on assumptions, and we can automate the database population of these test accounts, or set up the test accounts via the GUI or create them using a batch file.

Prioritize—Base Automation Requirements on a Prioritized Feature Schedule[3]

Software feature implementations need to be prioritized for each incremental software release, in the case of iterative development, or depending on the development lifecycle model used, and based on customer needs or the need to deliver some high-risk items first. Automated test procedure planning and development can then be based on priority and risk in addition to the software feature implementation schedule, since both can dictate the order in which features will be made available for testing.

It is therefore important that the software development schedule, including the feature implementation sequence, be determined and made available to the testing team so it can plan accordingly. This is especially important when time is limited, since you don't want to waste time developing tests for features that won't be available in the software until later releases. Our experience has shown that frequent changes to prioritized feature schedules have a direct impact on the stability of a release, requiring rework and affecting both development and testing. However, feature reprioritization is part of the lifecycle for some groups and is done for each iteration, for example, if there are changes to business scenarios and priorities or technology used. The automation team needs to be made aware of any reprioritizations to stay on top of the changes.

Feature prioritization especially applies to phased releases. In most cases, the development lifecycle should strive to deliver the most-needed—highest-priority—features first, and these should be tested first.

Feature lists can be prioritized based on various criteria that apply to lifecycles in general and not specifically to automated testing:

- **Highest to lowest risk:** It is important to consider the risks when developing a project schedule and the automated testing strategy. Focusing development of automated testing on the highest-risk features is one way to prioritize.

- **Highest to lowest complexity:** Like risk, prioritizing by complexity attempts to develop and test the most complex features first, thus minimizing schedule overruns.

- **Customer needs:** In most projects, feature delivery tends to be prioritized by customer needs, since this is usually required to fuel the marketing and sales activities associated with a product.

- **Budget constraints:** It's important to consider the testing budget allotted when prioritizing the features for test automation for a given release. Some features will be more important to the success of a program than others.

- **Time constraints:** Consider the time constraints when prioritizing the features for a given release. Again, some features will be more important to the success of a program than others.

- **Personnel constraints**: Consider available personnel and associated expertise when prioritizing the feature schedule. Key personnel required to implement a specific feature might be missing from the team, due to budget constraints or other issues. While prioritizing test automation features it's important to consider not only the "what" but the "who."

A combination of several of these approaches is typically necessary to arrive at an effective AST feature schedule. Examine each feature to determine its risk, complexity, customer need, and so on, then "score" the feature in each category to arrive at a total value, or "weight," for that feature. Once you have done this for each feature, you can sort the list by weight to arrive at a prioritized list of features. Feature prioritization can be done in many ways; this is just one example. If you are interested in the Agile or Scrum feature prioritization methods, refer to specific materials about them.

Defining the Test Objectives: An Example

Continuing with the testing of the DDS example used in Chapter 5, and after conducting our "what to automate" analysis, our test objectives may be identified as the following for the AUT:

- Automate testing of basic features of DDS as defined in test requirements 1.x through 5.x.

- Automate testing of enhanced features of DDS as defined in test requirements 6.x through 10.x.

- Automate testing of quality of service (QoS) parameters, per requirement *y.*

- Automate system performance testing and produce automated performance metrics and analysis.

- For phase I of the project, test only priority 1 test requirements (with 1 being the highest priority). For phase II of the project, test priority 2s, 3s, etc.

Given this example, the project team now has a defined set of high-level test objectives to design automated test cases, identify the testing approach, develop the automated testing framework, and assess results. The team at any time should be able to assess any task that they are working on and map it back to one of the test objectives. If they cannot, then chances are what they are working on is out of the scope of the project and can sidetrack the effort. Defining the test objectives will focus the automated test program.

6.3   Identify the Approach

At this point in developing a test strategy document (and based on the requirements discussion in Chapter 5), you have gathered a mountain of information, identified and listed various requirements, and clearly defined and stated your AST scope and test objectives. The next step is to develop an approach to achieving those objectives. The approach for implementing automated testing will be your methodology or line of attack for how the testing will be accomplished.

When identifying the automated testing approach, the previously defined scope and objectives need to be considered.

Designing and Developing the Test Cases

In order to effectively define the testing approach you will need to start designing and developing the test cases, which will help define the details of how you plan to accomplish the test objectives. At times when it comes to AST, manual test procedures might already have been designed and developed; in that case you would have to evaluate the existing test procedures for automation. The section entitled "Adapt Manual Procedures to Automation" discusses how there is often no one-to-one translation or reuse of manual test procedures for automation. Determining which of the manual tests lend themselves to automation and how this automation will be accomplished are some of the decisions to be made.

Identifying how you will test and verify the requirements by designing and developing the test cases will help derive some of the details the test approach will need to specify, such as

- Detailed description of test cases for each testing phase, such as functional, performance, security, and concurrency; types of testing techniques applied (see "Test Case Development Techniques" later in this chapter for further discussion); along with expected results, method of determining expected results, analysis of actual versus expected results, analysis of test outcome if not specific results but a range of data that needs to be analyzed, and more

- Reusable components and project-specific features required in the ASTF (see the ASTF architecture discussion for more detail on this)

- Type of test data to be used; how the test data will be derived or acquired

- Number and content of phases (or spirals, or iterations) of deliveries

- Reporting requirements

For the purpose of this exercise we will describe a typical manual test procedure template.

Figure 6-3 shows a typical example of a manual test procedure. The typical test execution starts with an operator sitting in front of a display. The operator follows the test steps, verifies the response of the action, and then records a pass or fail result. The manual procedure may define the testing steps to follow or serve as an outline. It may also define preconditions needed to run the test.

The primary elements of the standard test procedure (not all shown in Figure 6-3) are

- Test procedure ID: Use a naming convention when filling in the test procedure ID.

- Test name: Provide a longer description of the test procedure.

- Date executed: Fill in when the test procedure is executed.

Step	Action	Expected Result	Requirements	Pass/Fail	Comment
1	Select RAP Status from the MODE SELECTION window.	System State Manager mode is displayed.	R0100	Pass	
2	Select the Configuration tab, and then select Xap1.	Configuration tab is selected with Xap1.	R1729	Pass	
3	Expand Xap1 and using the right mouse, select Stop, and stop the following processes: a. XYZ b. Background PIP c. ABCTST	XYZ, Background PIP, and ABCTST processing has been stopped.	R14593	Pass	
4	Expand Xap2 and using the right mouse, select Stop, and stop the YStar process.	YStar processing has been stopped.	R0011	Pass	

Figure 6-3 Sample manual test procedure

- Test engineer initials: Provide the initials of the test engineer executing the test procedure.

- Test procedure author: Identify the developer of the test procedure.

- Test objective: Outline the objective of the test procedure.

- Related use case/requirement number: Identify the requirement identification number that the test procedure is validating.

- Precondition/assumption/dependency: Provide the criteria or prerequisite information needed before the test procedure can be run, such as specific data setup requirements. This field is completed when the test procedure is dependent on another test procedure that needs to be performed first. This field is also completed to support instances when two test procedures would conflict when performed at the same time. Note that the precondition for a use case often becomes the precondition for a test procedure.

- Verification method: This field may state certification, automated or manual test, inspection, demonstration, analysis, and any other applicable methods.

- User action: Here the goals and expectations of a test procedure are clearly defined. Completing this field allows for clarification and documentation of the test steps required to verify the use case.

- Expected results: Define the expected results associated with executing the particular test procedure.

- Actual result: This field may have a default value, such as "Same as expected result," that is changed to describe the actual result if the test procedure fails.

- Test data required: List the set of test data required to support execution of the test procedure. Test data requirements have been discussed in Chapter 5.

Nonfunctional (or additional SUT quality attributes, such as performance, concurrency, etc.) related test considerations are often an afterthought for many testing efforts. However, it is important that nonfunctional tests be considered from the beginning of the testing lifecycle. Ideally the test procedure is divided into sections to accommodate for functional testing steps, and the remainder for the nonfunctional areas of security, performance and scalability, compatibility, usability, and others.

Many manual test procedure standards exist and the test procedure example provided is typical of the manual testing effort, but automated test case generation needs to be approached slightly differently, such as following standards for design, determining the types of design techniques to be applied, and (following our principle of automating the automation) automatically generating the test case documentation and test code. Automated test case documentation needs to be streamlined:

- Include standards for design.
- Adapt manual procedures to automation.
- Automate your test procedure documentation.
- Automate your test code generation.

AST is software development. As for software development, standards for AST design need to be documented, communicated, and enforced so that everyone involved will conform to the design guidelines and produce the required information.[4] Generally those AST test design standards should be based on best coding practices, such as reusability, modularity, loose coupling, concise variable- and function-naming conventions, and other standards that a development team might follow. These practices are typically the same as those for general software development. For example, we might also want to include trace log information where we monitor the behavior of back-end components in an automated fashion; for example, during execution, Web system components will write log entries detailing the functions they are executing and the major objects with which they are interacting. These log entries can be captured as part of AST.

Test procedure creation standards or guidelines are necessary, whether the test team is developing manual test procedures or automated test procedures, but will look different for each.

Adapt Manual Procedures to Automation

An important point to note is that manual test procedures as written generally cannot straightforwardly be reused for automation. They generally need to be modified or adapted to allow for AST. For example, a manual test will take as input one test data element in one step and another in another step, each providing the respective expected result; however, AST needs to be designed in such a way that, for example, numerous test data elements can be tested via one

AST path and subsequent expected results can be evaluated as part of the streamlined process. AST will require a different design from the manual test template provided, and depending on the size of the application being tested. For example, instead of writing step-by-step instructions as to how to run a test, pseudo code for an algorithm for the AST software development could be provided. Also, writing extensive test procedures may be too time-consuming and even unnecessary; for example, the test procedure could contain only a high-level test procedure description. The automator then can take the high-level test procedure description and refine it further using an ASTF or AST tool automatically generating detailed test steps and test code as defined next.

Another important consideration for automated test procedure development is the "testability" that was built in to the AUT as discussed in Chapter 4. Test procedures need to be developed to take advantage of the testability features.

Automate Test Procedure Documentation and Test Code Generation

We have developed an effective way to document and develop AST procedures as part of our "automating the test automation" paradigm; an example of this is provided here, using a GUI test.

1. Document a high-level test procedure, describing the test objective verifying a requirement.

2. Armed with the understanding of what the test procedure will accomplish, use the capture/playback feature of the ASTF to run the specific test steps in order to meet the test objectives defined in step 1.

3. The ASTF in our case study is programmed to generate an automated test step entry in the test step documentation when a tester clicks through the test steps. This approach can be based on keywords that the automator can pick and choose for the ASTF tool to interpret. Based on the keyword chosen, specific test steps are automatically documented, and at the same time automated test code is generated.

4. The automated test code can be reused within the capture/playback tool during playback, or within the ASTF for other types of automated testing; no additional or only little additional coding is required.

Our goal for AST is to automate as much as is feasible. We have touched on this topic and how to accomplish this throughout the book.

Step	Action	Output		Test Results
		Type	Expected	Pass/Fail
1	Instruct the Test Fixture to **create a topic** "TOPIC-LATENCY-BUDGET."	Boolean	TRUE: Instruction executed successfully	
2	Instruct the Test Fixture to **create a Publisher** using the topic "TOPIC-LATENCY-BUDGET," and setting the QoS Latency_Budget policy duration to "**100ms**."	Boolean	TRUE: Instruction executed successfully	
3	Instruct the Test Fixture to **create a Subscriber** using the topic "TOPIC-LATENCY-BUDGET," and setting the QoS Latency_Budget policy duration to "**90ms**."	Boolean	FALSE: Instruction not executed— Incompatible QoS policies.	
4	Instruct the Test Fixture to **create a Subscriber** using the topic "TOPIC-LATENCY-BUDGET," and setting the QoS Latency_Budget policy duration to "**100ms**."	Boolean	TRUE: Instruction executed successfully	
5	Instruct the Test Fixture to **create a Subscriber** using the topic "TOPIC-LATENCY-BUDGET," and setting the QoS Latency_Budget policy duration to "**110ms**."	Boolean	TRUE: Instruction executed successfully	

Figure 6-4 Automated test procedure example

Figure 6-4 shows an example of binary steps in an automated test procedure. While the content looks similar to the manual test procedure, it has been generated in an automated fashion.

Test Case Development Techniques

As mentioned previously, a SUT cannot be 100% tested, nor can all tests be 100% automated. An analysis needs to take place and tests need to be prioritized as discussed previously in this chapter. Once the tests to be automated have been defined, testing techniques need to be applied to help narrow down a subset of test scenarios that if run still provide adequate testing coverage. AST does not remove the need to conduct the test analysis or the effort to derive a subset of test cases using various testing techniques. Various testing techniques exist, such as boundary value, risk-based, or equivalence partitioning, which have been described in previous chapters, and much literature is available describing the various testing techniques. One book that does a good job of explaining these techniques is *How We Test Software at Microsoft*.[5] Another technique, orthogonal array classification, can also be applied. We mentioned various tools available to help derive test data using orthogonal arrays in Chapter 1. For additional test case development you might want to consider "The 25 Most Dangerous Programming Errors" (see http://www.sans.org/top25errors/) and develop a test case for each.

6.4 Automated Software Test Framework (ASTF)

Now that we have defined the AST scope and objectives, and understand the types of tests we want to automate, we are ready to develop our ASTF requirements. Many open-source testing frameworks are available, such as FIT,[6] or Carl Nagle's Test Automation Framework,[7] or STAF/STAX,[8] and more, that can serve as a baseline to develop an ASTF, but you will need to evaluate the capabilities of each against your project-specific ASTF requirements.

As part of an ASTF you may want to be able to run various STL support tools; therefore, along with the ASTF requirements, automation test tool requirements need to be captured. These requirements describe what the new automation tool as part of ASTF needs to accomplish. They differ from the SUT requirements that describe the system being testing. These requirements describe the tool in support of the various testing phases, such as functional testing versus performance testing.

For the purpose of this case study we will use STAF/STAX as the baseline for developing our ASTF. We'll further assume we want to develop the STL AST as described in the previous section and illustrated in Figure 6-1, and we want to develop an infrastructure that ties all the STL components together to work as one entity with a central repository. As part of this effort, we will choose capture/playback tools that are compatible in a Linux environment along with a performance testing tool.

As we have mentioned, the ASTF development requires a software development lifecycle, and we start off with defining the ASTF requirements (Figure 6-5 provides a sample set of ASTF requirements); then we'll design the ASTF architecture, which is depicted in Figures 6-6 and 6-7. Once designed, it will need to be implemented, which requires software development skill. This section does not cover development/implementation; instead, armed with the design, we refer you to the respective development techniques and related books available. Once the ASTF has been developed it needs to be tested. Chapter 7 discusses ideas about how to test the ASTF framework and associated test cases.

ASTF Requirements

Figure 6-5 includes a requirement number, a categorization column, a high-level description, and a requirements priority column for a sample set of ASTF requirements. These types of requirements are necessary when initially developing the automated testing tool or if there are new requirements for an existing tool.

The framework example works through the entire testing process, implementing each step from requirements to test results. The example framework component interfaces with

- Requirements management and associated RTM
- Test cases/procedures documentation, run, results reporting
- Central control where all STL components are managed
- AUT
- Test results/defect tracking
- Configuration management

Req. #	Category	High-Level Description	Priority
. . .	. . .	. . .	. . .
3.0	Automated setup	Shall automate setup of each test.	1
4.0	Batch mode (e.g., overnight, etc.)	Shall be able to run a sequence of automated tests in batch mode.	1
5.0	Configuration change control	Shall be able to verify what, if any, changes in the system/network, application, etc., prior to starting a test.	3
6.0	IP version test	Shall be able to automate testing of IPv4 versus IPv6 configurations.	3
7.0	Test result reporting	Shall allow for centralized reporting of all STL components.	1
7.1		Shall automate the reporting of test results (pass/fail).	1
7.2		Shall automate the reporting of performance test results.	1
. . .	. . .	. . .	. . .

Figure 6-5   Sample ASTF requirements

In essence, the automated framework takes the test requirements listed in the RTM, automates the test procedures defined and hyperlinked in the RTM worksheet, executes the test procedures against the AUT, and produces test results, which in turn can be linked to a defect tracking tool. All of this will be under configuration management.

ASTF Architecture

Along with a written description of the automated testing framework and related ASTF requirements, include an architecture diagram in the testing strategy document. Figure 6-6 shows a high-level architecture diagram that is intended to provide an overall picture of the ASTF.

ASTF Design Components

Once the high-level architecture diagram has been designed, the various components need to be defined, as part of a detailed software design document. Figure 6-7 illustrates portions of an example of what the high-level software architecture design could look like. For example, the design would describe each architecture component and its related functionality, and the specific technologies used by each design component could be listed. The ideal ASTF is developed for reuse, but recognizing that there are many project-specific components given various requirements, the design should include an architecture of reusable (project-independent) and specific (project-dependent) components.

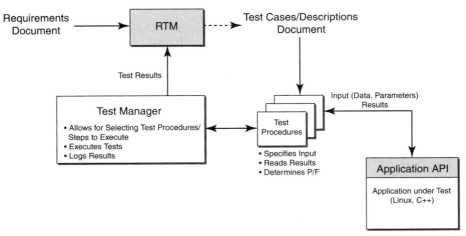

Figure 6-6 High-level architecture diagram

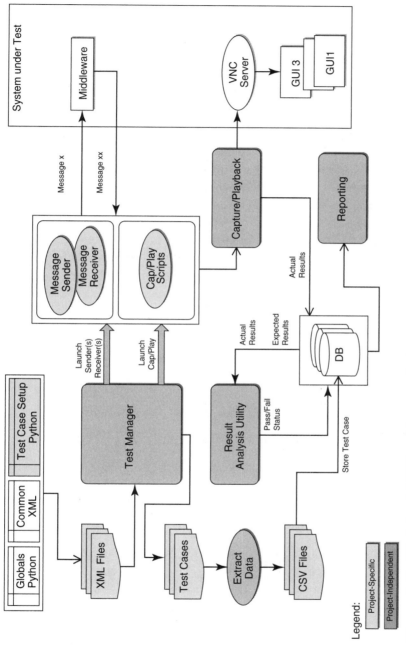

Figure 6-7 High-level ASTF architecture design

149

6.5 AST Environment/Configuration

Before evaluating tests to be automated, it is important to understand the test environment. As part of the requirements-gathering activity described in Chapter 5, we discussed the importance of considering test requirements as soon as the information is available. When setting up automated-test-accessible environments, environment preparers/automators should first identify any issues of security access, permissions and approvals required, or other organizational processes or practices that may require action. Firewalls and antivirus or disk encryption software, for example, may preempt or block automation from being implemented. It is important to find out what is required to get around those security lockdowns in a classified test lab, or any other lab where such security requirements exist.

As part of the AST strategy the test environment for automated testing is refined to ensure that all hardware requirements, software requirements, and other requirements, such as network requirements, are adequately met. Often test environments are set up with a minimal configuration that can run the application and various tests against it. However, in the real world, with real users and real data, the application will sometimes choke and crash. It may not be feasible to set up a test environment that is the same as the target environment. In Chapter 5 we discussed the use of a virtual test environment. Also, consider that for a functional verification/test a subset of the final environment is suitable, whereas for load or performance testing it is not, and final environment considerations are essential.

The automated testing environment should be separate from other environments, such as the development or production environments, and it should have the following characteristics:

- **Clean**

    The environment should be isolated, secure, controlled, and stable. Changes to the environment, such as to hardware, software (including the automated test framework), network, parameters, etc., are monitored and known. In a clean environment the AUT will not need to be modified during the testing process.

    Control of the test environment configuration is essential during any automated testing effort. In order for the automated tests to produce consistent results, the test environment needs to be under configuration management and a restorable test baseline needs to be established.

Before each test harness execution/run, checks of these configurations should be conducted in accordance with the required configuration components.

It is essential that any and all persons who are in a position to impact the test configuration understand that changes in the configuration must be accounted for in order to maintain the credibility of test results. The ability to validate the credibility of a test or exercise relies on the knowledge that the test was conducted with the appropriate hardware, software, documentation, and human elements.

- **Predictable and repeatable**

  Automated tests in this clean environment should behave as expected, and automated tests should have the ability to be rerun with known results. If tests are not predictable or not repeatable, then investigate possible configuration changes or framework errors.

- **Functionally equivalent**

  The environment should have functional components equivalent to those of the target environment. If target environment functionality cannot be met, then develop an approach that best mimics the component (e.g., use of simulators, etc.), but use extrapolation techniques sparingly.

- **Accounts for required test configurations**, as described next

Test Configurations

Test configurations need to be understood in order to finalize the AST environment, and they need to be specified using well-known entities. As an example, for a standard network communications testing configuration, systems capable of running a middleware data distribution service (DDS) are required. Typically with DDS, a system is needed to publish a message and receive a message. Depending on what you are testing, the test configuration can vary. Figure 6-8 shows three different types of network configurations that could be required for this example: Single Publish, Single Subscribe (A); Single Publish, Multiple Subscribe (B); and Multiple Publish, Single Subscribe (C). This is not meant to show complete test configuration coverage, but to provide a sample subset of test configurations.

Often duplicating the environment and covering all test configurations of complex systems can be a challenge. In those types of environments, specialized equipment, such as VMWare, simulation, and interfaces are required.

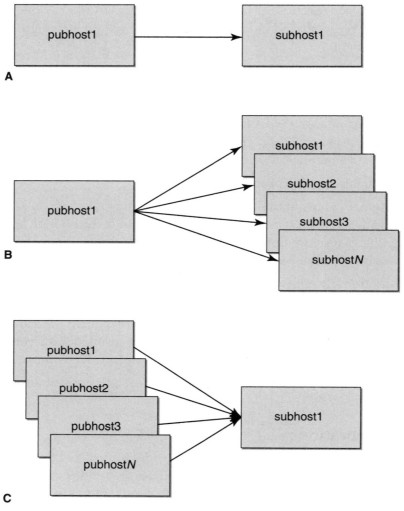

Figure 6-8 Sample DDS network configurations: (A) Single Publish, Single Subscribe; (B) Single Publish, Multiple Subscribe; (C) Multiple Publish, Single Subscribe

It is best to start with a configuration worksheet whose purpose is to capture all relevant hardware, software, and network components. Once this information is collected, begin to identify what is needed to produce your target environment. Table 6-1 is a sample configuration worksheet.

Table 6-1   Sample Configuration Worksheet

Name	OS	Function	IP Addr	Ports	Protocol	Display
testhost1	Solaris 5.8	Simulator	192.168.0.3	2525	UDP	Y
testhost2	Fedora 6	Publish Host1	192.168.0.19	3300	DDS	Y
testhost3	Fedora 6	Publish Host2	192.168.0.4	6818	UDP	N
testhost4	Fedora 6	Subscribe Host2	192.168.0.2	6819	UDP	N
testhost5	Win XP	Web Server	192.168.0.25	443	HTTPS	Y
testhost6	RedHat9	Analysis Host	192.168.0.20	6820	UDP	Y
testhost7	RedHat9	Database Server	192.168.0.17	6818	UDP	N
testhost8	LynxOS 4.0	Real-Time Simulator	192.168.0.6	1500	tbd	N
testhost9	Fedora 6	Subscribe Host1	192.168.0.5	2524	DDS	N
testhost10	Win XP	Client	192.168.0.33	7994	TCP/UDP	Y

Other Test Environment Automated Testing Requirements

This section of the test strategy document should list additional requirements, other than the hardware and software requirements, that may affect specific results of the automated testing effort. Other requirements might include, among others,

- Network constraints
- Specialized equipment
- Physical or environmental constraints

The purpose here is to identify and list items, other than when the system is operating normally, that will have a bearing on the automated testing results.

Automating the Test Environment Management— Automated CM

Once the test environment requirements have been identified, they are ideally managed in an automated fashion. This allows for a structured, automated approach to verifying that various baseline configuration parameters related to various settings—such as system and network configuration, including number and type of network agents, resulting latency and bandwidth, other network settings, etc.—have not changed from one state to the next. A well-constructed solution allows for baselining/backing up a snapshot of all relevant configurations and verifying that the configuration hasn't changed from one state to the next; it also includes an audit report on hardware, module, and software inventory and versions.

Automated configuration management technology expands baseline audits that have taken place and that have identified any nonstandard issues that have led to configuration updates, fixes, and improvements. Once the approved baseline has been established, the solution creates the baseline snapshot/backup for reuse and comparison to any newly introduced states to verify consistency. Figure 6-9 shows the process flow when system states change (e.g., operational versus nonoperational).

When implemented correctly, automated test environment management verifies that

- Only approved hardware and software are in place
- System settings and parameters are defined for the secure state (e.g., operator and user permissions, privilege settings for applications and systems code)

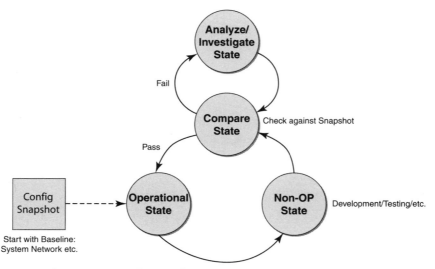

Figure 6-9 System state change flow

- No extraneous hardware or software has been introduced into the operational environment

- No required hardware or software has been removed

Automated test environment management can be set up differently depending on your particular environment and configuration. However, the general categories of data collection in the process are

- Hardware

- Software

- System

- Network

- Kernel

- Boot

- Volume management

- User

These categories capture a wide range of potential configuration changes of a system/network, whether intentional (warranted or malicious) or not. In this case, relying on the size and/or date stamp of a file is not enough; that type of information can be faked. A much more reliable method, which automated configuration management employs, is to determine the current MD5 checksum of the selected file and compare it to the value when the file was known to be clean. The MD5 checksum can also be used to determine alterations in device drivers and other file-based components.

Along with network-related information collected on the system, automated configuration management collects information regarding the network devices and routing specifics. A snapshot of network device configurations and network topology is created. Changes to the network are compared to the baseline. For example, consider if the following router configuration were changed:

```
access-list 103 permit ip any log
access-list 104 remark auto generated by SDM firewall configuration
access-list 104 remark SDM_ACL Category=1
access-list 104 permit udp any host 59.55.116.134
access-list 104 permit tcp any host 59.55.116.134
access-list 104 deny  ip 192.168.0.0 0.0.0.255 any
```

```
access-list 104 permit icmp any host 59.55.116.130 echo-reply
access-list 104 permit icmp any host 59.55.116.130 time-exceeded
access-list 104 permit icmp any host 59.55.116.130 unreachable
access-list 104 permit tcp any host 59.45.116.130 eq 443 <- incorrect address
access-list 104 permit tcp any host 59.55.116.130 eq 22
access-list 104 permit tcp any host 59.55.116.130 eq cmd
access-list 104 deny  ip 10.0.0.0 0.255.255.255 any
access-list 104 deny  ip 172.16.0.0 0.15.255.255 any
access-list 104 deny  ip 192.168.0.0 0.0.255.255 any
access-list 104 deny  ip 127.0.0.0 0.255.255.255 any
```

Automated test environment management would report the change when compared against the snapshot (e.g., as shown in the process flow in Figure 6-9) during the state transition.

Table 6-2 shows a subset of the categories of data collection, specific areas within the categories, and a sample of the type of data that will be collected and analyzed within one of the specific areas. *Note*: Depending on the configuration, there can be thousands of items to collect. The purpose of the "Detailed Example" column is to show a subset of the type of data in that category.

Implementing automated configuration management can ensure a clean testing environment as discussed earlier in this chapter.

Table 6-2 Subset of Data Collection Categories with Examples

Category	Specifics	Detailed Example (Snippet) of Data Collected

General	Nodename
	CPU speed
	OS name
	OS release
	etc.
		Info:
		`nodename: debian31`
		`model-id: i686`
		`hostid: 7f0100`
		`license:`
		`cpu_cnt: 1`
		`OS name: Linux`
		`OS release: 2.6.8-2-386`

Boot	Config
	Sysconfig
	Kernel/proc
	Run levels
	etc.
		Default rcS:
		`TMPTIME=0`
		`SULOGIN=no`
		`DELAYLOGIN=yes`
		`UTC=no`
		`VERBOSE=yes`
		`EDITMOTD=yes`
		`FSCKFIX=no`

(continues)

Table 6-2 Subset of Data Collection Categories with Examples *(Continued)*

Category	Specifics	Detailed Example (Snippet) of Data Collected

Hardware	Devices
	Meminfo
	Hwconf
	sysctl
	ioports
	etc.
		Dev sysctl
		<pre>dev.cdrom.info = drive speed: 40
		dev.cdrom.lock = 1
		dev.parport.default.spintime = 500
		dev.parport.default.timeslice = 200
		dev.parport.parport0.base-addr = 888 1912
		dev.parport.parport0.devices.active = none
		dev.parport.parport0.dma = 3
		dev.parport.parport0.irq = 7
		dev.parport.parport0.spintime = 500
		dev.rtc.max-user-freq = 64
		dev.scsi.logging_level = 0
		...</pre>

Software	cron
	Installed s/w
	Specific s/w
	Installed rpms
	Perl modules
	ipchain rules
	etc.
		Installed rpms:
		<pre>ftp 0.17-12 The FTP client
		g++ 3.3.5-3 The GNU C++ compiler
		g++-3.3 3.3.5-13 The GNU C++ compiler
		gcalctool 4.4.20-1 A GTK+ 2.0 desktop calculator
		gcc 3.3.5-3 The GNU C compiler
		gconf-editor 2.8.2-2 GConf configuration system
		gdb 6.3-6 The GNU Debugger
		gedit 2.8.3-4 Lightweight text editor
		...</pre>

Kernel	Parameters
	Modules
	sysctl
	etc.
		Sample parameters:
		<pre>CONFIG_MMU=y
		CONFIG_UID16=y
		CONFIG_GENERIC_ISA_DMA=y
		CONFIG_SWAP=y
		CONFIG_SYSVIPC=y
		CONFIG_POSIX_MQUEUE=y
		CONFIG_BSD_PROCESS_ACCT=y
		CONFIG_SYSCTL=y
		CONFIG_LOG_BUF_SHIFT=14
		CONFIG_ZFT_DFLT_BLK_SZ=10240
		CONFIG_FT_NR_BUFFERS=3
		CONFIG_FT_PROC_FS=y
		CONFIG_FT_NORMAL_DEBUG=y
		CONFIG_FT_STD_FDC=y
		CONFIG_FT_FDC_THR=8
		CONFIG_FT_FDC_MAX_RATE=2000
		CONFIG_FT_ALPHA_CLOCK=0
		...</pre>

(continues)

Table 6-2   Subset of Data Collection Categories with Examples *(Continued)*

Category	Specifics	Detailed Example (Snippet) of Data Collected

Network	Ports
	sysctl
	ipcs
	Network config files
	TCP/IP
	LAN data (router, switch)
	etc.
		Network sysctl:
		
		`net.core.optmem_max = 10240`
		`net.core.rmem_default = 110592`
		`net.core.rmem_max = 110592`
		`net.core.somaxconn = 128`
		`net.core.wmem_default = 110592`
		`net.core.wmem_max = 110592`
		`net.ipv4.conf.all.accept_redirects = 1`
		`net.ipv4.conf.all.accept_source_route = 0`
		`net.ipv6.route.gc_min_interval = 0`
		`net.ipv6.route.gc_thresh = 1024`
		`net.ipv6.route.gc_timeout = 60`
		`net.ipv6.route.max_size = 4096`
		`...`

System	Processes
	Security
	ldconfig
	etc.
		`ldconfig:`
		`(hwcap: 0x8000000000000000)`
		`ld-linux.so.2 -> ld-2.3.2.so`
		`libBrokenLocale.so.1 -> libBrokenLocale-2.3.2.so`
		`libSegFault.so -> libSegFault.so`
		`libanl.so.1 -> libanl-2.3.2.so`
		`libc.so.6 -> libc-2.3.2.so`
		`libcrypt.so.1 -> libcrypt-2.3.2.so`
		`libdl.so.2 -> libdl-2.3.2.so`
		`libm.so.6 -> libm-2.3.2.so`
		`libmemusage.so -> libmemusage.so`
		`libnsl.so.1 -> libnsl-2.3.2.so`
		`libnss_compat.so.2 -> libnss_compat-2.3.2.so`
		`...`

Volume Management	filesystem
	fstab
	Volume group
	Physical volume
	etc.
		`Mount info:`
		`/dev/hda1 on / type ext3 (rw,errors=remount-ro)`
		`devpts on /dev/pts type devpts (rw,gid=5,mode=620)`
		`proc on /proc type proc (rw)`
		`sysfs on /sys type sysfs (rw)`
		`tmpfs on /dev type tmpfs (rw,size=10M,mode=0755)`
		`tmpfs on /dev/shm type tmpfs (rw)`
		`usbfs on /proc/bus/usb type usbfs (rw)`

Users	passwd file
	Shadow file
	Group file
	etc.
		Password file:
		
		`bin:x:2:2:bin:/bin:/bin/sh`
		`daemon:x:1:1:daemon:/usr/sbin:/bin/sh`
		`root:x:0:0:root:/root:/bin/bash`
		`saned:x:108:108::/home/saned:/bin/false`
		`sshd:x:101:65534::/var/run/sshd:/bin/false`
		`sync:x:4:65534:sync:/bin:/bin/sync`
		`sys:x:3:3:sys:/dev:/bin/sh`
		`uucp:x:10:10:uucp:/var/spool/uucp:/bin/sh`
		`...`

6.6   Automating the RTM

As part of the requirements-gathering effort described in Chapter 5, we have already started initial development of an RTM. Our experience shows that it is best to use a methodology, process, or tool to check, verify, and track requirements during the design, coding, and testing phases. This section describes how to automate the RTM, another component of our AST strategy.

The SUT and in a separate effort the test tool or ASTF requirements are captured, categorized, and prioritized. This section focuses on the automated RTM related to SUT requirements. Within an RTM the SUT requirements can then be linked to all software development components, including design and development components; unit, integration, and system tests; and finally pass/ fail of the various tests to verify complete coverage. Figure 6-10 depicts the requirements check methodology, i.e., verifying there is design, code, and test coverage for each requirement.

As mentioned, the RTM on its own is a valuable document for the developers, testers, and others involved with the project. However, when fully integrated and implemented in an automated environment, it becomes much more than a stand-alone document. The RTM can be a powerful tool to verify and validate the entire STL effort. These are the steps for implementing the RTM in an automated environment:

*   Develop the RTM.
*   Require standard test case templates that are usable for your automation framework.
*   Hyperlink the test cases.

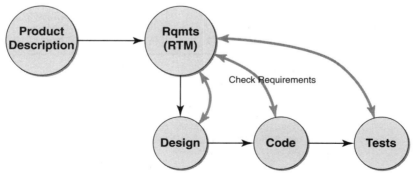

Figure 6-10   Requirements check methodology

- Update the test steps to include pass/fail results.
- Update the RTM to include pass/fail results.

Require Standard Test Case Templates That Are Usable for Your Automation Framework

Standardization of test case templates compatible with your automation framework can improve the efficiency of the overall test-case-building process. This is particularly true when you move from project to project, implementing your ASTF. Often we have found test procedures written in various formats (e.g., Microsoft Word, Excel, etc.) using various styles. We then need to convert them to our automated framework format. If, however, they were entered in the standard format from the beginning, then they could efficiently be converted or simply reused in our automated framework format. For automated GUI testing efforts, we have solved this issue of nonstandard test case documentation by autogenerating test case steps via a simple click within the SUT and subsequent AST code generation.

Hyperlink the Test Cases

Provide a mechanism to easily access the test cases within the RTM. Figure 6-11 illustrates a requirement taken from the sample RTM in Figure 6-5. The test case shown here in the "Test Case" column, "1.1.1 Pub-Sub_MixedDataTypes," is hyperlinked to the actual test case.

Req. #	Test Tool Requirements	Detailed Requirements	Test Case (hyperlink)	Test Result Status (filled in by test tool)	Priority
1.1	Basic feature	Shall demonstrate the ability of the DDS to send/receive (publish/subscribe) a message containing a data structure of mixed data types; i.e., message shall contain a combination of the basic data types: long, float (32/64 bit), integer, and text.	SubTestPlans\ 1.1.1 Pub-Sub MixedDataTypes .xls		1

Figure 6-11   Hyperlinked test case in an RTM

Update the Test Case Steps to Include Pass/Fail Results

As the test case steps are performed, develop a mechanism to automatically update the pass/fail status (see Figure 6-12).

Step	Action	Output		Test Results
		Type	Expected	Pass/Fail
1	Instruct the Test Fixture to **create a subscriber** using the topic "TEST-MIXED-DATA."	Boolean	TRUE: Instruction executed successfully	*Pass*
2	Instruct the Test Fixture to **create a publisher** using the topic "TEST-MIXED-DATA."	Boolean	TRUE: Instruction executed successfully	*Pass*
3	Instruct the Test Fixture to **read the message file** "sampleMixedDataTypes.msg."	Boolean	TRUE: Instruction executed successfully	*Pass*
4	Instruct the Test Fixture to **send the message** read in earlier using the previously created publisher.	Boolean	TRUE: Instruction executed successfully	*Pass*
5	**Wait x** ms to allow for the DDS to complete its task.	Boolean	TRUE: Instruction executed successfully	*Pass*
6	**Retrieve the message received** (if any) by the previously created subscriber.	Boolean	TRUE: Instruction executed successfully	*Pass*
7	**Verify** that a message was received and that it matches the message sent.	Boolean	TRUE: Instruction executed success-fully—Data message available and equates to sent message.	*Pass*

Figure 6-12 Pass/fail status shown in results field

Update the RTM to Include Pass/Fail Results

To tie it all together, develop a mechanism within your ASTF to allow for auto-mated update of the test case status in the RTM after a test run. Usually all steps in the detailed test case step need to "pass" in order to obtain a "pass" status for the requirement.

Figure 6-13 shows how a pass/fail status overview can be obtained via an ASTF-updated RTM. If there is a "fail" status, the ASTF should allow you to drill down by clicking on the test case hyperlink to determine exactly what test case or test step failed. Alternatively, log files generated during the testing can also be inspected to determine what failed and how; this is another feature that can be automated as part of the ASTF effort.

Req. #	Test Tool Requirements	Detailed Requirements	Test Case (hyperlink)	Test Result Status (filled in by test tool)	Priority
1.1	Basic feature	Shall demonstrate the ability of the DDS to send/receive (publish/subscribe) a message containing a data structure of mixed data types; i.e., message shall contain a combination of the basic data types: long, float (32/64 bit), integer, and text.	SubTestPlans\ 1.1.1 Pub-Sub MixedDataTypes .xls	*Pass*	1

Figure 6-13   Pass/fail status reported in RTM

You can develop the automated RTM in-house, but there are numerous tools with which to automate the generation and maintenance of the RTM, ranging from partial automation with simple spreadsheets to complete automation using specialized requirements management tools. Spreadsheets can be simple to set up and implement; however, they may require a great deal of manual effort and time-consuming maintenance. Specialized requirements management tools, on the other hand, make it easier to maintain and analyze traces. These tools may be helpful for medium-size to large projects. The International Council on Systems Engineering has compiled a very informative listing of requirements traceability tools on its Web site.[9]

Tracking that each requirement is covered is an important step in measuring the RTM's completeness. A few tools are available that can be used for requirements coverage. See Appendix C, Section C.1, Requirements Management, for additional examples of RM tools and RTM applications. Figure 6-14 shows an example of a tool that may be helpful for developers as they enter and continue with development and associated unit testing. This is an open-source tool called JFeature, which works with a well-known Java testing framework called JUnit. JFeature follows a two-step process:

1. Import/write requirements in your IDE environment (e.g., Eclipse, ANT).

2. Map the unit tests to requirements as the code and unit tests are developed.[10]

The tool helps developers map their code to specific requirements and also helps ensure that all requirements are actually covered. The tool accomplishes requirements coverage by

- Creating or importing a requirements file or files
- Associating the requirements file or files with the project
- Updating the requirements file or files to map the unit tests to the requirements

When the unit tests are run next, the tool can generate the requirements coverage report. The report can be configured to show

- Requirements successfully covered by code
- Requirements that are not covered
- Broken requirements—associated unit test(s) failed or tests did not execute

Figure 6-14 provides a screen shot of the JFeature requirements coverage tool. It is a good example of the type of tool you may want to research when thinking about requirements coverage for automation.

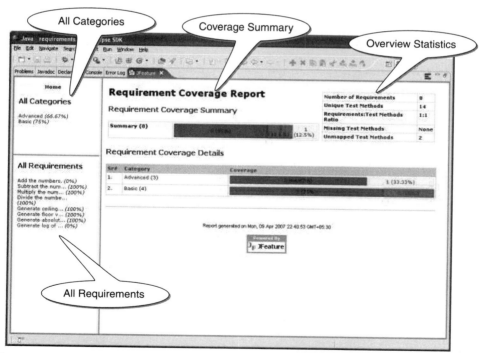

Figure 6-14   JFeature requirements coverage tool screen shot

6.7   Automated Defect Tracking

As part of our ASTF we also will have selected a defect tracking tool that will be integrated as part of the framework. See Appendix D for a list of example tools as part of the case study provided there. Although even the defect tracking portion of the STL can be automated, we will leave this as a high-level discussion and suggestion here; during a test run, if the expected result is not matched, an automated outline of a defect report can be generated that would produce, for example, the outline of a defect, including the requirements number, test step executed, the test priority, and even possibly a screen print of the system as the issue occurred. It is important that the defect tracking tool, such as the open-source Bugzilla, is not automatically populated with this defect; however, there should be an intermittent step that allows a test team member to evaluate the "proposed" defect before it is submitted to the defect or PTR tracking tool. This intermediate step will help avoid duplication of defects and avoids entry of false positives. The automation framework could allow defect generation with the push of a button once it's been determined a defect is real, or deletion of the proposed defect if it's determined otherwise.

Summary

This chapter introduced and defined the test strategy document and covered the sections that should be considered as part of one. An important aspect of the test strategy is identifying the approach to satisfy the overall test objectives. The AST strategy outlined will serve as your floor plan to implement your AST efforts. Once the test objectives are understood, it is important to decide on an overall testing framework, which can include coverage and automation of the entire STL, or simply automating a subset of tests. It can include various tools and automation capabilities, whether vendor-provided, open-source, or in-house-developed, such as requirements management, test management, unit, integration, and system testing, configuration management, automated testing frameworks, and defect tracking. Understanding your AST scope, and selecting the correct tool for the task at hand, is imperative, and in this chapter we described a how-to approach.

Notes

1. Adapted from Dustin, *Effective Software Testing*.

2. Adapted from Dustin et al., *Automated Software Testing*.

3. Adapted from Dustin, *Effective Software Testing*.

4. Dustin et al., *Automated Software Testing*, Section 7.3.4.

5. A. Page, K. Johnston, and B. Rollison, *How We Test Software at Microsoft* (Microsoft Press, 2008).

6. FIT is a tool developed to help with the writing of automated acceptance testing.

7. See http://safsdev.sourceforge.net/FRAMESDataDrivenTestAutomationFrame-works.htm.

8. See http://staf.sourceforge.net/.

9. www.incose.org/productspubs/products/setools/tooltax/reqtrace_tools.html.

10. www.technobuff.net/webapp/product/showProduct.do?name=jfeature.

Key 3: Test the Automated Software Test Framework (ASTF)

"Without counsel purposes are disappointed: but in the multitude of counselors they are established."

– Proverbs 15:22

Key 1: Know Your Requirements

Key 2: Develop the Automated Test Strategy

Key 3: Test the Automated Software Test Framework (ASTF)

Key 4: Continuously Track Progress—and Adjust Accordingly

Key 5: Implement AST Processes

Key 6: Put the Right People on the Project—Know the Skill Sets Required

We now understand the AST requirements and have designed and implemented an automated test strategy, including the required ASTF, support tools, test cases, and associated test data. Whether you have implemented only a few automated software tests or an entire ASTF, you now actually need to verify that it all works correctly and meets the goal; this is Key 3.

We are asked many times, "Do we need to test our automated tests?" The answer is yes, you do need to test and verify that what you have implemented works according to specifications. Although testing the ASTF and related artifacts seems redundant or possibly like an infinite/endless loop, testing the ASTF to verify that it behaves as expected is an important exercise. We need to be sure, for example, that the ASTF tests the SUT according to requirements, scales according to SUT and testing needs, and produces the correct results, without producing false positives or false negatives.

It would be ineffective as well as too time-consuming and cost-prohibitive to reproduce the efforts of an entire testing program to test the ASTF. Generally an ASTF with its associated artifacts is not delivered as a product to the customer and is used only in-house as part of the test program; in other cases, however, when the ASTF is delivered as a product to the customer, it has to be treated as such, requiring high quality. Generally, issues uncovered in an ASTF that is maintained and used internally can be quickly patched, but issues uncovered in an ASTF that is delivered externally as a product can lower the perception of its value. We contend, however, that whether used internally or externally, an ASTF requires high quality just like any other software development project.

Here we describe simple concepts that can be applied to gain adequate confidence that the ASTF you have developed works as expected. Either all ASTF testing tasks described here can be implemented, or a subset of those provided can be chosen, depending on the complexity of your ASTF implementation. Whether the ASTF is used internally only or is provided to a customer as a product, peer reviewing of test cases is an activity that should always take place.

We have broken down the recommended ASTF testing tasks as follows:

1. Verify that the ASTF meets specified requirements and that features behave as expected.

2. Peer-review all ASTF-related artifacts, including design, development, and associated test cases.

3. Verify SUT requirements and coverage.

4. Hold a customer review.

7.1 Verify That the ASTF Meets Specified Requirements and That Features Behave As Expected

Whether you have implemented your ASTF based on vendor-provided or open-source testing tools, chances are you will still need to develop additional features and enhancements to it in order to meet your testing needs. ASTF feature implementation might be an iterative and incremental exercise based on your incremental testing needs and ASTF requirements, and implementation will have to be prioritized accordingly. In Chapter 6 we provided a sample set of ASTF requirements; as part of this ASTF test you now need to verify that the ASTF project-specific and defined requirements have been implemented based on the various priorities. A mini RTM can be implemented to map ASTF requirement to actual feature implementation and evaluate coverage.

Once you have confirmed that an ASTF requirement has been implemented, it can be tested. The first test is to determine if any vendor-provided or open-source tools implemented as part of the ASTF behave as expected. Little time needs to be invested here, because most of the feature verification should have taken place during the tool evaluation, described in Appendix C. Testing of additional ASTF features (whether developed from scratch in-house or simply integrated from various existing tools) can be accomplished by ongoing peer review (which is described in Section 7.2) and then by actually running and exercising the ASTF feature. During the test run, for example, you could compare previously verified manual test outputs to the ASTF feature runs/outputs. If both results match, and any peer review issues have been resolved satisfactorily, there is a high probability that the ASTF feature works correctly. However, if you compare and receive the expected results, you will need to run a few more scenarios to be sure you are not receiving false negatives; if the test fails—expected results and actual results don't match—some analysis needs to be done as well, in order to exclude false positives and issues with the ASTF. Other requirements, such as ASTF scalability or handling a distributed test load as depicted earlier in Figure 1-1 (which illustrates the automated test and retest [ATRT] framework), for example, need to be tested and verified.

Verify That Effective ASTF Development Processes Have Been Applied

Often when we test overly buggy SUTs, we wish the developers had applied more effective development processes. In the course of developing our ASTF code, we have applied the following effective processes and recommend that you do the same:

- Use an Agile development process and verify that it is adhered to. For more on Agile see http://agilemanifesto.org/.

- Develop an automated unit test framework, using open-source unit testing tools, such as JUnit, NUnit, and so forth. Although we don't advocate automating any parts of the ASTF system test verification, the building of the ASTF needs to incorporate an automated unit test framework.

- Incorporate various automated testing tools into the ASTF development effort, such as code checkers, memory leak detection, or performance testing tools; see, for example, the PCLint example provided in Section 7.2.

- Use an automated build and configuration management process.

7.2   Peer-Review All ASTF-Related Artifacts, Including Design, Development, and Test Cases

The purpose of this section is to provide an overview of the important activity of peer review. Many publications discuss peer reviews in detail, and we will not repeat those specific proven strategies here. Instead, upon completion of this chapter you should have a firm understanding of how peer reviews can contribute to a high-quality ASTF outcome.

Peer Review As Part of the Software Development Lifecycle

Peer review in the software world is quite common and extremely beneficial. When peer reviews are performed correctly, software defects are caught early in the software development cycle, resulting in a higher-quality product. The concept of a peer review is one that can lend itself well to the AST world. As you will see in the following sections, peer reviews—specifically, reviews of test cases for automation—are just as important and valuable when implementing AST.

To begin a discussion of our ASTF peer reviews, let's first describe what a peer review is not. A peer review is not a judgment or a performance review of a peer's work. An effective peer review should

- Be designed to catch errors in the ASTF and related artifacts' design logic. In Chapter 6 we provided a case study of the ASTF design and architecture, then implementation. Ideally all artifacts of those efforts would be peer-reviewed, and adherence to all defined design standards should be verified.

- Evaluate ASTF requirements coverage as described in this section.

- Evaluate test cases and associated steps, including test logic and test coverage.

- Evaluate the test data to be used.

- Provide an environment where others can offer valuable suggestions for improvements.

IBM reported that each hour of inspection saved 20 hours of testing and 82 hours of rework effort that would have been necessary if the defects found by inspection had remained in the released product.[1]

Peer reviews should be built into the project schedule. Figure 7-1 is an excerpt from a project schedule that shows several peer reviews. One peer review meeting took place just prior to the test case review meeting with the customer. Other peer review meetings include those for requirements and AST design and code.

As shown in Figures 7-2 and 7-3, most software defects found early on, such as in the design and code software development lifecycle, are cheaper to fix. This is predictable and understandable; however, defects typically continue to be found in other phases, even post-release. As seen in Figure 7-3, defects found early are significantly less expensive to fix than defects found in the later stages. Post-release defects cost an average of $14,102 to fix compared to $25 per fix during pre-code. In fact, defects become increasingly more expensive to fix as development moves toward the post-release phase. The earlier a defect is found, the better for the overall project. Rework to fix defects is usually costly and often detrimental to projects.

The goal, then, apart from having fewer high-priority defects, would be to catch the defects as early as possible in the software development lifecycle. When implementing automation, test cases should be thought about and initial work done on them in the early stages. Test case peer reviews as part of the ASTF review should be performed early and, if possible, often.

Task Name
– Project X Automated Testing
– PROJECT REQUIREMENTS Phase
Kickoff Meeting
Gather Requirements
30-Day Follow-up Meeting
Test Strategy Doc—DRAFT
Preliminary Design Review (PDR)
Critical Design Review (CR)
Test Strategy Doc—FINAL
– Spiral 1
Spiral 1 Requirements (I/F & Test Tool)
Requirements Review Meeting
Test Case Development (RTM)
Test Case Peer Review Meeting
Spiral 1 Test Case Review Meeting
Deliver Phase 1 RTM
Interface Review Meeting
Design of Spiral 1 Components (detailed)
Code Development
Code Peer Review
Internal Demo
Customer Demo
Integration
Test Tool Software Delivery
Customer Presentation/Demo

Figure 7-1 Sample project schedule including peer review

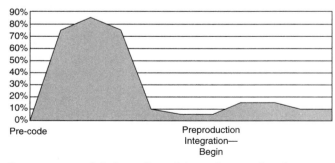

Figure 7-2 Percentage of defects found in software development phases[2]

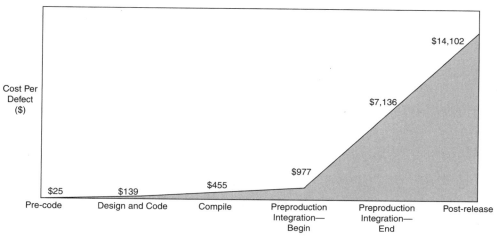

Figure 7-3 Defect correction costs in software under development[3]

Evaluate All ASTF Components

In Chapter 6 we discussed the ASTF architecture and design. As part of this review we now need to conduct a peer review of those components, asking questions such as, "Does the architecture meet all ASTF requirements? Do the design components meet the architectural requirements?" Architecture and design walk-throughs applied to general development efforts are necessary when these ASTF components are peer-reviewed.

Review Test Cases

Test cases are another component of the ASTF. Reviewing your work product, whatever it may be, is a practice that should be employed at any level of work. Reviewing test cases is no exception. In our experience, with the hurry to complete projects before looming delivery dates, thorough reviews unfortunately are often overlooked. Properly defined and executed test cases are critical to finding defects in the software product.

Review of the test cases could be broken up into various categories and examples as shown in Table 7-1. When conducting a peer review, devote ample time to the inspection of these areas.

Verifying that clear test steps have been implemented is beneficial in a multitude of ways. The most obvious is that those involved will have a clear understanding of what the test case is actually trying to accomplish. Clear test steps

Table 7-1 Sample Considerations for Test Case Review

Review Checklist	
☐ Review test steps	Verify that the test steps are legible, legitimate, and precise.
☐ Review test logic	Verify that the test case follows the correct logical flow.
☐ Review automated test code	Verify that the test code generated implements the test steps and logic.
☐ Review test coverage	Verify that the test is not a duplicate of an already existing test, that the test covers a new requirement, and that all requirements are covered.
☐ Review test template compliance	We discussed the need for a test template or standard for use within an AST framework in Chapter 5. Here we need to verify that the test case meets those template/framework requirements.
☐ Review test data	Verify that the test data is valid, covering the depth and breadth required, and that it supports the overall test coverage goals.

remove ambiguity. Whenever possible, each test step should be written in such a way as to have a Boolean result (e.g., true/false, yes/no, 0/1, etc.). The following is a test step taken from a test case used to test network communications with DDS middleware: "Instruct the test fixture to *create a subscriber* using the topic 'TEST-MIXED-DATA.'"

Here the Boolean result would be TRUE if the test fixture was able to create a subscriber using the topic "TEST-MIXED-DATA" and would be FALSE if the test fixture was not able to create a subscriber. The expected result for this step could be easily identified and captured.

During the test step review, check that the test steps are legible, legitimate, and precise. Table 7-2 provides such an example. It is clear that the result of each of these steps will be either TRUE or FALSE.

Along with the Boolean characteristics of each test step applicable to this scenario (note that not all test cases can be automated with a Boolean outcome), verify that each step is necessary, that there are no wasteful steps. Just as in software development, there are many ways to accomplish the same task. The peer review will weed out any unnecessary steps that result in added processing. One of the goals of automation is not only to automate the tests, but to automate wisely.

Table 7-2 Boolean Test Steps

Test Step	Description
1	Instruct the test fixture to ***create a subscriber*** using the topic "TEST-MIXED-DATA." [If TRUE, the test fixture created a subscriber using the topic "TEST-MIXED-DATA." *OR* If FALSE, the test fixture did not create a subscriber using the topic "TEST-MIXED-DATA."]
2	Instruct the test fixture to ***create a publisher*** using the topic "TEST-MIXED-DATA." [If TRUE, the test fixture created a publisher using the topic "TEST-MIXED-DATA." *OR* If FALSE, the test fixture did not create a publisher using the topic "TEST-MIXED-DATA."]

Review Test Logic

During the test logic review, check that the test case follows a logical flow. Similarly to reviewing the test steps, the peer review of the test logic is essential. Review that the test logic accurately captures the intent of the test case. Review that the logic is efficient and that it also holds true to the intent of the test case. Consider the test steps in Table 7-3.

Table 7-3 Test Logic Example

Test Step	Description
1	Instruct the test fixture to ***create a subscriber*** using the topic "TEST-MIXED-DATA."
2	Instruct the test fixture to ***create a publisher*** using the topic "TEST-MIXED-DATA."
3	Instruct the test fixture to ***read the message file*** "sampleMixedDataTypes.msg."
4	Instruct the test fixture to ***read the message file*** "sampleFixedDataTypes.msg."
5	Instruct the test fixture to ***send the message*** read in earlier using the previously created publisher.
6	***Wait x*** ms to allow the DDS to complete its task.
7	***Verify x*** ms passed prior to continuing.

(continues)

Table 7-3   Test Logic Example *(Continued)*

Test Step	Description
8	***Retrieve the message received*** (if any) by the previously created subscriber.
9	***Verify*** that a message was received and that it matches the message sent.

The intent of the test case from which these steps were taken is to test the DDS send/receive capability using mixed data types. A quick review of this logic shows that in step 4 a fixed-type data file is to be read immediately after a mixed-type data file (step 3). Although there is nothing inherently wrong with that step, it is not needed nor does it conform to the intent of the test case. If left in, it would be a wasted step. Step 7 is also not needed, because it is wasteful and does not serve a purpose.

Review Test Data

The topic of test data generation was discussed in Chapter 5. Here we'll discuss determining whether the test data is valid and whether it supports the overall test coverage goals.

Now that the test steps and test logic have been reviewed, move on to inspecting the test data. Without proper test data, even the best of test cases may produce unsuitable results or leave huge testing holes. Many test programs use test data generation tools, but regardless of the tools used, we emphasize including the test data in the peer review process. If you do, you can add a level of assurance that your test data is valid and supports the overall test coverage goals.

One of the areas to check when reviewing test data is boundary conditions. Boundary conditions were previously discussed in Chapter 5. Errors seem to congregate on and around the boundaries of valid and invalid input. Figure 7-4 is a worksheet where boundary test data values are used; however, not all boundaries are shown. Other approaches to test data generation have been discussed previously, such as equivalence partitioning or risk-based approaches. During the test data review, evaluate whether the data has sufficient breadth (all business data scenarios) and depth (large enough volume for performance testing, for example). (See Chapters 2 and 5 where test data recommendations have been discussed in detail.) Verify during the test data peer review that applicable recommendations have been implemented.

	Field Description						
Time of Transmission 64-bit FP/seconds/(0.0 to 86,401.0)	Latitude 64-bit FP/degrees/(−90.0 to +90.0)	Longitude 64-bit FP/degrees/(−180.0 to +180.0)	Vertical Position (32-bit FP/feet/−120,000.0 to +20,000.0)	Velocity North (32-bit FP/knots/−128 to +128)	Velocity East (32-bit FP/knots/−128 to +128)	Velocity Down (32-bit FP/knots/−128 to +128)	...
Tot	lat	lon	vp	nv	ve	vd	
−1	−90.1	−180.1	0	0	0	0	
0	−90.0	−180.0	−120,000	−128	−128	−128	
31	0	180	20,000	−129	−129	−129	
209	90.0	180.1	20,001	128	128	128	
316	90.1	180.0	−120,001	129	129	129	
...	...	0	...	...	...	...	

Figure 7-4 Sample test data worksheet

Review Automated Test Code

Peer review of the detailed test steps and the test logic will be futile if the automated test doesn't implement them correctly. We need to verify that the automated test code that's generated from all previously discussed artifacts actually implements all steps and meets all criteria accurately.

Figure 7-5 is a simple automated test case example showing the automated test step number, the action, type, expected output, and test result, which again needs to be verified as part of the peer review. Verify that all columns are filled in and meet the specified test criteria defined in the higher-level test case.

| Step | Action | Output | | Test Results |
		Type	Expected	Pass/Fail
1	Instruct the Test Fixture to **create a subscriber** using the topic "TEST-MIXED-DATA."	Boolean	TRUE: Instruction executed successfully	*Pass*
2	Instruct the Test Fixture to **create a publisher** using the topic "TEST-MIXED-DATA."	Boolean	TRUE: Instruction executed successfully	*Pass*
3	Instruct the Test Fixture to **read the message file** "sampleMixedDataTypes.msg."	Boolean	TRUE: Instruction executed successfully	*Pass*
4	Instruct the Test Fixture to **send the message** read in earlier using the previously created publisher.	Boolean	TRUE: Instruction executed successfully	*Pass*
5	**Wait *x* ms** to allow for the DDS to complete its task.	Boolean	TRUE: Instruction executed successfully	*Pass*
6	**Retrieve the message received** (if any) by the previously created subscriber.	Boolean	TRUE: Instruction executed successfully	*Pass*
7	**Verify** that a message was received and that it matches the message sent.	Boolean	TRUE: Instruction executed success-fully—Data message available and equates to sent message.	*Pass*

Figure 7-5   Sample automated test case steps

These test case steps are then converted into automated test code. The test code needs to be verified. Figure 7-6 is a code segment of this test case written in XML. The XML code to implement the test case is not shown in its entirety; our intent is to give you an idea of test case implementation in XML. For more details on XML, see the various Web sites where it is discussed in detail. A quick search on Google will bring up thousands of them.

```
<?xml version="1.0" encoding="UTF-8" standalone="no"?>
<!DOCTYPE stax SYSTEM "stax.dtd">

<!--
    TestCase_1.1.1.3.xml - definition file for STAX

    Job Description:

    This job executes a subscriber and publisher which will
    publish a TOPIC that contains mixed data.
-->

<stax>
  <!--
    -->
  <script>
    testCaseIdentifier    = 'TestCase_1.1.1.3'
    setCurrentJobName     = 1
    standaloneRun         = 1
  </script>

  <defaultcall function="startTestCase">{ 'pubMachList': PubMachList_tc_1_1_1_3, \
        'subMachList'             : SubMachList_tc_1_1_1_3, \
        'PubParams'               : PubParams_tc_1_1_1_3, \
        'ScsmPubParamList'        : PubParamsList_tc_1_1_1_3, \
        'dataFilesDir'            : dataFilesDir_tc_1_1_1_3, \
        'xlsPath'                 : originalXlsPath,\
        'dataFileList'            : dataFiles_tc_1_1_1_3, \
        'dataFilesSheetList'      : dataFilesSheetNames_tc_1_1_1_3, \
        'standaloneRun'           : standaloneRun, \
        'outputXlsPath'           : outputXlsPath, \
        'senderDataRatePerSec'    : senderDataRate_tc_1_1_1_3, \
        'periodLength'            : periodLength_tc_1_1_1_3 }
  </defaultcall>

  <function name="startTestCase" scope="local">
    <function-map-args>
      <function-optional-arg name="ScsmPubParamList" default="['local']">
        List of Publisher parameters for executing tm_scsm.
      </function-optional-arg>
      <function-optional-arg name="PubParams" default="['local']">
        List of Publisher parameters for executing tm_scsm.
      </function-optional-arg>
      <function-optional-arg name="pubMachList" default="['local']">
        List of machines where the publishers will be run.  The default is set
        to the local machine.
      </function-optional-arg>
      <function-optional-arg name="subMachList" default="['local']">
        List of machines where the subscribers will be run.  The default is set
        to the local machine.
      </function-optional-arg>
      <function-required-arg name="dataFilesDir">
        Path that contains the input data file(s) for this test case.
      </function-required-arg>
      <function-required-arg name="xlsPath">
        Path that contains the xls test case file(s).
      </function-required-arg>
      <function-required-arg name="dataFileList">
        List of data files that need to be published.
      </function-required-arg>
      <function-required-arg name="dataFilesSheetList">
        List of data file sheets in test case.
      </function-required-arg>
```

(continues)

Figure 7-6   Section of test case in XML format

```
    <function-optional-arg name="standaloneRun" default="1">
        Indicates that this test is one test case opposed to a job
        which is 1..n test cases.
    </function-optional-arg>
    <function-required-arg name="outputXlsPath">
        Path that contains the filled in test case.
    </function-required-arg>
    <function-optional-arg name="senderDataRatePerSec" default="1">
        Data rate for the sender to output data.
    </function-optional-arg>
    <function-optional-arg name="periodLength" default="5">
        Length of time to send data for.  The value is in seconds.
    </function-optional-arg>
    </function-map-args>
        <testcase name = "'%s' % (testCaseIdentifier)">
<sequence>
    <script>
        SubParams = ''
        runNumber = 0
                </script>
        <import machine="importMachine" file="importFile"/>
        <import machine="importMachine" file="importCniFile"/>
        <message>'Executing %s ...' % (testCaseIdentifier)</message>


                        .
                        . (note:  section deleted for brevity)
                        .


    <!--
        The following will create the CSV files as output.  The CSV files
        are used for reporting out the results the CSV format is recognized
        by excel and shows the output in a spreadsheet format.
    -->
    <call-with-map function="'generateFinalReport'">
        <call-map-arg name="'testCaseIdentifier'">testCaseIdentifier</call-map-arg>
        <call-map-arg name="'originalXlsDir'">xlsPath</call-map-arg>
        <call-map-arg name="'outputXlsDir'">outputXlsPath</call-map-arg>
        <call-map-arg name="'standaloneRun'">standaloneRun</call-map-arg>
    </call-with-map>
        <if expr="standaloneRun">
            <sequence>
                <call-with-map function="'incrementTestCaseCountVAR'">
                </call-with-map>
                <script>
                    import time
                    time.sleep(1)
                </script>

                <call-with-map function="'updateTaskDescription'">
                <call-map-arg name="'taskDescription'">"Test Complete!"</call-map-arg>
                <call-map-arg name="'incrementStepCount'">0</call-map-arg>
                </call-with-map>

                <call-with-map function="'updateDBTaskDescription'">
                <call-map-arg name="'taskDescription'">"Test Complete!"</call-map-arg>
                <call-map-arg name="'incrementStepCount'">0</call-map-arg>
                </call-with-map>
            </sequence>
        </if>
    </sequence>
    </testcase>
    </function>
</stax>
```

Figure 7-6   Section of test case in XML format *(continued)*

As an example, this XML section would be read by the automated testing framework that would then execute it. The actual results would be compared to stored expected results, which would then be analyzed. The test case status would be determined and reported back to the RTM. All related activities need to be peer-reviewed.

Various tools are available that can help check coding standards and even address security issues. Yes, even the ASTF needs to consider security concerns. For example, our ASTF is built on Eclipse, and we integrated PCLint[4] as part of our development efforts. One of the main features of PCLint is that it allows for static analysis of code and produces errors of various categories. Our first step in the PCLint-to-Eclipse integration was to produce PCLint error outputs within Eclipse. Figure 7-7 depicts an example outcome. This involved capturing the results output from the tool, storing the parsed data in a static data store visible to the entire plugin, and building a tabular view with the stored data to present to the user.

Incorporating various testing tools as part of your framework development will enhance its final quality.

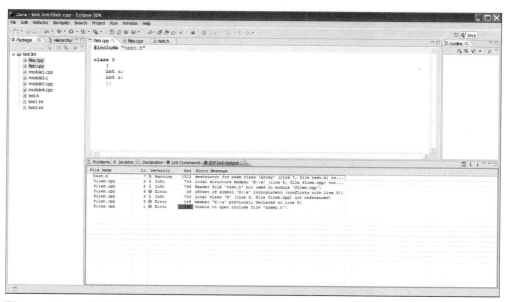

Figure 7-7 Eclipse and PCLint error output

7.3   Verify Requirements and Coverage

Various effective SUT requirements-gathering techniques have been developed and are available in books and discussions on the Internet. In this section we do not discuss how to develop effective SUT requirements, but rather how to verify, as part of ASTF verification and peer review, that all SUT requirements (each covered by one or more tests) have been thoroughly and effectively tested. This exercise is part of the test case review discussed previously. First ensure that the requirements are reflected in the test cases. Spend the time and effort to check the requirements again, in detail, before proceeding too far down the test case development path. Verify that they are clear and understood. Time and resources are often wasted and quality is compromised when test case development and automation start hastily without thorough requirements understanding. Check requirements to minimize rework and to help keep the ASTF project on track. Two important areas that need to be checked and rechecked are requirements coverage and requirements traceability, as shown in Table 7-4.

Table 7-4   Basic Requirements Considerations

Requirements Check	
☐ Requirements coverage	Do the test cases accurately and effectively test the given requirements?
☐ Requirements traceability	Do the test cases and status accurately map back to requirements?

Traceability

Do the test cases accurately map the status back to the requirements document? Are the requirements actually being satisfied? Requirements traceability can be defined in the following way:

> "Requirements traceability refers to the ability to define, capture and follow the traces left by requirements on other elements of the software development environment and the trace left by those elements on requirements."[5]

In other words, traceability is being able to define and trace the relationship between two software development objects or components. When speaking of requirements, the second object is derived from the first. Hence you should be able to trace the second object back to the first in the various elements or phases of the software development environment.

Coverage

The next question to ask is, "Do the test cases accurately test the stated requirements, and is there a test case for each requirement?"

The coverage of requirements is a fundamental necessity to ensure the success of a project. As discussed in earlier chapters, specifically Chapter 5, requirements are the building blocks of a given project. At every step of the lifecycle, it is imperative to keep the requirements in check to make sure the end goal is reached. Far too much time and resources are spent developing test cases and code that really do not meet the specified requirements.

Approaches to automating the RTM are covered in Chapter 6.

7.4 Hold a Customer Review

It is often beneficial to review automation strategy, requirements, test case approaches, and implementation with your customer, whether internal or external. Successful customer reviews should uncover potential problems and issues with the quality of the product. The product, after all, is what is delivered to the customer. Therefore, to help ensure you are delivering what the customer is expecting regarding test automation and an ASTF, we suggest two areas to cover in a customer review: clarifying any assumptions by the interested parties, and documenting agreements that have been mentioned (see Table 7-5).

Table 7-5 Customer Review Considerations

Customer Review	
❑ Assumptions	Clearly communicate automation goals and objectives. Write down and review any potential assumptions.
❑ Approach	Once defined, present the AST approach, whether it involves simple automated test development or elaborate ASTF development. Involve the customer in all peer reviews, as desired.
❑ Agreement	Capture in written form any agreements between you and the customer.

During the customer review, state the automation goals. Answer questions such as

- How much automation is planned (e.g., what is the scope of automation; is everything being automated or only a certain percentage)?
- What features of ASTF are to be developed? Involve the customer in reviews of all artifacts.
- What metrics are being used to measure automation success?
- Are there any existing test cases that are being automated, and if yes, which ones? Involve the customer in peer review of all test cases to be automated.
- What type of reporting will be done?

We suggest establishing assumptions and agreements as exit criteria for the customer review. Sometimes we have found that automation conjures up different images for different people. Customer reviews will help mitigate potential misunderstandings.

Summary

High-quality automated testing benefits from the careful examination and inspection of all automation artifacts, to include the ASTF and any related artifacts. In this chapter we guided you through the importance of verifying the quality of the AST efforts, including peer reviews and the use of automated test support tools and processes to accomplish the goal of a high-quality product.

The end goal is to create a quality AST work product. Reviews should not be an afterthought, but rather built into the project schedule. Choosing the best approach for your environment and spending the time to implement reviews will have a positive impact on your results.

Notes

1. Dick Holland, "Document Inspection as an Agent of Change," *Software Quality Professional* 2, no. 1 (1999): 22–33.

2. G. D. Everett and R. McLeod Jr., *Software Testing: Testing across the Entire Software Development Life Cycle* (Wiley, 2007).

3. Ibid.

4. www.gimpel.com/.

5. F. A. C. Pinheiro and J. A. Goguen, "An Object-Oriented Tool for Tracing Requirements," *IEEE Software* 13, no. 2 (1996): 52–64.

Chapter 8

Key 4: Continuously Track Progress—and Adjust Accordingly

"When you can measure what you are speaking about, and can express it in numbers, you know something about it; but when you cannot measure it, when you cannot express it in numbers, your knowledge is of a meager and unsatisfactory kind."

—Lord Kelvin

Key 1: Know Your Requirements

Key 2: Develop the Automated Test Strategy

Key 3: Test the Automated Software Test Framework (ASTF)

Key 4: Continuously Track Progress—and Adjust Accordingly

Key 5: Implement AST Processes

Key 6: Put the Right People on the Project—Know the Skill Sets Required

Most of us have worked on at least one project where the best-laid plans went awry and at times there wasn't just one reason we could point to that caused the failure. People, schedules, processes, and budgets can all contribute.[1] Based on such experiences from the past, we have learned that as part of a successful automated testing program it is important that the right people with the applicable skills be hired (covered in Chapter 10), goals and strategies be defined (as discussed in Chapter 6), then implemented, and that steps be put in place to continuously track, measure, and adjust, as needed, against these goals and strategies. Chapter 9 defines the high-level AST processes to be implemented with associated quality gates to measure the process implementation, and Appendix A provides a checklist to be used during verification of those process steps, but here we'll continue to discuss the importance of tracking the AST program, to include various defect prevention techniques, such as peer reviews, touched on throughout the book. We'll then focus on the types of AST metrics to gather so that we can measure progress, gauge the effectiveness of our AST efforts, and help keep them on track and/or make adjustments, if necessary. Finally, we will discuss the importance of a root cause analysis if a defect or issue is encountered.

Based on the outcome of these various efforts, adjustments can be made where necessary; e.g., the defects remaining to be fixed in a testing cycle can be assessed, schedules can be adjusted, and/or goals can be reduced. For example, if a feature is left with too many high-priority defects, a decision can be made to move the ship date, to ship the system as is (which generally isn't wise, unless a quick patch process is in place), or to go live without that specific feature.

Success is measured based on achieving the goals we set out to accomplish relative to the expectations of our stakeholders and customers.

8.1 AST Program Tracking and Defect Prevention

In Chapter 5 we discussed the importance of valid requirements and their assessment; in Chapter 6 we discussed the precautions to take when deciding what to automate; and in Chapter 7 we discussed in detail the importance of peer reviews. Here we'll provide additional ideas that aid in defect prevention efforts, including technical interchanges and walk-throughs; internal inspections; examination of constraints and associated risks; risk mitigation strategies; safeguarding AST processes and environments via configuration management; and defining and tracking schedules, costs, action items, and issues/defects.

Conduct Technical Interchanges and Walk-throughs

As already suggested in Chapter 7, peer reviews, technical interchanges, and walk-throughs with the customer and the internal AST team represent evaluation techniques that should take place throughout the AST effort. These techniques can be applied to all AST deliverables—test requirements, test cases, AST design and code, and other software work products, such as test procedures and automated test scripts. They consist of a detailed examination by a person or a group other than the author. These interchanges and walk-throughs are intended to detect defects, nonadherence to AST standards, test procedure issues, and other problems.

An example of a technical interchange meeting is an overview of test requirement documentation. When AST test requirements are defined in terms that are testable and correct, errors are prevented from entering the AST development pipeline that could eventually be reflected as defects in the deliverable. AST design component walk-throughs can be performed to ensure that the design is consistent with defined requirements—e.g., that it conforms to OA standards and applicable design methodology—and that errors are minimized.

Technical reviews and inspections have proven to be the most effective forms of preventing miscommunication, allowing for defect detection and removal.

Conduct Internal Inspections

In addition to customer technical interchanges and walk-throughs, internal inspections of deliverable work products should take place, before anything is even presented to the customer, to support the detection and removal of defects and process/practice omissions or deficiencies early in the AST development and test cycle; prevent the migration of defects to later phases; improve quality and productivity; and reduce cost, cycle time, and maintenance efforts.

Examine Constraints and Associated Risks

A careful examination of goals and constraints and associated risks should take place, leading to a systematic AST strategy and producing a predictable, higher-quality outcome and a high degree of success. Combining a careful examination of constraints together with defect detection technologies will yield the best results.

Any constraint and associated risk should be communicated to the customer and risk mitigation strategies developed as necessary.

Implement Risk Mitigation Strategies

Defined processes, such as the one described in Chapter 9, allow for constant risk assessment and review. If a risk is identified, appropriate mitigation strategies can be deployed. Require ongoing review of cost, schedules, processes, and implementation to ensure that potential problems do not go unnoticed until too late; instead, processes need to ensure that problems are addressed and corrected immediately. For example, how will you mitigate the risk if your "star" developer quits? There are numerous possible answers. Software development is a team effort and it is never a good practice to rely on one "star" developer. Hire qualified developers, so they can integrate as a team and each can be relied on in various ways based on their respective qualifications. One team member might have more experience than another, but neither should be irreplaceable, and the departure of one of them should not be detrimental to the project. Follow good hiring and software development practices (such as documenting and maintaining all AST-related artifacts) and put the right people on the project; see Chapter 10 for more on hiring. Additional risks could be missed deadlines or being over budget. Evaluate and determine risk mitigation techniques in case an identified risk comes to fruition.

Safeguard the Integrity of the AST Process and Environments

Experience shows that it is important to safeguard the integrity of the AST processes and environment. In Chapter 6 we discussed the importance of an isolated test environment and having it under configuration management. For example, you might want to test any new technology to be used as part of the AST effort in an isolated environment and validate that a tool, for example, performs to product specifications and marketing claims before it is used on any AUT or customer test environment. At one point we installed a tool on our Micron PC used for daily activities, only to have it blue-screen. It turned out that the tool we wanted to test wasn't compatible with the Micron PC. To solve the problem, we actually had to upgrade the PC's BIOS. An isolated test environment for these types of evaluation activities is vital.

The automator should also verify that any upgrades to a technology still run in the current environment. The previous version of the tool may have performed correctly and a new upgrade may perform fine in other environments, but the upgrade may adversely affect the team's particular environment. We had an experience when a new tool upgrade wasn't compatible with our e-mail software package any longer. It was a good thing we caught this issue, because otherwise an upgrade install would have rendered the tool useless, as we heavily relied on e-mail notification, for example, if a defect was generated.

Additionally, using a configuration management tool to baseline the test repository will help safeguard the integrity of the automated testing process. For example, all AST automation framework components, script files, test case and test procedure documentation, schedules, cost tracking, and other related AST artifacts need to be under configuration management. Using a configuration management tool ensures that the latest and most accurate version control and records of AST artifacts and products are maintained. For example, we are using the open-source tool Subversion in order to maintain AST product integrity; we evaluate the best products available to allow for the most efficient controls on an ongoing basis.

Define, Communicate, and Track Schedules and Costs

It is not good enough to base a schedule on a marketing-department-defined deadline. Instead, schedule and task durations need to be determined based on past historical performance and associated best estimates gathered from all stakeholders. Additionally, any schedule dependencies and critical path elements need to be considered up front and incorporated into the schedule. Project schedules need to be defined, continuously tracked, and communicated.

In order to meet any schedule—for example, if the program is under a tight deadline—only the AST tasks that can be successfully delivered in time are included in the schedule iteration. During AST Phase 1, test requirements are prioritized; see the process description in Chapter 9. This prioritization allows including up front and prioritizing the most critical AST tasks to be completed as opposed to the less critical and lower-priority tasks, which can then be moved to later in the schedule, accordingly. After AST Phase 1, for example, an initial schedule is presented to the customer for approval and not before the SUT AST requirements and associated level of effort are understood.

During the technical interchanges and walk-throughs, schedules are evaluated and presented on an ongoing basis to allow for continuous communication and monitoring. Potential schedule risks should be communicated well in advance and risk mitigation strategies explored and implemented, as needed; any schedule slips should be communicated to the customer immediately and adjustments made accordingly.

By closely tracking schedules and other required AST resources, we can also ensure that a cost tracking and control process is followed. Inspections, walkthroughs, and other status reporting allow for closely monitored cost control and tracking. Tracking costs, schedules, and so forth allows for tracking of the project's performance.

Track Actions, Issues, and Defects

A detailed procedure needs to be defined for tracking action items to completion. Templates should be used that describe all elements to be filled out for action item reports.

Additionally, a procedure needs to be in place that allows for tracking issues, STRs, or defects to closure, known as a defect tracking lifecycle. See Chapter 9 for a sample defect tracking lifecycle used in the open-source defect tracking tool Bugzilla. Various defect tracking lifecycles exist; adapt one to your environment, tool, and project needs. Once defined, put measures in place to verify that the defect or action item lifecycle is adhered to.

If an issue or defect is uncovered, a root cause analysis should be conducted. See Section 8.3 for more on root cause analysis.

8.2   AST Metrics

Metrics can aid in improving your organization's automated testing process and tracking its status. Much has been said and written about the need for using metrics carefully and not letting metrics drive an effort—i.e., don't measure for the sake of measuring. As with our recommended lightweight and adjustable process described in Chapter 9, we recommend using these metrics to enhance the AST effort, not to drive it. Our software test teams have successfully used the metrics and techniques discussed here. As the beginning chapter quote implies, if you can measure something, then you have something you can quantify.

As time proceeds, software projects become more complex because of increased lines of code as a result of added features, bug fixes, etc. Also, tasks must be done in less time and with fewer people. Complexity over time has a tendency to decrease the test coverage and ultimately affect the quality of the product. Other factors involved over time are the overall cost of the product and the time in which to deliver the software. Carefully defined metrics can provide insight into the status of automated testing efforts.

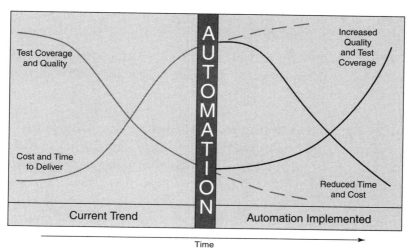

Figure 8-1 AST goal examples comparing current trend with automation implementation

When implemented properly, AST can help reverse the negative trend. As represented in Figure 8-1, automation efforts can provide a larger test coverage area and increase the overall quality of a product. The figure illustrates that the goal of automation is ultimately to reduce the time of testing and the cost of delivery, while increasing test coverage and quality. These benefits are typically realized over multiple test and project release cycles.

Automated testing metrics can aid in making assessments as to whether coverage, progress, and quality goals are being met. Before we discuss how these goals can be accomplished, we want to define metrics, automated testing metrics, and what makes a good automated test metric.

What is a metric? The basic definition of a *metric* is a standard of measurement. It can also be described as a system of related measures that facilitate the quantification of some particular characteristic.[2] For our purposes, a metric can be seen as a measure that can be used to display past and present performance and/or predict future performance.

Metrics categories: Most software testing metrics (including the ones presented here) fall into one of three categories:

- **Coverage:** meaningful parameters for measuring test scope and success.

- **Progress:** parameters that help identify test progress to be matched against success criteria. Progress metrics are collected iteratively over time. They can be used to graph the progress itself (e.g., time to fix defects, time to test, etc.).

- **Quality:** meaningful measures of testing product quality. Usability, performance, scalability, overall customer satisfaction, and defects reported are a few examples.

What are automated testing metrics? Automated testing metrics are metrics used to measure the performance (past, present, and future) of the implemented automated testing process and related efforts and artifacts. Here we can also differentiate metrics related to unit test automation versus integration or system test automation. Automated testing metrics serve to enhance and complement general testing metrics, providing a measure of the AST coverage, progress, and quality, not replace them.

What makes a good automated testing metric? As with any metrics, automated testing metrics should have clearly defined goals for the automation effort. It serves no purpose to measure something for the sake of measuring. To be meaningful, a metric should relate to the performance of the effort.

Prior to defining the automated testing metrics, there are metrics-setting fundamentals you may want to review. Before measuring anything, set goals. What is it you are trying to accomplish? Goals are important; if you do not have them, what is it that you are measuring? It is also important to track and measure on an ongoing basis. Based on the metrics outcome, you can decide whether changes to deadlines, feature lists, process strategies, etc., need to be adjusted accordingly. As a step toward goal setting, questions may need to be asked about the current state of affairs. Decide what questions to ask to determine whether or not you are tracking toward the defined goals. For example:

- How many permutations of the test(s) selected do we run?

- How much time does it take to run all the tests?

- How is test coverage defined? Are we measuring test cases against requirements (generally during system testing), or are we measuring test cases against all possible paths taken through the units and components (generally used for unit testing)? In other words, are we looking at unit testing coverage, code coverage, or requirements coverage?

- How much time does it take to do data analysis? Are we better off automating that analysis? What would be involved in generating the automated analysis?

- How long does it take to build a scenario and required driver?
- How often do we run the test(s) selected?
- How many people do we require to run the test(s) selected?
- How much system and lab time is required to run the test(s) selected?

In essence, a good automated testing metric has the following characteristics:

- It is objective.
- It is measurable.
- It is meaningful.
- Data for it is easily gathered.
- It can help identify areas of test automation improvement.
- It is simple.

A few more words about metrics being simple: Albert Einstein once said, "Make everything as simple as possible, but not simpler." When applying this wisdom to AST and related metrics collection, you will see that

- Simplicity reduces errors.
- Simplicity is more effective.
- Simplicity brings focus.

It is important to generate a metric that calculates the value of automation, especially if this is the first time an automated testing approach has been used for a project. Chapter 3 discusses ROI measurement in detail and provides various worksheets that can serve as a baseline for calculating AST ROI. For example, there we mention that the test team will need to measure the time spent on developing and executing test scripts against the results that the scripts produce. If needed, the test team could justify the number of hours required to develop and execute AST by providing the number of defects found using this automation that would likely not have been revealed during a manual test effort. Specific details as to why the manual effort would not have found the defect can be provided; some possible reasons are that the automated test used additional test data not previously included in the manual effort, or the automated test used additional scenarios and path coverage previously not touched manually. Another way of putting this is that, for example, with manual testing you might have been able to test *x* number of test data combinations; with automated testing you are now able to test *x* + *y* test data combinations. Defects that were uncovered in the set of *y* combinations are the defects that manual testing may have never uncovered. Here you can also show the increase in testing coverage for future software releases.

Another way to quantify or measure automation benefits is to show that a specific automated test could hardly have been accomplished in a manual fashion. For example, say that during stress testing 1,000 virtual users execute a specific functionality and the system crashes. It would be very difficult to discover this problem manually, using 1,000 test engineers or possibly even extrapolation as it is still very commonly used today.

AST can also minimize the test effort, for example, by the use of an automated test tool for data entry or record setup. Consider the test effort associated with the system requirement that reads, "The system shall allow the addition of 10,000 new accounts." Imagine having to manually enter 10,000 accounts into a system in order to test this requirement! An automated test script can easily support this requirement by reading account information from a file through the use of a looping construct, or simply via a batch file. The data file can easily be generated using a data generator. The effort to verify this system requirement using test automation requires far fewer man-hours than performing such a test using manual test methods.[3] The ROI metric that applies in this case measures the time required to manually set up the needed records versus the time required to set up the records using an automated tool.

What follows are additional metrics that can be used to help track progress of the AST program. Here we can differentiate between test case and progress metrics and defect and defect removal metrics.

Percent Automatable or Automation Index

As part of an AST effort, the project is either basing its automation on existing manual test procedures, or starting a new automation effort from scratch, some combination, or even just maintaining an AST effort. Whatever the case, a percent automatable metric or the automation index can be determined.

Percent automatable can be defined as the percentage of a set of given test cases that is automatable. This could be represented by the following equation:

$$PA\,(\%) = \frac{ATC}{TC} = \left(\frac{\textit{Number of test cases automatable}}{\textit{Total number of test cases}} \right)$$

PA = Percent automatable

ATC = Number of test cases automatable

TC = Total number of test cases

When evaluating test cases to be developed, what is to be considered automatable and what is to be considered not automatable? Given enough ingenuity and resources, one can argue that almost anything can be automated. So where do you draw the line? Something that can be considered "not automatable," for example, could be an application area that is still under design, not very stable, and mostly in flux. In cases such as this, you should evaluate whether it make sense to automate. See Chapter 6 for a detailed discussion of how to determine what to automate. There we discussed that we would evaluate, given the set of test cases, which ones would provide the biggest return on investment if automated. **Just because a test is automatable doesn't necessarily mean it should be automated.**

Prioritize your automation effort based on the outcome of this "what to automate" evaluation. Figure 8-2 shows how this metric can be used to summarize,

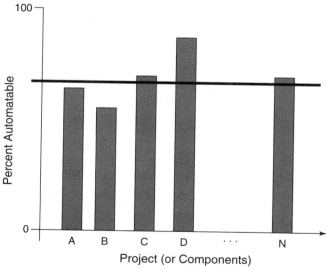

Figure 8-2   Example of percent automatable (automation index) per project (or component)

for example, the percent automatable of various projects or components within a project and to set the automation goal. Once we know the percent automatable, we can use it as a baseline for measuring AST implementation progress.

Automation Progress

Automation progress refers to the number of tests that have been automated as a percentage of all automatable test cases. Basically, how well are you doing against the goal of automated testing? The ultimate goal is to automate 100% of the "automatable" test cases. This can be accomplished in phases, so it is important to set a goal that states the deadlines for when a specific percentage of the ASTs should be automated. It is useful to track this metric during the various stages of automated testing development.

$$AP\,(\%) = \frac{AA}{ATC} = \left(\frac{Number\ of\ test\ cases\ automated}{Number\ of\ test\ cases\ automatable} \right)$$

AP = Automation progress

AA = Number of test cases automated

ATC = Number of test cases automatable

The automation progress metric is a metric typically tracked over time. In the case of Figure 8-3, the time is weeks.

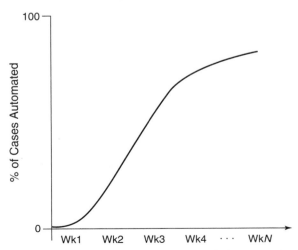

Figure 8-3   Test cases automated over time (weeks)

Test Progress

A common metric closely associated with the progress of automation, yet not exclusive to automation, is *test progress*. Test progress can simply be defined as the number of test cases (manual and automated) executed over time.

$$TC = \frac{TC}{T} = \left(\frac{\textit{Number of test cases executed}}{\textit{Total number of test cases}} \right)$$

TP = Test progress

TC = Number of test cases executed

T = Total number of test cases

The purpose of this metric is to track test progress, and it can be used to show how testing is tracking against the overall project plan.

A more detailed analysis is needed to determine test pass/fail, which can be captured in a more refined metric; i.e., we need to determine not only how many tests have been run over time and how many more there are to be run, but also how many of those test executions actually pass consistently without failure so that the test can actually be considered complete. In the test progress metric we can replace *Number of test cases executed* with *Number of test cases completed*, counting only those test cases that actually consistently pass.

Percent of Automated Test Coverage

Another AST metric we want to consider is *percent of automated test coverage*. This metric determines what percentage of test coverage the automated testing is actually achieving. Various degrees of test coverage can be achieved, depending on the project and defined goals. Also depending on the types of testing performed, unit test automation coverage could be measured against all identified units, or functional system test coverage could be measured against all requirements, and so forth. Together with manual test coverage, this metric measures the completeness of the test coverage and can measure how much automation is being executed relative to the total number of tests. However, it does not say anything about the quality of the automation. For example, 2,000 test cases executing the same or similar data paths may take a lot of time and effort to execute, but they do not equate to a larger percentage of test coverage. Test data techniques discussed in earlier chapters need to be used to effectively derive the number of test data elements required to test the same or similar data path. Percent of automated test coverage does not indicate anything about the effectiveness of the testing taking place; it is a metric that measures its dimension. For a related discussion on code coverage testing, see Appendix B, Section B.5.

$$PTC\,(\%) = \frac{AC}{C} = \left(\frac{Automation\ coverage}{Total\ coverage} \right)$$

PTC = Percent of automated test coverage

AC = Automation coverage

C = Total coverage (i.e., requirements, units/components, or code coverage)

There is a wealth of material available regarding the sizing or coverage of systems. A useful resource is Stephen H. Kan's book *Metrics and Models in Software Quality Engineering.*[4]

Figure 8-4 provides an example of test coverage for Project A versus Project B over various iterations. The dip in coverage for Project A might reveal that new functionality was delivered that hadn't yet been tested, so that no coverage was provided for that area.

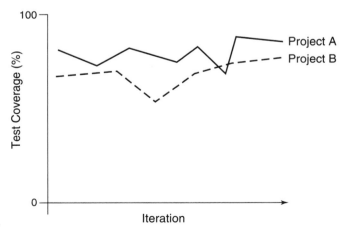

Figure 8-4   Test coverage per project over various iterations

Defect Density

Measuring defects is a discipline to be implemented regardless of whether the testing effort is automated or not. *Defect density* is another well-known metric that can be used for determining an area to automate. If a component requires a lot of retesting because the defect density is very high, it might lend itself to automated testing. Defect density is a measure of the total known defects divided by the size of the software entity being measured. For example, if there is a high defect density in a specific functionality, it is important to conduct a causal analysis. Is this functionality very complex, and therefore is it to be expected that the defect density would be high? Is there a problem with the design or implementation of the functionality? Were the wrong (or not enough) resources assigned to the functionality, because an inaccurate risk had been assigned to it and the complexity was not understood? It also could be inferred that the developer responsible for this specific functionality needs more training.

$$DD = \frac{D}{SS} = \left(\frac{Number\ of\ known\ defects}{Size\ of\ software\ entity} \right)$$

DD = Defect density

D = Number of known defects

SS = Size of software entity

We can't necessary blame a high defect density on large software component size; although the thinking is generally that a high defect density in a large component is more justifiable than in a small component, the small component could be much more complex than the large one. AST complexity is an important consideration when evaluating defect density.

Additionally, when evaluating defect density, the priority of the defect should be considered. For example, one application requirement may have as many as 50 low-priority defects and still pass because the acceptance criteria have been satisfied. Still another requirement may have only one open defect, but that defect prevents the acceptance criteria from being satisfied because it is a high priority. Higher-priority defects are generally weighted more heavily as part of this metric.

Defect Trend Analysis

Another useful testing metric in general is *defect trend analysis.* Defect trend analysis is calculated as

$$DTA = \frac{D}{TPE} = \left(\frac{Number\ of\ known\ defects}{Number\ of\ test\ procedures\ executed} \right)$$

DTA = Defect trend analysis

D = Number of known defects

TPE = Number of test procedures executed over time

Defect trend analysis can help determine the trend of defects found over time. Is the trend improving as the testing phase is winding down, or does the trend remain static or is it worsening? During the AST testing process, we have found defect trend analysis to be one of the more useful metrics to show the health of a project. One approach to showing the trend is to plot the total number of defects over time, as shown in Figure 8-5.[5]

Effective defect tracking analysis can present a clear view of the status of testing throughout the project.

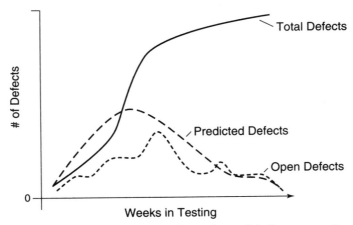

Figure 8-5   Defect trend analysis: total number of defects over time (here after weeks in testing)

Defect Removal Efficiency

One of the more popular metrics is *defect removal efficiency* (DRE); this metric is not specific to automation, but it is very useful when used in conjunction with automation efforts (Figure 8-6). DRE is used to determine the effectiveness of defect removal efforts. It is also an indirect measurement of product quality. The value of the DRE is calculated as a percentage. The higher the percentage, the greater the potential positive impact on the quality of the product. This is because it represents the timely identification and removal of defects at any particular phase.

$$DRE = \frac{DT}{DT + DA} = \left(\frac{\text{Number of defects found during testing}}{\text{Number of defects found during testing} + \text{Number of defects found after delivery}} \right)$$

DRE = Defect removal efficiency

DT = Number of defects found during testing

DA = Number of defects found after delivery

The highest attainable value of DRE is 1, which equates to 100%. In practice, we have found that an efficiency rating of 100% is not likely. According to Capers Jones, world-class organizations have a DRE greater than 95%.[6] DRE should be measured during the different development phases. For example, low

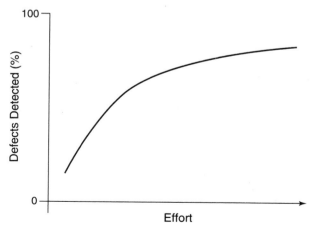

Figure 8-6 Defect removal efficiency over the testing lifecycle effort

DRE during analysis and design may indicate that more time should be spent improving the way formal technical reviews are conducted.

This calculation can be extended for released products as a measure of the number of defects in the product that were not caught during the product development or testing phases.

Automated Software Testing ROI

As we have discussed, metrics help define the progress, health, and quality of an automated testing effort. Without such metrics, it would be practically impossible to quantify, explain with certainty, or demonstrate quality. Along with quality, metrics also help with demonstrating ROI, covered in detail in Chapter 3 of this book. ROI measurement, like most metrics, is an ongoing exercise and needs to be closely maintained. Consider the ROI and the various testing metrics when investigating the quality and value of AST. As shown in Figure 8-7, metrics can assist in presenting the ROI for your effort. Be sure to include all facets in your ROI metric as described in Chapter 3.

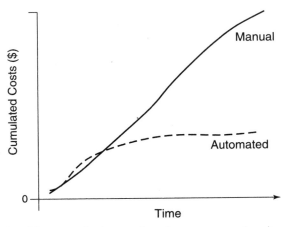

Figure 8-7   AST ROI example (cumulated costs over time)

Other Software Testing Metrics

Along with the metrics mentioned in the previous sections, there are a few more common test metrics useful for the overall testing program. Table 8-1 provides a summary and high-level description of some of these additional useful metrics.

Table 8-1 Additional Common and Useful Software Test Metrics[7]

Metric Name	Description	Category
Error discovery rate	Number of total defects found/Number of test procedures executed The *error discovery rate* is used to analyze and support a rational product release decision.	Progress
Defect aging	The date a defect was opened versus the date the defect was fixed The *defect aging* metric indicates turnaround of the defect.	Progress
Defect fix retest	The date a defect was fixed and released in a new build versus the date the defect was retested The *defect fix retest* metric indicates whether the testing team is retesting the fixes fast enough, in order to get an accurate progress metric.	Progress
Current quality ratio	Number of test procedures successfully executed (without defects) versus the number of test procedures. The *current quality ratio* metric indicates the amount of functionality that has successfully been demonstrated.	Quality
Problem reports by priority	The number of software problem reports broken down by priority The *problem reports* metric counts the number of software problems reported, listed by priority.	Quality

8.3 Root Cause Analysis

It is not good enough to conduct a lessons learned evaluation after the AST program has been implemented. Instead, as soon as a problem is uncovered, regardless of the phase or the type of issue—whether it's a schedule, budget, or software defect problem—a root cause analysis should be conducted, so that corrective actions and adjustments can be made. Root cause analysis should not focus on determining blame; it is a neutral investigation that determines the cause of the problem. For example, a root cause template could be developed where stakeholders can fill in their respective parts if a defect is uncovered in production. The template could list neutral questions, such as, "What is the exact problem and its effect? How was it uncovered and who reported it? When was it reported? Who is/was affected by this problem? What is the priority of the problem?" Once all this information has been gathered, stakeholders need to be involved in the discussion and determination of the root cause, how to resolve the issue (corrective action to be taken) and understand the priority of solving and retesting it, and how to prevent that sort of issue from happening in the future.

Defects will be uncovered despite the best-laid plans and implementations; corrective actions and adjustments are always needed—i.e., expect the unexpected—but have a plan for addressing them. Effective AST processes should allow for and support the implementation of necessary corrective actions. They should allow for strategic course correction, schedule adjustments, and deviation from AST phases to adjust to specific project needs, to support continuous process improvement and an ultimate successful delivery.

Root cause analysis is a popular area that has been researched and written about a great deal. What we present here is our approach to implementing it. For more information on root cause analysis and a sample template, review the Six-Sigma discussion on "Final Solution via Root Cause Analysis (with a Template)."[8]

Summary

To assure AST program success, the AST goals need to be not only defined but also constantly tracked. Defect prevention, AST and other software testing metrics, and root causes analysis implementation are important steps to help prevent, detect, and solve process issues and SUT defects. With the help of these steps the health, quality, and progress of an AST effort can be tracked. These activities can also be used to evaluate past performance, current status, and future trends. Good metrics are objective, measurable, meaningful, and simple, and they have easily obtainable data. Traditional software testing metrics used in software quality engineering can be applied and adapted to AST programs. Some metrics specific to automated testing are

- Percent automatable
- Automation progress
- Percent of automated testing coverage
- Software automation ROI (see Chapter 3 for more details)
- Automated test effectiveness (related to ROI)

Evaluate the metrics outcome and adjust accordingly.

Track budgets, schedules, and all AST program-related activities to ensure that your plans will be implemented successfully. Take advantage of peer reviews and inspections, activities that have been proven useful in defect prevention.

As covered in Chapter 6, in the test case requirements-gathering phase of your automation effort, evaluate whether it makes sense to automate or not. Given the set of automatable test cases, determine which ones would provide the biggest ROI. Consider that just because a test is automatable doesn't necessarily mean it should be automated. Using this strategy for determining what to automate, you are well on your way to AST success.

Notes

1. E. Dustin, "The People Problem," www.stpmag.com/issues/stp-2006-04.pdf; "The Schedule Problem," www.stpmag.com/issues/stp-2006-05.pdf; and "The Processes and Budget Problem," www.stpmag.com/issues/stp-2006-06.pdf.

2. www.thefreedictionary.com/metric.

3. Adapted from Dustin et al., *Automated Software Testing*.

4. Stephen H. Kan, *Metrics and Models in Software Quality Engineering, 2nd ed.* (Addison-Wesley, 2003).

5. Adapted from www.teknologika.com/blog/SoftwareDevelopmentMetricsDefect-Tracking.aspx.

6. C. Jones, keynote address, Fifth International Conference on Software Quality, Austin, TX, 1995.

7. Adapted from Dustin et al., *Automated Software Testing*.

8. www.isixsigma.com/library/content/c050516a.asp.

Chapter 9

Key 5: Implement AST Processes

Lightweight processes and ongoing tracking of them are other keys to success.

Key 1: Know Your Requirements

Key 2: Develop the Automated Test Strategy

Key 3: Test the Automated Software Test Framework (ASTF)

Key 4: Continuously Track Progress—and Adjust Accordingly

Key 5: Implement AST Processes

Key 6: Put the Right People on the Project—Know the Skill Sets Required

Our experience has shown, and the results of the IDT survey described in Chapter 2 also indicate, that many AST efforts fail because of a lack of process.

Implementing a successful AST effort requires a well-defined, structured, but lightweight technical process, using minimal overhead—a process that we describe here. The AST technical process—the automated testing lifecycle methodology (ATLM)—is based on proven system and software engineering processes.[1] It consists of six phases, each requiring that a "virtual" quality gate be passed before the next phase is entered. Many companies throughout the industry have implemented the ATLM as part of their AST processes and have

209

adapted it to their environments. Figure 9-1 provides an example of the IDT-modified ATLM. The "virtual" gates as part of the ATLM help enforce building quality into the entire AST implementation, thus preventing late and expensive rework. (See Figure 9-3.)

   The overall process implementation can be verified via inspections, quality checklists, and other audit activities, each of which has been discussed in detail in Chapter 8.

   The proposed AST technical process needs to be flexible enough to allow for ongoing iterative and incremental improvement feedback loops, including adjustments to specific project needs. For example, if test requirements and test cases already exist for a project, we will evaluate the existing test artifacts for automation. Once it has been determined that the test cases lend themselves to automation (using the criteria described in Chapter 6), we mark them as "to be automated." The goal is to reuse existing components and artifacts whenever possible, modify them as appropriate, and build upon existing artifacts, avoiding duplication of effort and instead fostering reuse.

   AST phases and selected best practices need to be adapted to each task at hand and revisited and reviewed for effectiveness on an ongoing basis. We describe an approach to doing this here.

   The very best standards and processes are not useful if stakeholders don't know about them or don't adhere to them. Therefore, AST processes and pro-

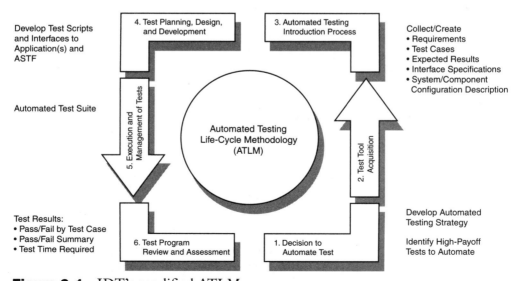

Figure 9-1   IDT's modified ATLM

cedures are documented, communicated, enforced, and tracked. AST process training needs to take place.

Our process spans all phases of the AST lifecycle. For example, in the requirements phase an initial schedule is developed and is then maintained throughout each phase of the AST implementation (e.g., the test progress metric and other metrics as described in Chapter 8 are updated to allow for program status tracking). To help enforce the virtual quality gates, the various review activities described in Chapter 8 are implemented.

It is the goal of this section to provide program management and all other AST program stakeholders a high-level summary of AST technical process practices and recommendations (each of which has been discussed in detail in various chapters throughout the book). The goal here is to ultimately improve the quality of the AST program, increase productivity with respect to schedule and work performed, and aid successful AST efforts, avoiding failures.

9.1 AST Phases and Milestones

Independent of the SUT's specific need, the ATLM or a modified version of it will bring a structured technical process and approach to automated testing and a specific set of phases and milestones to each program. Suggested phases in the IDT-modified ATLM are

- AST Phase 1: requirements gathering—analyze automated testing needs, develop high-level automated test strategies (see Chapters 5 and 6)

- AST Phase 2: test case design and development (see Chapter 5)

- AST Phase 3: automation framework and test script development (see Chapters 6 and 7)

- AST Phase 4: automated test execution and results reporting (see Chapter 8)

- AST Phase 5: program review and assessment (see Chapter 8)

Our proposed overall project approach mirroring the ATLM is summarized in the following sections.

9.2 AST Phase 1: Requirements Gathering—Analyze Automated Testing Needs

Phase 1 generally begins with a kickoff meeting. The purpose of the kickoff meeting is to become familiar with the AUT's background, related testing process, automated testing needs, and schedules. Any additional information regarding the AUT is also collected for further analysis. This phase serves as the baseline for an effective AST program; the test requirements serve as a blueprint for the entire AST effort. Requirements-gathering techniques are described in detail in Chapter 5.

It is desirable for the following information to be available or eventually developed for each AST effort:

- SUT test requirements
- SUT architecture and design documents
- Test cases
- Test procedures
- Expected results
- Test environment requirements
- Interface specifications

In the event that needed information is not available, the automator works with the customer to derive and/or develop it as needed. Various techniques describing how to develop information that's not available have been described in Chapter 5.

Additionally, during this phase AST efforts generally follow this process:

1. Evaluate the AUT's current manual testing process.
   a. Determine areas for testing technique improvement.
   b. Determine areas for automated testing.
   c. Determine the current quality index of the AUT, as applicable.
   d. Collect the initial manual test timelines and duration metrics (to be used as a comparison baseline for one of the many inputs to the AST ROI calculation; see Chapter 3 for details on other inputs to the AST ROI calculation).

    e. Determine the automation index (see Chapter 8 for a definition of the automation index).

2. Analyze the existing AUT test requirements for the automation index (this exercise is further defined in Chapter 6).

    a. If program requirements or test requirements are not documented, the AST effort will need to include documentation of the specific requirements that need to be automated to allow for a requirements traceability matrix (RTM).

    b. Requirements are automated based on various criteria (see Chapter 6 for the detailed test automation criteria checklist), such as

        i. Most critical feature paths
        ii. Most often reused (automating a test requirement that has to be run only once might not be cost-effective)

        iii. Most complex, which is often the most error-prone

        iv. Most data combinations, since testing all permutations and combinations manually is time-consuming and often not feasible

        v. Highest-risk

        vi. Most time-consuming, for example, test performance data output and analysis

3. Evaluate the test automation ROI of the test requirement (further defined in Chapter 3); ideally you can then prioritize test automation implementation based on the largest ROI.

4. Analyze the AUT's current lifecycle tool use and evaluate AST reuse of existing tools (see a discussion of selecting the correct tool in Appendix C); i.e., assess and recommend any additional tool use or in-house development required.

A key technical objective is to demonstrate an increase in testing execution efficiency and eventually a significant reduction in regression test time using AST. Therefore, this phase involves a detailed assessment of the time required to manually execute and validate results. The assessment includes measuring the actual test time required not only for manually developing the tests, but also for setting up the test environment, executing the tests, and validating the results. Depending on the nature of the application and tests, validation of results can often take significantly longer than executing the tests and is often an area for which automation needs to be considered.

Based on understanding the AUT requirements and the automation index, you would then develop a list of requirements for testing tools and products most compatible with the AUT. This important step—acquiring a temporary license and evaluating the tools and products on the AUT—is often overlooked, and tools are simply bought up front without consideration for the application's technology or architecture or even testing needs. The result is less than optimum results in the best case and simply not being able to use the tools in the worst case.

At this time you would also identify and develop additional software as required to support AST. This AST software could provide interfaces and other utilities to support any unique requirements not supported by, for example, an already selected open-source framework or vendor-provided tool, while maximizing the use of those freely available components and commercial off-the-shelf (COTS) testing tools and products.

The final step for this phase is to include procurement requirements and installation of the recommended testing tools and products, along with the additional software utilities' development requirements. The products of this AST Phase 1 typically are the following:

1. Report on test improvement opportunities, as applicable, such as use of more effective testing techniques, use of an isolated test environment, and so forth

2. Automation index to include a report on recommendations for tests to automate (test requirements to be automated)

3. AST test requirements walk-through with stakeholders, resulting in agreement

4. Initial summary of the high-level test automation approach

5. Report on the test tool requirements, initial evaluation, and/or in-house AST development needs and associated recommendations to include software utilities required

6. Summary of the test environment and procurement needs

7. Initial estimated costs, schedules, and timelines

8. Summary of the current manual testing level of effort to be used as a baseline for automated testing ROI measurements

Once the stakeholders agree to the list of test requirements to be automated, the requirements should be entered in the requirements management (RM) tool and/or test management (TM) tool for documentation and tracking purposes.

9.3 AST Phase 2: Test Case Design and Development

Armed with the test requirements to be automated as defined during Phase 1, you can now develop the test case outline in preparation for the automated test case development. Keep in mind that if test cases already exist, they should be analyzed, then mapped as applicable to the automated test requirements so that information can be reused. However, there is rarely a one-to-one translation of manual test cases to automated test cases, as discussed in Chapter 6, "Adapt Manual Procedures to Automation." Generally, as a best practice, before any test can be automated its purpose and outline need to be documented and vetted with the customer (internal or external) or other representative stakeholder to verify their accuracy and that your understanding of the test requirement is correct. This can be accomplished via a test case walk-through, as discussed in Section 7.2.

Deriving effective and correct (i.e., they actually verify the test requirement) test cases is important for AST success; automating inefficient test cases will result in poor AST program performance.

In addition to the test procedures, other documentation, such as the design documentation and interface specifications (sample documentation that can support automation effort is discussed in Chapter 5), should be evaluated in support of AST test case development. Understanding the architecture and design of the SUT will allow you to determine the scenarios and paths the automated test scripts need to take. Phase 2 additionally includes continuation of maintaining the requirements and test cases in the test manager and/or RM tool as applicable, an effort started in Phase 1. The end result is a populated RTM that links requirements to test cases. This central repository provides a mechanism for organizing and tracking test results by test cases and requirements. The test case, related test procedure, test data input, and expected results from each test case are also collected, documented, organized, and verified at this time. The expected results provide the baseline that AST will use to determine the pass or fail status of each test. How to verify test procedures and related expected results has been discussed in Chapter 7 in detail.

The products of AST Phase 2 are typically the following:

1. Documented test cases to be automated, to serve as the AST requirements baseline

2. AST test case walk-through and priority agreement

3. AST test case implementation by phase/priority and timeline

4. Automated and populated RTM

5. Any software trouble reports associated with manual test execution (see Chapter 7)

6. First draft of the AST project strategy document (as described in Chapter 6)

9.4 AST Phase 3: Automated Software Testing Framework (ASTF) and Test Script Development

Chapter 6 describes the detailed considerations that need to go into the AST framework and test script development. This phase needs to allow for the development of new frameworks and scripts, plus analysis and evaluation of existing frameworks and AST artifacts. It is expected that for each subsequent AST implementation, there will be software utilities and test scripts that can be reused from previous tasks.

Our process for developing the AST framework and associated test scripts is essentially the same as the process for developing a software application: A mini development lifecycle is applied, including requirements gathering (Key 1), developing the AST strategy to include the design and architecture and subsequent implementation (Key 2), and testing the AST framework (Key 3). This technical approach to developing test scripts is that AST implementations are based on generally accepted development standards.

The products of AST Phase 3 are typically the following:

1. New or modified automated test framework; new, modified, and/or reusable test scripts (as applicable); and review for technology obsolescence and/or deprecation of automation tool functions

2. Test case automation—newly developed test scripts, based on AST standards

3. High-level walk-through of automated test cases with the customer (this can include a demonstration)

4. Automated test coverage report as part of a finalized AST project strategy and document

5. Updated RTM

9.5 AST Phase 4: Automated Test Execution and Results Reporting

Next, the tests are executed using AST and the framework and related test scripts that were developed. Pass/fail status is captured and recorded using the automated framework, such as in a test manager. Defects are reported, tracked, and measured. A defect tracking lifecycle needs to be in place and adhered to; as mentioned in Chapter 8, define a defect tracking lifecycle that suits your environment. Figure 9-2 provides such a defect tracking lifecycle used within the open-source defect tracking tool Bugzilla, for example.[2] An analysis and comparison of manual and automated test times and results found (pass/fail) is conducted and then summarized in a test presentation report.

Depending on the nature of the application and tests, an analysis that characterizes the range of performance for the application is completed. Coverage and progress metrics are applied, as described in Chapter 8. The quality index (QI) is determined.

The products of AST Phase 4 are typically the following:

1. Test report, including pass/fail status by test case and requirement (including updated RTM)

2. Test execution times (manual and automated), initial ROI reports

3. Test summary presentation

4. IDT-provided AST training, as required

5. Various automation metrics collected, including QI

6. Root cause analysis documentation, as applicable

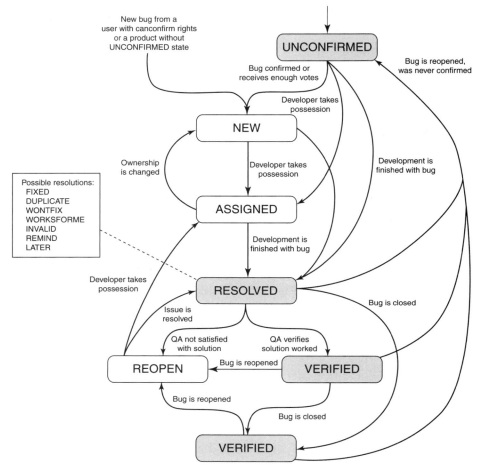

Figure 9-2   Example of Bugzilla's defect tracking lifecycle

9.6   AST Phase 5: Program Review and Assessment

One of the goals of AST implementations is to allow for continued improvements. During this phase the performance of the AST test program is reviewed in order to determine where improvements can be implemented.

Throughout the AST efforts various test metrics are collected, many during the test execution phase. It is not beneficial to wait until the end of the AST effort to document insights gained into how to improve specific procedures;

instead, detailed procedures should be altered during the test program when it becomes apparent that such changes are necessary to improve the efficiency of an ongoing activity.

Another focus of the test program review includes an assessment of whether AST efforts satisfy completion criteria and the AUT automation effort has been completed. The review could also include an evaluation of additional progress measurements and other metrics collected, as required by the program.

The evaluation of the test metrics should examine how well original test program time/sizing measurements compare with the actual number of hours expended and test procedures developed to accomplish the AST effort. The review of test metrics should conclude with improvement recommendations, as needed.

It is just as important to document the activities that AST efforts performed well and were done correctly in order to be able to repeat these successful processes.

Once the project is complete, proposed corrective actions will surely be beneficial to the next project, but the corrective actions applied during the test program can be significant enough to improve the final results of the test program.

AST efforts ideally incorporate a culture of ongoing iterative "lessons learned" activities. This approach encourages AST implementers to take the responsibility to raise corrective action proposals immediately, when such actions potentially have significant impact on the test program performance. It is our experience that it is one of the best practices to promote such leadership behavior in each AST stakeholder.

The product of AST Phase 5 is the final test report. It will include a reference to all test artifacts and outcomes discussed so far.

9.7 Virtual Quality Gates

In our experience the ideal quality assurance process allows for internal controls to ensure the quality and timelines of all services performed as well as products delivered. Additionally, these processes include methods for tracking and controlling costs. A detailed description of this process is provided here, and more details of each practice are described in Chapters 7 and 8.

The ideal quality processes and internal controls in place are repeatable. Repeatability is achieved by documenting and communicating the processes to all stakeholders, while continuously fine-tuning and improving them. The quality process is geared toward producing repeated quality and increased efficiency.

Our experience has shown that internal controls and quality assurance processes verify that each phase has been completed successfully, while keeping the stakeholders involved.

We call these controls "virtual quality gates." Some of the activities of the various phases can run in parallel, but ideally the process is sequential, and successful completion of the activities prescribed by the process should be the only approved gateway to the next phase. Those approval activities or quality gates include technical interchanges, walk-throughs, internal inspections, examination of constraints and associated risks, configuration management, tracked and monitored schedules and costs, corrective actions, and more as Chapter 8 describes. Figure 9-3 reflects typical virtual quality gates that apply to the AST milestones.

We recommend that process controls verify that the output of each stage represented in Figure 9-3 is fit to be used as the input to the next stage. Verification that output is satisfactory may be an iterative process, and it is accomplished by customer review meetings, internal meetings, and comparing the output against defined standards and other project-specific criteria, as applicable. Evaluate and apply the respective review activities described in Chapter 8 to accomplish this goal.

9.8   Process Measurement

The ATLM modified process is checked and measured to ensure that activities are being performed in accordance with defined plans. As a result, the test lead, for example, verifies on an ongoing basis that the process has been properly implemented. Applicable criteria include the following:

- **Performance of the process:** Evaluate process performance. Are any steps missing? Is the process adding too much overhead? Additionally, are the tools and procedures that are in place effective in accomplishing what was intended? Adjust accordingly.

- **Process adherence:** Is project personnel aware of, trained in, or given the tools needed for executing the process? Consistent execution of the process is required. Is the process being executed as defined?

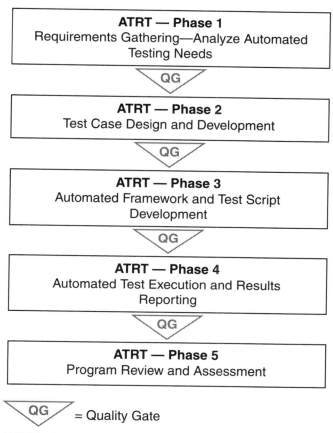

Figure 9-3 ATRT phases, milestones, and virtual quality gates

Summary

AST is software development and requires a mini software development lifecycle that runs in parallel to the actual software development efforts. As with any effective software development lifecycle, effective processes need to be defined, implemented, and adhered to. This chapter provided a summary of the IDT-modified automated testing lifecycle methodology (ATLM); its original version was described in the book *Automated Software Testing*.[3] When implementing AST it is important that a lightweight process be used such as the one described here, which is broken down into five phases with resulting artifacts. While some parts of the phases can run in parallel, virtual quality gates could be in place to assure that the products of one phase are completed satisfactorily and are of high enough quality to feed into the next phase.

Review and evaluation activities such as the ones described in Chapter 8 can be applied as input to measure the completeness of those virtual quality gates.

A process is only as good as the people implementing it and requires continuous review of process performance and adherence.

Appendix A provides a checklist that can be used when implementing this process and for measuring adherence to it.

Notes

1. This process is based on the ATLM described in Dustin et al., *Automated Software Testing*.
2. https://bugzilla.mozilla.org/.
3. Dustin et al., *Automated Software Testing*.

Chapter 10

Key 6: Put the Right People on the Project— Know the Skill Sets Required

An effective AST program requires a mix of skills, expertise, and experience

Key 1: Know Your Requirements

Key 2: Develop the Automated Test Strategy

Key 3: Test the Automated Software Test Framework (ASTF)

Key 4: Continuously Track Progress—and Adjust Accordingly

Key 5: Implement AST Processes

Key 6: Put the Right People on the Project—Know the Skill Sets Required

So far we have covered the whats, what nots, and whys of AST plus five important keys to a successful AST program. We now need people with various skills who clearly understand their roles and responsibilities, and can implement the respective tasks effectively to make this AST program a success. People are at the core of the successful implementation of those keys, and the corollary is true that people are at the core of project anomalies that may lead to failure. Hiring competent and qualified people with the matching skill set is critical to the success of the AST program.

For example, as we have already mentioned, don't believe the vendor hype that anyone can pick up a capture/playback tool and develop AST; development skills are required. It is also not good practice, for example, to design your hiring practices around getting the lowest labor costs, or filling most positions with interns or recent college graduates. You need the most experienced people for the most complex or critical tasks, if only to mentor more junior personnel. There are specific tasks applicable to junior members of a testing team, but making hiring decisions based solely on keeping costs down could be detrimental to the success of the project. Recent research from the Gartner Group and other reliable sources shows that more than 90% of all IT projects will not be completed on time or on budget; unqualified resources surely contribute to that dismal statistic.

For automated testing programs to be implemented successfully, companies need to evaluate and rethink their hiring practices in order to attract and retain the best-qualified people. Requiring professional industry-respected certifications[1] and solid references, removing middlemen, and performing background checks are means of weeding out unqualified candidates.

It is also important to look at the interviewer's skills. Are nontechnical managers interviewing for technical positions? Nontechnical managers can evaluate a candidate's ability to work well with others, attention to detail, and other soft skills, but hardly a candidate's ability to perform detailed technical work. A highly technical resource from the project should have the authority to participate in interviews to be able to scrutinize the candidates' knowledge of design and other technical expertise.

People skills are important. At a previous company, we had a development manager who was unrealistically demanding and only deadline-driven. He wanted to hear only that the date could be made; any attempt to tell him the truth was squelched with a demeaning remark. When the going got tough and the development manager demanded progress, developers stopped telling the truth about the lack of progress. Thus *perceived progress* was born. Empty promises were made. The development manager, for example, promised the automation team that once developers had completed their tasks, they would help out with the automated testing. Since the developers never finished the development effort, this promise couldn't be fulfilled. No team can rely on this type of promised support.

Effective people skills will help avoid the perceived progress phenomenon. It is important to keep the channel of honest communication open. It doesn't make sense to dictate impossible deadlines. A manager needs to derive, monitor, and manage toward realistic deadlines. A manager needs to not only manage up (provide realistic deadlines) but also manage down (keep an honest conversation flow).

As described in Chapter 4, many myths and misperceptions exist about what is required to successfully implement an AST program. When people think of AST, they often think the skill set required is one of a "tester," and that any manual tester can pick up and learn how to use an automated testing tool. Although the skills and talents of someone who implements testing techniques, derives test cases, and has subject matter expertise are still needed to implement AST, a complement of skills similar to the broad range of skill sets needed to develop the software product itself is needed.

In addition, even if only a vendor-provided testing tool is used, to varying degrees the automated test tools require software development skills. Some tools require less expertise than others, but given that the product being tested is software, that the automation tools helping to conduct the testing are software, and that software is being developed to work with automation tools, software development experience and skills are needed. We recommend that proven techniques be used to produce efficient, maintainable, and reusable automated test scripts and software.

The development of a software product includes a project schedule, requirements development, design and implementation of the software, configuration management of the product baseline, and quality assurance participation throughout the project. In this case, the product is AST and happens to be used for testing. In fact, one of the primary reasons automation efforts get in trouble is that they do not treat AST as a software development project.

As we discussed in earlier chapters, a schedule for the AST project should be developed up front and tracked throughout. The requirements to be tested need to be developed and verified. Software needs to be designed and developed, and just as the team developing the product to be tested is expected to use good techniques and practices, the expectation for the AST software team should be the same. The AST software must be robust and testing activities implemented as described in Chapter 7; otherwise it will be of marginal value to the project.

The primary differences between the skill sets needed for AST and those needed for development of the software product are that the AST team also needs an in-depth knowledge of automated test tools, knowledge of the available

ASTFs and approaches to implementing them, and an understanding of the applicability of test techniques and how to implement an AST program (described throughout this book). Appendix C describes a sample of the various automation tools currently available commercially and the vendors that provide them, plus some useful open-source testing tools.

The AST team needs to have the experience and background to not only understand that these types of tools are available, but also to be able to evaluate which ones work best for which types of applications and tests and are compatible with the software product being tested.

When developing the ASTF, associated test scripts, and software, the AST team should be skilled in implementing the various keys described throughout this book, plus the following software development techniques and selected best practices. In Chapter 4 we discussed the need for the software developers to build in testability and determined that AST is software development. The automators will need to follow various software development guidelines and keep in mind selected best practices, such as the ones provided in Chapter 6 and here:

- **Know the types of ASTFs available and understand approaches to implementing an ASTF.**

  Be familiar with the various types of AST frameworks offered, and the approaches one can take to develop such ASTF efforts, using in-house-developed and/or open-source tools such as the ones described in Chapter 6. Understand the difference between keyword-driven and data-driven framework approaches, for example. For the *keyword-driven* approach, keywords that define the common test steps are developed. The framework uses those keywords, independent of the ASTF technology used, to execute the steps and the test script code associated with the keyword actions. *Data-driven* means that the data values are either read in from spreadsheets or tool-provided data pools or external databases, rather than being hard-coded values in the test procedure script. This approach is always preferable; hard-coded values are rarely justifiable. As we mentioned in previous chapters, testing with different data, datasets, and data volume, with realistic depth and breadth, is key to defect detection. Another reason for externalizing the input data is to reduce data maintenance and increase flexibility. Whenever there is a need to rerun a test procedure with a different set of data, the data source can simply be updated or changed as necessary, and the related expected result is also updated. The article "Choosing a Test Automation Framework" at www.ibm.com/developerworks/rational/library/591.html provides a good explanation of the keyword-driven approach.

- **Apply modular ASTF architecture and design.**

  Chapter 6 provides an example of modular ASTF design. Keep all ASTF components separate, and build a "pluggable" framework to allow for ease of maintenance, whether new components need to be added or old ones need to be removed. Also keep in mind that if the ASTF will support various projects, project-independent and project-dependent components can be developed. Evaluate and assess component implementation accordingly.

- **Implement modular script development.**

  For all ASTF and related AST script development efforts, software development best practices need to be applied. For example, a common software development technique used to increase maintainability and readability of source code is to divide the code into logical modules that perform separate pieces of the job. These pieces, or modules, can then be reused from multiple points in a script or the test software so that code does not have to be rewritten each time. This is especially important when a change occurs to one of the modules—the change is limited to only that module, which reduces maintenance costs. Modular script development is a software development best practice that needs to be applied to AST. In general, any sort of software development best practices need to be applied to an AST effort.

- **Implement modular user interface/GUI navigation.**

  An especially important aspect of test scripts and software that should be modularized is navigation of the application's graphical user interface (GUI). In order to achieve higher reusability of the test scripts, a test engineer needs to use a GUI navigation method that is least susceptible to changes in the application's user interface. Navigation functions should be kept in a separate module as part of the test library.

- **Develop libraries of reusable functions.**

  Test scripts and software will typically perform many similar actions when dealing with the same product, or even when dealing with different products of the same type, e.g., Web applications. Factoring these common actions into shared script libraries that are reusable by all test engineers in the organization can greatly enhance the efficiency of the test effort. In addition, functional decomposition will help control changes to test scripts when an application changes, as described previously in the discussion of modular script development.

- **Reuse prebuilt libraries.**

  Prebuilt libraries of functions are available on the Internet for certain testing tools. For example, there are libraries that contain templates for test scripts, extensions of the test script language, and standardized test procedures for GUI testing. Additionally, there are component reuse sites, such as www.koders.com and www.krugle.com. Capitalizing on existing components and fragments and assembling them into custom-built sources of information can be an effective way to developing an ASTF.

- **Apply version control.**

  This might be obvious to some, but version control is a vital part of any software development project. All ASTF code, test script software, and other AST artifacts should be stored in a version control tool to allow for configuration management and ensure that the artifacts are protected from simultaneous changes by multiple test engineers, and that a history of changes to each file is maintained. Without a version control tool, it is all too easy for multiple ASTF and script developers to change the same code, and then be in the position of manually merging their changes, which is an error-prone task. In addition, keeping track of which scripts and test software work with which software builds is much easier when using a version control tool, since sets of scripts can be "labeled" into a single unit that can be retrieved at any time in the future.

- **Automatically generate your ASTF code.**

  Use various input types (such as IDL and C-style header files) to generate ASTF code that then can become the glue/API to your SUT. Appendix D provides an example of how this can be accomplished. The benefits of doing this are various, such as predictable test software that is scalable and portable, where you can fix problems in one place and reuse the same approach across projects. We have found that using this approach cuts down on AST development time per project, which makes automating tests more effective.

- **Automatically generate your test case code.**

  We conducted a market analysis of automated test generation products and found that various tools exist that allow for test generation based upon models, rules checking, algorithms, and test descriptions, but few products are actually built, e.g, Telelogic Rhapsody ATG, Teradyne TestMaster, Conformiq Test Generator, T-VEC. The limitations most often are that the tests have to be generated within the vendor-provided software. Therefore, we decided to develop this capability in-house, taking advantage of open-source tools and applying the following techniques to develop our automatically generated test case code (this is further described in the case study provided in Appendix D):

  - Use a .csv parser to put the test case in standard format, if a test case already exists, but is not standardized.

  - A standardized test case format facilitates automated step procedure extraction.

  - Each step in the test case procedure has associated code generated to execute its behavior.

  - XML is used to define the extracted test step information as input into the autogeneration process.

  - StringTemplates[2] provide for a common code set as well as project-unique sets.

Figure 10-1 includes some of the building blocks and skills needed for a successful AST implementation.

In this chapter we will discuss the types of skills needed to successfully implement AST and some of the keys discussed in the previous chapters, as well as in the introduction here. We'll provide examples of how these skills are used in each of the AST process areas described in Chapter 9. This section will help clarify roles and responsibilities, which is an important activity; people need to know what tasks they are responsible for and what is expected of them. If roles and responsibilities are defined and communicated, performance can be assessed in relation to them.

The roles and responsibilities and associated tasks are organized into the following areas, which our experience shows are key to implementing a successful AST program. Depending on your environment, areas may not always be separated; for example, the CM role may be the responsibility of all involved.

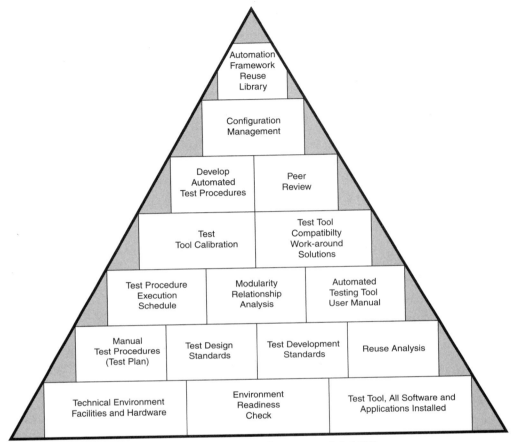

Figure 10-1   Example building blocks of a successful AST program

- Program management
- Systems engineering
- Software development
- Configuration management
- Quality assurance
- Subject matter expertise

One person may have several skills, or one task may be covered by several people; mapping skills to people is not a one-to-one exercise. There are also varying degrees of experience. What is important is that the AST implementation team collectively has all skills covered. But experience also shows that the least experienced person should never be put on the most complex task. This sounds like a simple rule; however, in practice it's not always applied.

Soft Skills

Earlier we mentioned the need for people skills, and while specific technical skills are required to implement an automated testing program successfully (these are described in the next sections), other soft skills are required to enhance the chances for success. We call them "soft" skills because few tests can predict whether a person demonstrates those skills, as opposed to "hard" skills, which are generally determined via a test or quiz.

Here are a few examples of soft skills to consider when recruiting personnel for an automated test program.

Automated testing team members need to be adaptable; that is, experience has shown that automated testing will need to be performed in a variety of different technical environments—on different platforms, using different technologies, and with a variety of subject matter expertise. Therefore, the team members should be able to learn quickly and are ideally already familiar with new technologies, various processes, tools, and methodologies. It is advantageous if the automated test team members possess the following additional skills:

- Be quick learners who enjoy performing a variety of tasks, learning new things, and touching many different products

- Have an aptitude for conceptualizing complex activities

- Understand complex test requirements, be able to formulate test planning and design approaches to support requirements, and be able to perform multiple responsibilities concurrently

- Be able to develop work-around solutions to problems encountered during test development and execution

- Be creative, with the ability to think of a multitude of ways to exercise a system or application to ensure that it works in all circumstances, and to be able to identify all conditions under which the software or system could fail

- Be diplomatic and discrete, especially when having to report major defects, and be able to work closely and effectively with a variety of stakeholders

- Possess strong verbal, written, and grammatical skills, with the ability to communicate any issues and articulate ideas to the customer/stakeholders

- Be detail-oriented, be able to identify difficult-to-find glitches, and have a strong interest in improving the quality of a software product, including being self-motivated and trying to find all defects possible

- Be process-oriented and skilled in the ability to understand inputs, logical sequence of steps, and expected output

Sometimes a project team is inherited. In this case, evaluate the current skill sets of the team and then map the skills back to the projects in the pipeline to ensure that the skills needed are available—before the project starts. Then create a gap analysis of skills needed by the group. You can then create a training plan to acquire these skills or hire for them. It is important to note that a successful automation team consists of a mix of skills and levels of experience and expertise. **It is a mistake to think that software developers alone can implement a successful automated testing program.**

In the next sections we will map the process steps described in Chapter 9 to the respective skills required.

10.1 Program Management

The traditional program management role includes leading the overall project, acting as the customer point of contact, establishing schedule and cost budgets, tracking schedule and cost against budgets, and resolving issues or assessing and mitigating program risks. Key skills include good leadership and communication skills, planning, the ability to identify milestones, including a well rounded technical understanding of the project.

From the specific perspective of implementing AST, these skills are applied throughout the ATLM process described in Chapter 9. Following are the responsibilities of the program manager for each phase of ATLM; the soft skills are not discussed. Skills required can be derived from the assigned tasks, such as general program management experience, AST technical skills, and most importantly people skills. We don't require our program managers to be PMP-certified, for example, as in our experience this specific certification, like so many, is too generic for what we are trying to accomplish in our AST programs; certification is not necessarily a plus, and experience weighs much more than any certification. Program managers should be proficient in Microsoft Project or similar software packages, such as open-source equivalents, for developing reports, presentations, and detailed schedules for the project.

AST Phase 1: Requirements Gathering—Analyze Automated Testing Needs

1. Project kickoff and organization

2. Knowing the processes to be followed and helping enforce them via constant assessment and measurement (as defined in Chapters 7 and 8)—ensuring that an RTM is started and tracked, for example

3. Understanding the AST program lifecycle, testing phases, and schedule for the SUT to be tested and when AST needs to be available

4. Developing the initial proposed schedule, staffing, and budget for AST requirements; knowing the main inputs that need to go into a project schedule, for example, activities, constraints, resources, and historical information (there are many different techniques used to measure and track task durations and cost, such as the earned value metric described in detail in *Automated Software Testing*[3], which covers how to apply this method to the software testing effort); knowing what goes into the budget, such as various items required to implement the AST strategy as defined in Chapter 6, such as procurement of test environment components, tools required, and more

5. Coordinating the collection and review of information needed (i.e., requirements, test cases, test procedures, expected results, and interface specifications) and knowing the tools used to do so

6. Leading the evaluation of the current manual testing level of effort and estimating the ROI of using automation, while understanding all measurements that go into the ROI calculation (as described in Chapter 3)

7. Developing recommendations on specific test requirements to automate, knowing the process to follow to help derive those automatable requirements as described in Chapter 4

AST Phase 2: Test Case Design and Development

1. Providing the updated baseline schedule, staffing, and budget for AST implementation, continuously tracking progress, and making adjustments as needed

2. Coordinating meetings and reviews of requirements and test cases as required with the team developing the software product to be tested

3. Documenting action items and issues to be resolved and tracking them to closure

4. Understanding the types of testing to be performed, i.e., functional, performance, security, concurrency, etc. (examples are provided in Appendix B)

5. Leading the development of the automated testing strategy using selected best practices as described in Chapter 6, and obtaining buy-in from stakeholders

AST Phase 3: Automated Software Testing Framework (ASTF) and Test Script Development

1. Continuously assessing project performance against the baseline schedule, staffing, and budget

2. Coordinating various meetings and reviews of ASTF architecture and design overview, test case techniques, and automation as required with the team developing the software product to be tested

3. Procuring automation software test tools and frameworks as required

4. Understanding the licensing requirements related to open-source use and the customer's expectation

5. Verifying that the ASTF has been tested as described in Chapter 7

6. Ensuring that the isolated test environment and other AST requirements are implemented and ready for test execution

7. Ensuring that test entry criteria have been developed, communicated, and agreed to by stakeholders (entrance and exit criteria are discussed in Chapter 2)

8. Removing all roadblocks to allow for seamless AST execution

AST Phase 4: Automated Test Execution and Results Reporting

1. Continuing assessment of project performance against the baseline schedule, staffing, and budget

2. Working closely with the entire AST team to derive the various effective testing metrics as described in Chapter 8

3. Ensuring that the defect tracking lifecycle defined is implemented and adhered to, and that defect tracking tools are in place to support this effort

4. Coordinating development of the test summary presentation

5. Ensuring root cause analysis is conducted as issues arise, as described in Chapter 8

6. Understanding and communicating the exit criteria, i.e., a defined list of criteria that need to be met so that test execution can be considered complete; for example, a criterion that all high-priority defects need to be fixed on all functionality that is to be developed (for more on exit criteria, see Chapter 2)

AST Phase 5: Program Review and Assessment

1. Coordinating and leading the program review and assessment activities

2. Providing assessment of project performance against the baseline schedule, staffing, and budget

3. Assessing whether the AST implementation meets the automated testing strategy developed at the beginning of the project

4. Leading development of the final report

5. Tracking any defects that actually slipped into production, and conducting root cause analysis, to be sure this information is tracked for historical purposes, to allow for future AST program adjustments, to avoid repeating the same mistake

Once the budgets, schedules, and all activities have been decided upon, they need to be tracked and reviewed continuously.

The program manager should be proficient in using Microsoft Office and Project or similar software packages for developing reports, presentations, and detailed schedules. Ideally, the program manager is also proficient in executing the AST upon completion. Knowledge of the available automation tools is also critical.

10.2   Systems Engineering

Systems engineering roles typically are associated with subject matter expertise regarding the project or system, development and management of requirements from the highest to the lowest level, providing the technical lead for how the system works and why it was designed to work that way, development of the test plan and tests to confirm that the design meets the requirements, and providing the customer with a technical point of contact. Strong communication skills, subject matter expertise, knowledge of how the product or system is used, the ability to develop and document requirements, and the ability to design tests to validate requirements are all important skills for a systems engineer.

For each phase of ATLM, systems engineering skills are needed. Key responsibilities are identified here.

AST Phase 1: Requirements Gathering—Analyze Automated Testing Needs

1. Developing a strong understanding of the requirements of the software product to be tested by reviewing the requirements documentation, functional description, and interaction with product development team

2. Verifying that SUT requirements are correct and testable

3. Understanding the SUT's architecture and design, which will serve as a baseline for effective test path development

4. Understanding various testing techniques, such as boundary value, equivalence partitioning, risk-based testing, orthogonal classification, and other effective testing techniques (referred to throughout this book)

5. Reviewing and understanding the test cases and test procedures currently used to manually test the software product, if they exist, including what the tests do, the traceability to requirements, the system configuration used for testing, and any special equipment used

6. Analyzing expected results for the test cases and test procedures provided, including the magnitude of results to be evaluated (i.e., are there 10 records, 1,000 records, or 1,000,000 records to be evaluated?), the type of evaluation or comparison that is required to determine if results are correct, and how deterministic the expected results are

7. Reviewing and understanding the GUI interfaces and internal system interfaces (APIs, etc.) to the software product to be tested, including the protocol required, the size and timing requirements, and any special equipment needed for these interfaces

8. Supporting the evaluation of the current manual testing level of effort and estimating the ROI of using automation

9. Supporting the development of recommendations for which test requirements to automate

10. Identifying isolated test environment requirements and needs

11. Identifying various test configuration requirements; examples are provided in Chapter 7

AST Phase 2: Test Case Design and Development

1. Reviewing specific test cases associated with the test requirements to be automated

2. Providing analysis of the test requirements to be automated for which there are currently no manual test cases

3. Leading the effort to prioritize the test cases to be automated

4. Designing and documenting test cases as required (i.e., test requirements to be automated for which there are no documented test cases available)

5. Validating that test cases produce the expected results

6. Completing the RTM

7. Supporting development of the automated testing strategy

8. Defining the types of testing to be performed, i.e., functional, performance, security, concurrency, etc. (examples are provided in Appendix B).

AST Phase 3: Automated Software Testing Framework (ASTF) and Test Script Development

1. Participating in reviews of the ASTF software design and related automated test cases

2. Participating in reviews of any software developed to support the automation framework and test cases developed

3. Developing an approach and plan for testing the automated test cases

4. Leading the testing of automated test cases

5. Updating the RTM as required

AST Phase 4: Automated Test Execution and Results Reporting

1. Leading the automated test execution

2. Collecting, organizing, and reporting test results (such as pass/fail status)

3. Collecting, organizing, and reporting test execution times in support of the ROI comparison of manual to automated testing

4. Leading the development of training materials needed to implement AST

5. Leading the development of the test summary presentation

6. Supporting any root cause analysis as issues arise

AST Phase 5: Program Review and Assessment

1. Supporting the program review

2. Providing assessment of test metrics, in particular in comparison to manual testing

3. Supporting development of the final report

4. Providing process improvement recommendations

5. Supporting any root cause analysis if defects are uncovered in production, documenting them for historical purposes and to allow for a feedback loop into upcoming projects

Systems engineers should be proficient in the use of any RM tools used on the project such as DOORS, RequisitePro, or Focal Point, to name just a few. Some projects also use Microsoft Excel to organize and manage requirements. It is also critical for the systems engineers to be able to use any tools or products for documenting the test case outlines that feed into the ASTF. They need to know how the ASTF works and should also be familiar with the scripting and development languages used on the project. These could range from C++, to Perl or Java, to Python, and .NET—just a small sample of the possibilities. Expertise in the use of the available automated tools is also essential for the systems engineers so that they can provide recommendations for what tests can be automated and a technical approach for implementing the automation. They need to be able to test the ASTF.

10.3 Software Development

Software development responsibilities include the design and development of the ASTF and associated test software, as well as subject matter expertise regarding the processes, languages, and tools used during AST development. Critical skills include strong communication skills, the ability to understand requirements and then design software based on the requirements, software programming skills, and knowledge of the software development lifecycle processes.

These are the key software development responsibilities in each phase of ATLM:

AST Phase 1: Requirements Gathering—Analyze Automated Testing Needs

1. Reviewing and understanding the software architecture of the SUT to be tested

2. Identifying the operating systems and programming languages used by/within the software product to be tested

3. Identifying any software test tools already in use during manual testing and evaluating reuse for AST efforts

4. Reviewing and understanding the types of test cases and test procedures currently used to manually test the software product

5. Reviewing the types of expected results to be evaluated and the magnitude of the expected results for the test cases and test procedures provided

6. Reviewing and understanding the software interfaces (internal and external) to the software product to be tested, including the protocol required, details of the information format and content, any size and timing requirements, as well as whether special equipment or software is needed for these interfaces

7. Supporting the evaluation of the current manual testing level of effort and estimating the ROI of using automation

8. Developing an initial recommendation for ASTF design and development and related automated testing tools to be used and identifying any additional software that may have to be developed

9. Supporting the development of recommendations as to which test requirements to automate

AST Phase 2: Test Case Design and Development

1. Reviewing the completed RTM and developing a strategy for automating maintenance of it

2. Developing a detailed understanding of how the manual tests are conducted through participation in the process of validating that the test cases produce the expected results, and evaluating whether they can be reused for automation

3. Supporting the development of the automated testing strategy

AST Phase 3: Automated Software Testing Framework (ASTF) and Test Script Development

1. Designing and developing the software or software modifications to implement the ASTF; software skills and experience need to be consistent with the languages and operating system used by the project

2. Leading reviews of any software developed to support the automation framework

3. Designing and developing the software test scripts

4. Leading reviews of the software test scripts

5. Participating in the testing of ASTF and test case automation; incorporating fixes as needed

6. If updated, reviewing the automated RTM

7. Knowing the types of testing to be performed, i.e., functional, performance, security, concurrency, etc. (examples are provided in Appendix B)

AST Phase 4: Automated Test Execution and Results Reporting

1. Supporting automated test execution as required

2. Supporting the development of training materials needed to implement AST

3. Supporting the development of the test summary presentation

4. Supporting any root cause analysis as issues arise

AST Phase 5: Program Review and Assessment

1. Supporting the program review

2. Reviewing the assessment of test metrics, in particular in comparison to manual testing

3. Supporting the development of the final report

4. Providing process improvement recommendations

5. Supporting any root cause analysis if defects are uncovered in production, documenting them for historical purposes and to allow for a feedback loop into upcoming projects

The AST implementation needs at a minimum to be able to interface with the languages and operating systems used for the product to be tested, so it is very helpful for the software developers to be experienced with those same programming languages and operating systems. The software developers also need to be proficient in the scripting languages and development languages used on the project. Finally, they need to be experts in the use of the automation tools and automation frameworks or development of those that support the types of testing to be implemented.

10.4 Configuration Management

The configuration management (CM) role includes management of all aspects of the product baseline, including version control, product release, and problem reports. Necessary skills include strong communication skills, subject matter expertise in the technical skills to support version control and product release, including programming, and proficiency with CM tools, problem reporting tools, and the software development lifecycle process.

CM doesn't necessarily need to be a separate activity from the rest of the roles described so far, and actually each role described so far—program management, systems engineering, and software development—is responsible for CM of their specific tasks and activities. However, in some organizations the CM role is separate.

From the specific perspective of implementing AST, the primary CM responsibilities during each phase of ATLM are the following:

AST Phase 1: Requirements Gathering—Analyze Automated Testing Needs

1. Developing the configuration management plan for AST implementation for the project

2. Bringing under configuration control all documentation and artifacts provided for the software product to be tested (reviewed during this phase by the AST team)

3. Understanding the AST processes, software product lifecycle, and CM system used, and helping to enforce their implementation

4. Developing the initial plan for how AST implementation should be delivered

5. Supporting the evaluation of the current manual testing level of effort and estimating the ROI of using automation

6. Supporting the development of recommendations for which test requirements to automate

AST Phase 2: Test Case Design and Development

1. Coordinating the review of any software trouble reports associated with manually executing tests so they can feed into the "what to automate" evaluation activities

2. Bringing the RTM and test cases to be automated under configuration control

3. Supporting the development of the automated testing strategy

4. Assuring all AST artifacts are maintained under CM control.

AST Phase 3: Automated Software Testing Framework (ASTF) and Test Script Development

1. Bringing any automated software tools purchased under configuration control

2. Bringing the ASTF and other software developed for framework and test scripts under configuration control

3. Bringing test plans for testing automation and test results under configuration control

4. Building and maintaining the automated software test baseline from CM

AST Phase 4: Automated Test Execution and Results Reporting

1. Bringing test reports under configuration control

2. Bringing training materials under configuration control

3. Bringing the test summary presentation under configuration control

AST Phase 5: Program Review and Assessment

1. Supporting the program review

2. Bringing the final report under configuration control

3. Providing process improvement recommendations

In addition to being familiar with the CM tools used on the project, the configuration manager should be familiar with the scripting languages and development languages used on the project. Some expertise in the use of the available automated tools is also necessary for the configuration manager to be able to develop CM procedures and build scripts. For more information on CM and CM tools, see Appendix C, Section C.3, Configuration Management.

10.5   Quality Assurance

Quality assurance provides independent verification and validation that the planned processes are being followed and ongoing evaluation of product quality. Skills that are needed include strong communication skills, subject matter expertise in quality assurance methodologies, understanding of the system requirements and functionality to be able to assess performance, proficiency in the software programming languages being used on the project, CM and QA tools, STR reporting tools, and the software development lifecycle process.

Here is a summary for each phase of ATLM of key quality assurance responsibilities:

AST Phase 1: Requirements Gathering—Analyze Automated Testing Needs

1. Identifying and understanding the current metrics used to assess software product quality

2. Reviewing current test reports and documenting how test results from AST are to be reported

3. Supporting the evaluation of the current manual testing level of effort and estimating the ROI of using automation, as defined in Chapter 6

4. Supporting the development of recommendations for which test requirements to automate

AST Phase 2: Test Case Design and Development

1. Participating in the requirements and test case reviews

2. Analyzing software trouble reports associated with manually executing tests and associated test reports

3. Reviewing the test summary report from manual test execution, if it exists

4. Supporting development of the automated testing strategy

AST Phase 3: Automated Software Testing Framework (ASTF) and Test Script Development

1. Participating in software design and development reviews

2. Assessing and developing the various test data inputs required

3. Helping determine the various test data scenarios that need to be run to allow for best test coverage

4. Understanding test data derivation techniques, such as orthogonal array testing

5. Understanding test case development techniques, such as boundary analysis, equivalence partitioning, risk-based testing, etc.

6. Support the testing of the ASTF and related artifacts

AST Phase 4: Automated Test Execution and Results Reporting

1. Reviewing test reports and the ROI analysis

2. Reviewing training materials

3. Verify AST process adherence

AST Phase 5: Program Review and Assessment

1. Supporting the program review

2. Reviewing the assessment of test metrics, in particular in comparison to manual testing

3. Providing process improvement recommendations

QA engineers should be familiar with the software programming languages being used on the project. In addition, they should be highly proficient in QA tools and problem reporting tools. Familiarity with the automated test tools being used is also needed in order to support analysis for which the engineers are responsible.

10.6   Subject Matter Experts (SMEs)

At some point the AST team can acquire the introductory skills of an SME, but at times the SUT's subject matter and related business logic can be very complex, and a few weeks spent becoming familiar with it will not replace an SME's knowledge. It is therefore important to note that the SME plays an important role when automating any somewhat complex SUT.

Training

Once the roles and responsibilities and related tasks have been defined, it is important that they be communicated so that everybody involved understands who is responsible for what. AST program implementation is a team effort, and at times a person can have multiple roles and be responsible for a variety of tasks. It is important that team members work toward a common goal, and that it is clear that all are held accountable for the success of the AST program, without anyone person being held responsible for its success or failure.

Task overview meetings and discussions of roles and responsibilities need to take place. Training sessions should be held to allow for cross-training to make people most effective. A process isn't valuable unless it has been documented, is communicated, and training has been provided. The same is true of a tool or automation framework: It can end up on a shelf if the tester is not trained on how to use or maintain it. AST training efforts can include test tool or automated script training. For example, the AST implementation personnel and other stakeholders need to view test automation activities within the scope of a separate development effort complete with strategy and goal planning, test requirement definition, analysis, design, and coding. This way they can learn to appreciate the fact that effective automated test development requires careful design and planning just like any other software application development effort.

The outcome of this training is that all stakeholders understand the AST phases and milestones and the processes, roles and responsibilities, and tasks associated with them. All stakeholders will know how to use the AST-recommended tool suite and will be familiar with the AST program and its implementation; for example, they would know how to run the ASTF and automated testing scripts, so if needed they could demonstrate or maintain the automated tool suite.

Only when roles and responsibilities have been communicated and tasks are understood can personnel's performance be evaluated against them.

Summary

As we have described in this chapter, the AST team needs to comprise diverse skill sets, including software development and knowledge of automated testing methodologies and tools. We have reviewed the skills required based on the roles and responsibilities and associated tasks required, by major discipline and in the context of the ATLM. The AST team members are not expected to neatly and precisely fit into a specific discipline area; sometimes people have to wear many hats to get the job done, but it is important that all the needed skills be present on the team. The list below could be used as a defined set of roles and responsibilities for each team member and serve as a top-level assessment of the skill sets of the AST team in order to assess against and identify technical strengths and weaknesses. We encourage you to consider additional tasks that will need to be completed for your specific AST project. If there are tasks listed for which no one on the AST team currently has the requisite skills, either someone with those skills should be added to the team, or additional training should be provided for someone on the team to develop the skills.

- Analyzing system requirements for testability
- Deriving test requirements and test strategy
- Determining the SUT automation index
- Evaluating ASTFs and automated test tools
- Verifying automated test tool compatibility with the AUT
- Finding work-around solutions to test tool incompatibility problems
- Planning for test tool introduction on a project
- Planning AST activities
- Identifying the kinds of tests to be performed (see Appendix B for examples) using effective testing techniques
- Planning, tracking, and managing test environment setup activities
- Developing ASTF architecture and design and related automated test designs
- Knowing best development practices to follow
- Developing test data and refreshing the test database during test execution
- Performing test readiness reviews

- Documenting, tracking, and obtaining closure on trouble reports
- Performing test activities within the same technical environment planned for the project
- Checking software into/out of the CM tool

Notes

1. Few testing certificates are well respected in the industry. Instead focus on some of the more accepted and respected Microsoft certifications or security certifications, as applicable.
2. www.stringtemplate.org/.
3. Dustin et al., *Automated Software Testing*, Section 9.3.1, "Earned Value Management System."

Appendices

Appendix A

Process Checklist

To help enforce the AST technical process and associated quality gates throughout AST implementations, we have developed a high-level quality checklist for each phase of AST. The AST phases were described in detail in Chapter 9 and consist of the following:

- AST Phase 1: Requirements Gathering—Analyze Automated Testing Needs, Develop High-Level Automated Test Strategies
- AST Phase 2: Test Case Design and Development
- AST Phase 3: Automated Software Testing Framework (ASTF) and Test Script Development
- AST Phase 4: Automated Test Execution and Results Reporting
- AST Phase 5: Program Review and Assessment

This quality/testing checklist can serve as a baseline of sample (not comprehensive) process steps for a process gap analysis but is not to serve as a rigid guide for process steps you must stick to; instead, evaluate your process needs, and choose from applicable process steps as shown in the following sections, as they are deemed applicable to your environment.

A.1   AST Phase 1: Requirements Gathering— Analyze Automated Testing Needs

Checklist

✓ The kickoff meeting and SUT overview have taken place.

✓ Current SUT testing processes have been evaluated to determine improvement opportunities.

✓ SUT requirements are testable and automatable.

✓ An assessment of what can be automated has taken place.

✓ ASTF requirements have been communicated via technical interchange meetings and clear processes.

✓ Manual test timelines and duration metrics have been collected (to be used as a comparison baseline for AST ROI).

✓ SUT's current lifecycle tool use and AST reuse of existing tools have been analyzed.

✓ The need for additional AST and testing support tools has been assessed and recommendations made for this effort.

✓ Stakeholders have been identified.

✓ The test environment has been defined and discussed, including procuring or scheduling the test environment

✓ Test types and related requirements, such as functional, security, concurrency, performance, and soak testing, have been defined and communicated.

✓ AST program entrance and exit criteria have been developed.

Products

1. Report on test improvement opportunities, as applicable

2. AST test requirements walk-through with stakeholders, resulting in agreement

3. Report on recommendations for tests to automate (test requirements to be automated)

4. Initial summary of the high-level test automation approach

5. Report on the test tool or in-house development needs and associated recommendations

6. Identification of open-source and/or freeware components

7. AST software utilities

8. Initial test data requirements

9. AST configuration for the application

10. Summary of the test environment

11. Initial timelines

12. Test types and related requirements

13. Summary of the current manual testing level of effort to be used as a baseline for automated testing ROI measurements

14. First draft of "Automated Software Testing Project Strategy," which includes a summary of some of the products listed here

15. AST program entrance and exit criteria

A.2   AST Phase 2: Test Case Design and Development

Checklist

✓ The task at hand is understood and has been communicated along with the related test automation goal (i.e., the SUT architecture and underlying components and related technical issues are understood).

✓ The risks have been considered and risk mitigation strategies are in place.

✓ Manual test cases and procedures, if they exist, have been evaluated for reuse or automated test conversion.

✓ ASTF architecture and design have been defined.

✓ Automated test cases as part of the ASTF have been developed using various effective testing techniques.

✓ Test data has been defined and developed or acquired.

✓ Test requirements and related test cases and other AST artifacts have been linked for RTM tracking.

✓ The AST test case/procedure walk-through has taken place and an agreement on priority has been reached.

Products

1. Documented high-level test cases to be automated, along with detailed test steps
2. Test case walk-through and priority agreement
3. Test case implementation by phase/priority and timeline
4. ASTF architecture and design walk-throughs
5. Populated RTM
6. Any software trouble reports associated with manual test execution to feed into the AST effort
7. Updated timelines—finalized schedule
8. Second draft of "Automated Software Testing Project Strategy" document.

A.3 AST Phase 3: Automated Software Testing Framework (ASTF) and Test Script Development

Checklist

✓ The existing automation framework and test scripts have been analyzed for reuse, and reusable items have been identified to determine implementation delta.

✓ The automation framework has been modified as required, and new scripts have been developed to meet test case requirements.

✓ Schedule and performance are being tracked.

✓ ASTF has been tested.

Test Environment

• The test data being used has been verified to be effective; i.e., the depth and breadth of the test data have been considered.

- The datasets for touching various business rules or access permissions are correct.

- The specific configuration of the test environment has been determined and lead times for ordering hardware have been considered.

- The test environment mirrors the production environment for performance testing activities, for example, or it has been determined that using a virtual environment (such as VMWare) to conduct initial functional testing is effective. Acceptable extrapolation methods have been considered.

- Access and security permissions are correct such that software can be installed and test automation software can be executed, along with application software and application components such as .NET or XML.

- Test configurations are defined.

Products

1. Implemented and/or modified ASTF
2. Test case automation—newly developed test scripts
3. High-level walk-through of automated test cases with customer
4. Walk-through of test environment configuration
5. Automated test coverage report
6. Updated RTM
7. Test configurations

A.4   AST Phase 4: Automated Test Execution and Results Reporting

Checklist

- ✓ Entrance and exit criteria are understood and are being followed.
- ✓ The test environment has been isolated from the development environment.

✓ The automation framework and test scripts have been executed.

✓ The pass/fail status of each test run has been recorded.

✓ Software trouble reports are produced, the defect tracking lifecycle is being adhered to, and defects are tracked to closure, as applicable.

✓ Manual versus automated testing times have been compared to start building the ROI.

✓ Performance and schedule are being tracked.

Products

1. Test report including pass/fail status by test case and requirement (including updated RTM)

2. Test execution times (manual and automated), initial ROI reports

3. Test summary presentation

4. AST training, as required, including an ASTF user's guide, as applicable

A.5 AST Phase 5: Program Review and Assessment

Checklist

✓ AST efforts have satisfied exit criteria.

✓ The AUT automation effort has been completed.

✓ Lessons learned have been documented.

✓ Any root cause analysis has taken place and appropriate actions have been taken.

Products

1. Final AST program report that includes all relevant artifacts discussed so far, such as status metrics, various testing outcomes, root cause analysis, and so forth.

Appendix B

AST Applied to Various Testing Types

Based on our definition provided in Chapter 1, AST can be applied throughout the software testing lifecycle. Our experience has shown that AST provides important benefits, like repeatability, in addition to lower-level, bottom-up testing in the case of unit testing, for example, or static or dynamic code analysis in the case of security testing. In this appendix we discuss some of the major testing types that lend themselves to automation. All of the ones described here, with the exception of unit testing (which is generally done by development) and test coverage (which is a measure of test completeness and effectiveness), are considered tests of nonfunctional requirements (NFRs), because they don't test the system's functional requirements specifically, but rather the associated quality attributes, such as performance, security, concurrency, soak testing, and so forth. This appendix is not meant to serve as an exhaustive list of testing types, but as a sample set. We provide references and tools for each type, so you can conduct research and drill into each topic further, as needed.

B.1 Security Testing

Security is considered an NFR, and security testing is the process for ensuring that vulnerabilities do not exist in an application. Automating this testing, through source code analysis, for example, provides the following major payoffs:

257

- Reduction in the overall security test effort, i.e., reducing the need for manual and labor-intensive code walk-through
- Minimization of missed vulnerabilities

A *vulnerability* is a weakness in the software that allows the application's, and maybe the system's, integrity to be compromised by an attack. Some examples of vulnerabilities are buffer overflow and SQL injection. All types of vulnerability testing are best accomplished via model checking or with static and dynamic analysis tools or fuzzers or penetration tools, i.e., via test automation. Examples of static and dynamic tools and a description of fuzzers and penetration tools are provided in Appendix C.

A *buffer overflow* condition is one in which an application attempts to store data beyond the bounds of the destination buffer. The overwritten data could contain alternative data or even alternative program flow control data. This could lead to corrupted data, application crash, or even execution of malicious code that could affect the system.

The code in Figure B-1 represents an application that could be exploited via a buffer overflow. If the process is executed with a well-formatted IPv4 address (like "192.168.0.100") passed in on the command line, then the application would simply execute through the normal path in the code. If the IPv6 address were something like "3ffe::1900:4545:3:200:f8ff:fe21:67cf," then the application would crash from a segmentation violation due to the return address on the call stack being overwritten by the `strcpy` call on line 3.

```
1: void f(char *ip){
2:        char buf[15];
3:        strcpy(buf,ip);
4:        printf("ip: %s\n",buf);
5: }
6:
7: void main(int argc,char** argv){
8:        char string[128];
9:        f(argv[1]);
10:}
```

Figure B-1   Example of code that can be exploited via buffer overflow

The *SQL injection vulnerability,* as the name suggests, affects an application at its database layer. This exploit takes place when user input/data is not validated. This vulnerability is prevalent in Web-based applications. The resulting effect could be anything from a deletion of a database table to a modification of critical data. The validation mechanism generally takes on a few forms, like filtering escape characters. If the user input is not checked for escape characters (such as " ' "), then the SQL statement could be manipulated by an attacker.

```
'"SELECT * FROM users WHERE usr = '" + usr + "'and passwd = '" +
passwd + "'";
```

Figure B-2   Example SQL query

Take the example SQL query in Figure B-2 that would be used in a login for some Web site. This query could be used to authenticate a user's access to some secured site. A malicious attack could be launched by a user passing in the values for the usr and passwd variables, respectively, shown in Figure B-3.

```
marcus' OR 'x' = 'x
none' OR 'x' = 'x
```

Figure B-3   Values for usr and passwd variables

The resulting SQL statement would look like Figure B-4.

```
"SELECT * FROM users WHERE usr = 'marcus' OR 'x' = 'x' and
passwd = 'none' OR 'x' = 'x'";
```

Figure B-4   SQL injection outcome

Because of the injection of the OR statements in the conditionals, the query would return a row every time. This is a simplified example, but a more complex statement could be built to execute other database commands like insertions or deletions.

Scrubbing software manually for security vulnerabilities is cumbersome and prone to error. A manual effort would require a line-by-line inspection of the entire application. The effort involved in this analysis is a function of the size of the application and could also be affected by the criticality of the system's integrity. For many SUTs, such as in a bank account system, for example, security testing needs to be rigorous. A Web site for such a system needs to be 100% secure to protect the bank customers' account information. There is a resource hit involved in reviewing source code line by line, and a margin of error associated with the human error factor; and the review team needs to be well versed in all types of security vulnerabilities and some of the common source code holes. If no one on the review team is familiar with SQL injections and what things to look for, then holes in the source code would go unnoticed prior to deployment. The team needs to understand how to apply static and dynamic analysis tools. For a detailed discussion of security testing and various tools available, see the section on security testing tools in Appendix C, the section on tools at www.softwaresecuritytesting.com/ for a few examples, and the book *The Art of Software Security Testing* for many more details and types of vulnerabilities.[1]

Code analysis tools such as PREFast, Fortify, or PCLint (which was demonstrated in Chapter 7) allow for verifying secure coding practices and pinpointing any security holes.

This book focuses on automated *software* testing, but during the security testing phase other areas need to be tested for security, such as the test environment's networks; a *port-scanning tool,* for example, allows the user to scan a host or range of hosts to determine whether the hosts are exposing services (server processes) on some of them or all ports. Because some of these services contain known security problems, a port scanner allows an outside user to determine whether a potential entry point on a server may be used to gain access to the system. Several port-scanning tools are available as shareware or as freeware; it is best to use a few different port scanners, as each offers different feature sets. Another useful tool is a network monitor, or *sniffer,* which is a tool that supports the detailed examination of packets being transmitted across a network. There are also *security concerns for operating system configuration* to be researched, but not covered in detail here, such as

- Unnecessary user accounts
- File and directory permissions, especially critical configuration files

- Networked disk volumes, such as Network File System (NFS) or Windows shared directories
- Log files
- Registry on Windows NT/2000 machines
- Unnecessary background processes
- Password policy

For a summary of an example secure software development lifecycle to apply, see www.devsource.com/c/a/Techniques/The-Secure-Software-Development-Lifecycle/.

B.2   Soak Testing

Soak testing involves significantly loading a system for an extended period of time and assessing its behavior under an increasing load. (Soak testing is also referred to as load testing.) Soak testing is also considered an NFR, and automating this testing provides the following major payoffs:

- Ease of creating the necessary system load
- Data collection
- Data reduction for large data results sets
- Data analysis

Significantly loading a system means submitting it to an amount of stimuli above its expected normal amount. See www.perftestplus.com for a great resource for anything related to soak or performance testing (performance testing is also discussed in this appendix). An example of soak testing would be to simulate twice the number of ATM transactions that a bank account database software is expected to handle on average. The key to this type of testing is not only the increased load but the length of the test period. A true test of a system's stability needs to include a longevity run at some point in the lifecycle prior to deployment. The longer the run, the more likely problems will be seen that would not normally be uncovered in shorter runs. This includes things like memory leaks, race conditions, or compromised data integrity. In the bank accounts example, the possibility of detecting an error in the system that could lead to an account's data being corrupted more than supports the importance of this type of testing.

Manually creating a significant load, as described above, would require a tremendous amount of resources, for example (continuing with the bank account software example), having to manually simulate thousands of ATM transactions, say, by using some form-driven interface. Even if that were feasible within the scope of a project's resource pool, extending the manual simulation for the necessary length of time would possibly test its limits, but it would also increase the probability of human input error, which could cause nonrepeatable error conditions.

Data collection and analysis is another integral piece in a test like this. When an error condition is reached, it is often necessary to have some level of data collected, such as log files, to analyze. Depending on the length of time between the start of the test and the time of error, these collection files could become large enough to perturb any manual analysis effort. Automation could solve the issues. Inputs would be predictable, increasing repeatability. Tests could be run unmanned for a majority of the execution time. Even data analysis could be streamlined to any desired degree, such as scanning for error outputs or reducing the data to enable filtering.

Various tools are available that can support this type of load or soak testing; see the performance testing section for available tools. Generally, tools that can be used for performance testing can often be used for load or soak testing. One of the most popular performance testing tools is HP/Mercury's Loadrunner. However, there are also open-source performance testing tools available; refer to http://opensourcetesting.org for additional information.

As part of soak testing, you also want to consider the use of memory leak detection tools, in case that feature is not built into your performance testing tool. Tools in the memory leak detection category are used for a specific purpose: to verify that an application is properly using its memory resources and not failing to release memory allocated to it, among other things, such as runtime error detection. Since memory issues can be the reason for many program defects, including performance issues, it is worthwhile to test an application's memory usage frequently. Some of the tools on the market that allow for memory leak detection are AutomatedQA's AQtime, IBM's Rational Purify, and Compuware's BoundsChecker.

B.3 Concurrency Testing

Concurrency testing is considered another NFR and is conducted in order to determine any resource issues, when the SUT's resources are accessed concurrently. Automating this testing provides the following major payoffs:

- Simulating a concurrent run to determine any resource issues
- Allowing for extended runtime to overcome the inability to inject concurrent vulnerabilities
- Reducing the manpower needed to execute the tests

One difference is that a disruption in the liveness of a concurrent application could cause a system failure. *Liveness* is the ability of a concurrent application to fulfill its functional requirements within some finite window of time. These failure types are described by three categories: deadlock, livelock, and starvation. In a deadlock situation, multiple threads within an application are blocked at some point in their code while trying to execute. Consequently, the application is unable to complete its execution, or unable to satisfy its functional requirement(s).

Refer to the example shown in Figure B-5. In this scenario, both threads could hit a deadlock after their critical section 1 segments if they reach the lock statement simultaneously. With both threads blocked, the application would be unable to complete execution and would be in a passively hung state. In a livelock failure, the threads are not blocked and inactive; they are stuck in a nonprogressing code cycle. Each thread's actions are driven by the other's. A real-world example

```
threadA{                              threadB{
    lock semaphore A                      lock semaphore B
    // critical section 1                 // critical section 1
    lock semaphore B                      lock semaphore A
    // critical section 2                 // critical section 2
    unlock semaphore B                    unlock semaphore A
    // critical section 3                 // critical section 3
    unlock semaphore A                    unlock semaphore B
}
```

Figure B-5 Potential deadlock example

would be when two people approach each other in a narrow hallway. One person decides to be polite and move to the left to attempt avoidance. The other person also opts for politeness and slides to the right. Both threads, or people, are stuck going back and forth, and neither advances forward. In a starvation failure, a resource contention among threads occurs. It is similar to deadlock except the affected threads are not blocked. This situation is best represented by the "dining philosophers problem" thought up by Edsger Dijkstra in 1971:

> The dining philosophers problem is summarized as five philosophers sitting at a table doing one of two things: eating or thinking. While eating, they are not thinking, and while thinking, they are not eating. The five philosophers sit at a circular table with a large bowl of spaghetti in the center. A fork is placed in-between each philosopher, and as such, each philosopher has one fork to his or her left and one fork to his or her right. As spaghetti is difficult to serve and eat with a single fork, it is assumed that a philosopher must eat with two forks. The philosopher can only use the fork on his or her immediate left or right . . . The philosophers never speak to each other, which creates a dangerous possibility of deadlock when every philosopher holds a left fork and waits perpetually for a right fork (or vice versa).[2]

These types of concurrency issues can be difficult to identify because of their nondeterministic nature. In a sequential flow, race conditions don't exist within the context of an application; behavior is expected to be the same when executed with the same inputs. Consequently, sequentially executing applications are not subject to the same pitfalls as concurrent applications. Some of these pitfalls can have a big impact on the application's functional requirements satisfaction, such as with safety issues. Some of these pitfalls don't occur predictably, such as race conditions. In the banking account example from Section B.2, a concurrent component of that system should be tested extensively, and over an extended period of time, to ensure that the integrity of the account data is not compromised because a concurrent component of the system fails. The testing should also be done on an enumerated set of target hardware configurations. An example hardware property that could affect a concurrent application is hyper-threading. Using the described approach, this would verify the system's functional readiness across multiple platforms prior to deployment.

The shortcomings of manually implementing concurrency tests are apparent. Testers attempting to inject liveness issues, such as inducing a thread dead-lock, would be hard-pressed to effect the execution of an application's thread outside of a debugging environment. They would therefore be relegated to iterating a set of test cases or steps over some amount of time, hoping to uncover any issues. The big question is, how long is long enough? How long should the testing be done before there is confidence that any concurrency issues have been weeded out? Automating the test would remove the need for continuing lab coverage. Additionally, the system could be put under a load geared toward increasing the number of concurrent code path executions. For testing across platforms, automation would help facilitate a parallel testing effort to cut down on the overall test time.

Various tools that can support concurrency testing are available. CHESS is an automated tool from Microsoft Research for finding errors in multithreaded software by systematic exploration of thread schedules.[3] It applies a combination of model checking and dynamic analysis techniques to the concurrency testing effort. CHESS can detect deadlocks and races (using the Goldilocks lockset algorithm).

There is also the Intel Thread Checker, which is a dynamic analysis tool for finding deadlocks (including potential deadlocks), stalls, data races, and incorrect uses of the native Windows synchronization APIs (see http://go.microsoft.com/fwlink/?LinkId=115727). The Thread Checker needs to instrument either the source code or the compiled binary to make every memory reference and every standard Win32 synchronization primitive observable.

B.4   Performance Testing

Performance testing is part of concurrency testing, and it is a means by which a system's performance specifications and/or performance service-level agreements are tested. This is considered another NFR. Automating this testing would provide the following major payoffs:

- Repeatable test inputs
- Complete data collection and analysis
- Accomplish what manual testing can do with difficulty or not at all

For example, how many users on average will there be on the system, or what is the response time for a set of transactions on the system? Performance testing involves subjecting the system to a realistic load in an environment that is as close to the target environment as possible. Remaining as close as possible to the target environment is vital to avoid an external variable affecting the test execution and obtaining unusable data. This testing is used to get a measure of a system's quality attributes: speed, scalability, and stability.

The speed quality refers to the time it takes for the system to respond to some stimulus. The stimulus could, for example, be a form submittal or an account query. Usually a maximum allowable amount of time is defined as an NFR. For example, in the bank account example, there could be a requirement that a new account must be added within five seconds.

The `accountObject` in Figure B-6 would represent the component responsible for initiating the "add account" action. This could be a graphical user interface, or a batch script, for example. The `accountManager` would handle the transaction request from the `accountObject`. Some internal actions are performed in addition to invoking the "save new account" action on the `databaseManager` which is responsible for storing the account information and returning a status to the `accountManager`. Then, finally, a status is returned to the `accountObject` indicating that the account has been added.

The scalability quality refers to the system's behavior when the load (number of users, number of transactions, etc.) is increased. The behavior in this context could refer to anything from its speed, to network utilization for distributed systems, to database transaction frequency. In the bank account example, there would more than likely be an NFR that the system's response time for an ATM

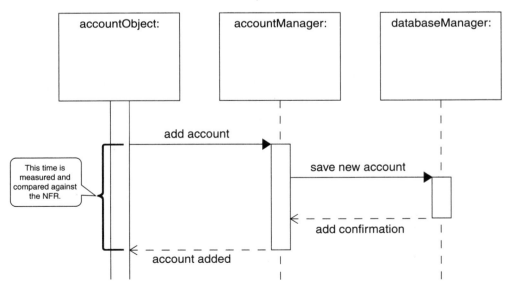

Figure B-6 Example of performance measure for adding an account

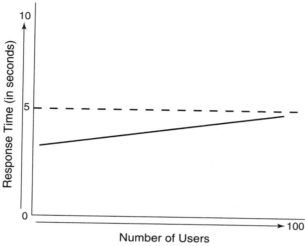

Figure B-7   Graph example of response time versus number of users

transaction shall not exceed five seconds. Ideally, the results from a performance run would then look like the graph in Figure B-7. The system's response time in this analysis does increase along with the number of users, but the maximum response time is not exceeded.

The stability quality refers to the system's ability to execute under a normal, or slightly exaggerated, load for an extended period of time without crashing. This type of testing is closely related to endurance testing, except during endurance or soak testing the system needs to continue to execute without fail. Failures could occur for various reasons, resource depletion being the more common one.

Performance testing is used to measure the system's performance against the NFRs. This is useful in areas like regression testing and system integration. Performance testing could also be used to compare different target configurations. The environment with the best results could be identified, for example, to use for recommendations to customers. As with other types of testing, human error makes performance testing harder. To truly test a system's performance across multiple platforms, the inputs in each case would have to be identical. Otherwise the results are invalid. Depending on the complexity of the inputs to the system, executing the test manually would not be conducive to getting a true sense of its behavior. Additionally, in some tests, gathering the necessary data to analyze could also be hindered during a manual execution. If, for instance, the network throughput needs to be monitored to satisfy some NFR for a distributed system, then the tester will need to execute a tool or set of tools to collect the data by hand. In an automated scenario, the required tools would be kicked off without a tester's intervention, ensuring that the correct, and the same, data is recorded for each test run.

Finally, a shortcoming of executing this type of test manually lies in the data analysis and results reporting. Consider a test that runs for 48 or 72 hours. Manually sifting through three or more days' worth of network traffic data or timestamped log entries for each transaction executed would be cumbersome at best. An extension to the automated testing could provide tools for parsing the data to provide error filtering and report generation capabilities.

For more details on performance testing for Web applications, see "Performance Testing Guidance for Web Applications" at www.codeplex.com/PerfTestingGuide.

A summary of what to look for during performance testing is described here:[4]

- **Variance in test results:** This is indicative of an unstable application. The variance in test results can be understood by calculating the standard deviation of results.

- **CPU utilization:** Low CPU usage could be a sign of concurrency bugs such as deadlocks and synchronization overheads. Conversely, a high CPU utilization does not necessarily indicate success, as livelocks result in high CPU utilization.

- **Garbage collections:** For managed applications, too many memory management operations can hinder actual work execution and could point to faulty design or implementation.

- **Total thread execution time:** This enables you to approximate the total execution time if the program were to be executed sequentially. Comparing the total thread execution time to the elapsed time of sequential implementation of the same algorithm program is a way to understand the parallelization overheads (and to note whether the test is valid).

- **Total memory usage:** Measuring total memory usage can be valuable in understanding the memory profile of the application. For managed applications, the garbage collector plays a significant role in altering the total memory usage of the application and should be taken into consideration while evaluating the memory usage.

B.5   Code Coverage Testing

Code coverage testing is a technique that involves measuring the percentage of a system's code that is being tested by a test suite. Automating this testing provides the following major payoffs:

- Personnel resources who otherwise spent time on inspections and reviews can spend time on higher-priority testing tasks

- Reduction in missed findings related to human errors

- Allowance for measurement of SUT testing coverage, i.e., identifies areas that are not covered by a test (almost impossible to conduct manually)

Code coverage testing interfaces with the code directly; therefore, it is a type of white-box testing. A test suite is a collection of test cases that are used to validate a component's code functionality. The test cases are generally implemented as unit test cases (see Section B.6). The coverage testing is helpful in finding parts of the application that are not being tested. It also helps bolster confidence in the parts of an application that get exercised via a test frequently. There are certain instances in which code coverage is not only important but could also be required. A safety-critical application (one in which a failure would have dire consequences) could have an NFR that its code coverage testing results will reveal that 100% of its code is tested, such as with our bank account example. If a failure in that system went undetected because some code wasn't tested, the result could be a loss of the bank's customer account information.

The code coverage tests will compare the results percentages against some set of criteria. Some examples of these criteria are function coverage, statement coverage, and condition coverage. In a test of function coverage, 100% success would indicate that every function/method in an application has been called by the test suite, ensuring that all functions are exercised to some degree. In a test of statement coverage, 100% success would indicate that every line of code in an application has been tested. In a test of condition coverage, 100% success would indicate that for each conditional statement, all outcomes have been tested. Some coverage test criteria will overlap. Path coverage testing (testing all paths through the code) will implicitly test statement coverage and function coverage, and statement coverage will implicitly test function coverage.

Figure B-8 shows sample output from an open-source Java code coverage tool called Emma[5] that was executed in Sun's javac Java compiler.

```
[EMMA v2.0.4015 (stable) report, generated Sat May 15 12:02:28 CDT 2008]

OVERALL COVERAGE SUMMARY:

[class, %]       [method, %]       [block, %]           [line, %]            [name]
85% (157/185)!   65% (1345/2061)!  60% (44997/74846)!   64% (8346.3/13135)!  all classes

OVERALL STATS SUMMARY:

total packages:         8
total classes:          185
total methods:          2061
total executable files: 62
total executable lines: 13135

COVERAGE BREAKDOWN BY PACKAGE:

[class, %]    [method, %]      [block, %]           [line, %]          [name]
25% (1/4)!    25% (3/12)!      40% (3012/7446)!     25% (3/12)!        com.sun.tools.javac.v8.resources
94% (16/17)!  49% (41/83)!     48% (1111/2292)!     45% (201.1/450)!   com.sun.tools.javac.v8
88% (45/51)!  61% (242/397)!   54% (3070/5729)!     52% (809.6/1563)!  com.sun.tools.javac.v8.tree
83% (19/23)!  60% (134/224)!   54% (2746/5063)!     56% (580.1/1041)!  com.sun.tools.javac.v8.util
100% (1/1)    40% (2/5)!       58% (25/43)!         49% (5.9/12)!      com.sun.tools.javac
77% (33/43)!  59% (310/529)!   60% (10584/17674)!61% (2077.2/3396)!   com.sun.tools.javac.v8.code
91% (39/43)!  75% (521/698)    66% (19701/29863)!70% (3606.9/5138)!   com.sun.tools.javac.v8.comp
100% (3/3)    81% (92/113)     70% (4748/6736)!     70% (1062.4/1523)! com.sun.tools.javac.v8.parser
```

Figure B-8 Sample output from an open-source Java code coverage tool called Emma

Manually executing a code coverage test would involve a visual inspection of the code as well as the test suite. Depending on the size of the application, this would require a decent amount of personnel resources: individual review time (multiplied by the number of reviewers) and formal review meeting time. Even then, there is still a high probability that something will get missed. The number of reviewers could be increased to minimize the impact, but in some cases that wouldn't be practical and would still leave room for error. Automation is the natural solution. Reports, like the example in Figure B-8, can be created in a fraction of the time they would take manually, and with more confidence in a low margin of coverage testing error. These tests could easily be rerun during regression testing following source code modifications and prior to system integration.

B.6   Unit Testing

Unit testing is used to validate that the individual units in an application's source code are behaving correctly. Automating this testing provides the following payoffs:

- Finer control over unit isolation

- Repeatability of test cases

- Supports automated build processes, such as when all components have been checked into the source control system and are automatically built; automated unit test will help quickly detect any build issues

In this context, a unit is the lowest testable piece of the application. In an object-oriented paradigm this would equate to a class method. Each unit's test case should be independent of all other test cases. The idea is to isolate the units under test to ensure that they provide the expected functionality. Since a lower level of understanding of the code is needed to test at the unit level, the onus of writing and executing the unit test cases generally falls on the software developers. The developers will not only arrive at conclusions as to whether or not the units behave as expected but can also verify the satisfaction of the application's requirements that are not verifiable by means of demonstration (usually through some graphical user interface). Assuming the software's design is stable, this bottom-up approach can help developers find implementation bugs early on in the software lifecycle and minimize functional errors further down the road.

Unit test case development can be facilitated by using a testing framework. Several unit test frameworks are available in multiple languages. A family of unit test frameworks, called xUnit, shares similar properties. The xUnit idea was originally developed by Kent Beck for Smalltalk.[6] Frameworks that are a part of the xUnit family are expected to provide the following components:

1. **Test fixtures:** used to create a state in which multiple test cases are executed

2. **Test suites:** an aggregate of tests associated with the same test fixture

3. **Test execution:** execution of a unit test with initialization and cleanup capabilities, producing test results

4. **Assertion mechanism:** a means of determining the success or failure of the unit under test

One of the more stable xUnit frameworks for Java is JUnit.[7] This framework, which was created by Kent Beck and Erich Gamma, has gained wide popularity in test-driven development. It comes as part of the standard Java software development kit. The Eclipse IDE[8] bundles usually have JUnit-specific functionality already included.

Figure B-9 is an example of what a unit test case looks like using JUnit. In this example, the class `HelloWorld` has a method with the signature shown in Figure B-10.

This method is expected to multiply both actual parameters and return the result. In our simplified unit test case, then, we are testing this method with an assertion: `assertEquals`. In the assertion we are verifying that the method returns a correct result. The test framework provides not only the assertion mechanism but also the execution and monitoring of the test run. Executing this test within Eclipse produces the display shown in Figure B-11.

In addition to the visual control, the test results can also be exported as XML for inclusion in a software design artifact as part of a software process.

A major drawback of attempting to execute unit tests manually is the difficulty of isolating a unit. Manually, a unit test would be composed of nothing more than a set of step-by-step instructions for an operator to follow. This approach does not allow for the granularity that the unit test case needs. In some cases, such as the example in Figure B-9, it would be difficult to get to the unit level manually. Automated testing frameworks provide the glue for developers to

```
public class HelloWorldTest {
    private HelloWorld hw_;

    /**
     * @throws java.lang.Exception
     */
    @Before
    public void setUp() throws Exception {
        hw_=new HelloWorld();
    }

    /**
     * @throws java.lang.Exception
     */
    @After
    public void tearDown() throws Exception {
    }

    /**
     * Test method for
     * {@link mbmb.pkg.HelloWorld#multiply(int, int)}.
     */
    @Test
    public void testMultiply() {
        assertEquals("multiply", 144, hw_.multiply(12,12));
    }

}
```

Figure B-9   Example unit test case using JUnit

```
public int multiply(int l, int r)
```

Figure B-10   Example signature

use between their code and their unit test cases. They allow the test cases to be written correctly and provide the execution environment. Many of them, like JUnit, are freely available.

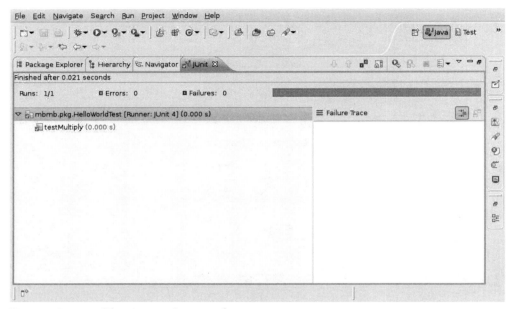

Figure B-11   Test execution result

Notes

1. C. Wysopal, L. Nelson, D. Zovi, and E. Dustin, *The Art of Software Security Testing* (Addison-Wesley, 2006).
2. http://en.wikipedia.org/wiki/Dining_philosophers_problem.
3. http://channel9.msdn.com/shows/Going+Deep/CHESS-An-Automated-Concurrency-Testing-Tool/.
4. http://msdn.microsoft.com/en-us/magazine/cc546569.aspx.
5. http://emma.sourceforge.net/.
6. www.xprogramming.com/testfram.htm.
7. http://junit.org/.
8. www.eclipse.org/.

Appendix C

The Right Tool for the Job

The best tool on the market depends on your need; i.e., evaluate the tool specific to your context.

As we have defined AST in Chapter 1 and throughout this book, it can cover the entire software testing lifecycle (STL). We selected and describe here a subset of tools to support the STL effort, including requirements, unit testing, configuration management, defect tracking, security testing, and functional automated testing tools. Additionally, we'll present support tools, such as VMWare, for test environment support, test data generators, test case generators, and more. We provide sample evaluations and what to consider when choosing a tool. This appendix is not meant to be an exhaustive list, but rather a sample subset of the available tools. For more details on available tools, refer to the following Web sites:

For open-source testing tools, see http://opensourcetesting.com/.

For general open-source tools, see http://sourceforge.net/.

For various Web testing tools, see www.softwareqatest.com/ qatweb1.html#FUNC; this site includes popular Web testing tools such as Watir and Selenium.

For a sample of Agile testing tools, see http://functionaltestingtools.pbwiki.com/FrontPage.

An interesting collaborative functional testing tool is described at http://studios.thoughtworks.com/twist-agile-test-automation/test-automation.

For a discussion of various popular software testing tools, see www.qaforums.com.

For software component reuse sites, see www.koders.com and www.krugle.com.

For additional vendor-provided testing tools, see specific vendor Web sites.

Each STL category described in this appendix will include a list of specific tool evaluation criteria, and for some tools we'll assign a weight and rank, based on our example needs. Each section will provide a baseline evaluation approach for the specific tool covered.

It is important to note that before evaluating any type of tool, you must understand the goal you are trying to accomplish; that is, you need to be clear about the problem you are trying to solve. Before embarking on a tool evaluation effort, know the types of tools that are available[1] in order to narrow down the choices. There are as many types of tools for the STL as there are testing types and phases. Also, keep in mind that the best tool for the job is the one that works specifically in your testing environment. We therefore recommend that you always evaluate tools using your specific AUT or SUT.

C.1 Requirements Management (RM)

When assessing the many RM tools on the market today, it is difficult to find one that fits all program needs. This section is to be used as a guide to assist you in making the best decisions when acquiring an RM tool. The program's RM team needs to define its RM tool requirements. Requirements management is commonly thought of as organizing, documenting, and tracking requirements, design components, test cases, procedures, and so forth, with the end state of providing traceability to all defined artifacts, i.e., providing an RTM. An RTM will help determine any missing pieces of the development or testing process.

In order to build reliable systems, reliable and cost-effective software testing should begin in the requirements phase.[2] Automating requirements helps improve the testing phase. If requirements are unambiguous, consistent, and contain all the information a test engineer needs in a testable form, the requirements are said to be test-ready or testable. Requirements tools provide an environment for, and central database approach to, managing large numbers of requirements related in potentially complex ways (traceability). Requirements tools provide continuity through time, across projects, through staff and contractor changes. In a program setting, an RM tool can be used in a number of contexts:

- Planning the scope of a release or a series of releases (key in iterative, incremental releases)

- Managing plan execution, such as who is responsible for what, by when, etc.

- Tracking requirements design, implementation, and testing status (i.e., the entire RTM cycle)

- Changing control of the scope, particularly when evaluating the impact of proposed changes (this is where traceability of requirements is critical)

There are many tools on the market that can be used to help document testable requirements. Test-ready requirements minimize the test effort and cost of testing. Requirements that are in test-ready condition help support the preparation of an efficient test design and requirements to test design/test procedure traceability. This better traceability in turn helps to provide the project team greater assurance that the AUT will perform correctly because all requirements have test cases associated with them (full functional testing coverage).

Traceability verifies that each requirement is identified in such a way that it can be linked to all parts of the system where it is used. For any change to requirements, it is possible to identify all parts of the system where this change has an effect. Ideally, each requirement has been considered as a separately identifiable, measurable entity. Now it is necessary to consider the connections between requirements to understand the effect of one requirement on other components of the system. This means there must be a way of dealing with a large number of requirements and the complex connections between them. Rather than trying to tackle everything simultaneously, it is better to divide the requirements into manageable groups. This could be a matter of allocating requirements to subsystems, or to sequential releases based on priority.

Traceability also provides information about individual requirements and other parts of the system that could be affected if a requirement changes, such as test cases that are affected. The tester will be informed of the requirement

Figure C-1 Example HP Quality Center: test procedures generated directly
from requirements

change, for example, via a flag used in the tool and then can make sure that all
affected areas are adjusted.

Most requirements tools include a requirements and test case tracking facility,
allowing for generation of an RTM, and tracking of manual versus automated
test cases or procedures, automating test cases, test case pass and fail status, plus
often a defect tracking capability, among many other features. Additionally, test
procedures can be generated directly from requirements, as shown in the Hewlett-
Packard (HP) Quality Center example (Figure C-1).

Automating Requirements Management

Generally, in almost all testing efforts, test cases are based on requirements.
Generally, an RTM is generated that maps each requirement to one or more test
cases, to allow for test coverage measurement.

Maintaining an RTM in a manual fashion, such as in a Word document or
Excel spreadsheet, can be tedious and is error-prone; for example, sometimes a
requirement change is not communicated to the testing team. Often the test
engineer stumbles onto the change by finding a false positive during a test run, such

as uncovering a PTR when following the test procedure steps, yet further research and analysis determine that it is the requirement that has changed. An RM tool such as Test Director, RequisitePro, or DOORS will flag any types of changes to alert the stakeholder, in this case the test engineer, that a requirement has changed and that a test case/procedure has to be changed accordingly.

Table C-1 lists requirements for our case study application, "SeaClear," and maps the associated test cases. This RTM is very tedious to maintain manually. An RM tool or TM tool can help automate the RTM generation and maintenance.

Table C-1 Manual RTM Example

Requirement ID	Requirement Description	Requirement Type	Priority	Test Case ID
1	The SeaClear system shall allow the user to view all charts available on a local drive.	Functional	P1	1
1.1	The SeaClear system shall make available the following types of charts:	Functional	P1	N/A
1.1.1	USA chart file		P1	3
1.1.2	Europe chart file*		P1	2
...	...	...		
1.2	The charts should appear within 3 sec of the user hitting the select button.	Performance	P1	X
201	The SeaClear system shall allow the user to search for any chart name.		P2	201
201.1	The SeaClear system shall allow the user to search for chart name xyz.†	Functional		
...	...	...		
401	The SeaClear system shall allow the user to print each chart and have it display correctly in the printout.	Functional		401
401.1	The chart xyz shall display in the abc fashion.	...	...	

* Depending on the requirements structure, generally a data dictionary is referenced that will lay out the different types of chart files.

† The different types of searches required could be laid out in a data dictionary as well.

Figure C-2 shows how, for example, in Test Director, requirements to test mapping can be reported, thus automatically creating the RTM. Test cases and requirements can be flagged for follow-up, allowing for updates and automatic status and coverage reporting.

As with many programs, the tracking and maintaining of requirements requires discipline and constant management. The ability to control and obtain information from a program's documents, and maintain them in a centralized location, is essential to the success of a program.

It can be argued that many of the RM tools that are available today perform similar functions. The need to import documents in different formats (such as a Word file or .pdf) and enable requirement searching, tracking, and providing a central repository for all requirements maintenance are key RM tool requirements. The RM tool needs to be adaptable to a program's systems engineering process, to allow for integration of a program's process and its requirements.

Deciding which tool is best for your program can make all the difference in the success or failure of a program. Many programs have large document repositories, with thousands of requirements, which can certainly be challenging for both the systems and software engineers. Tools being developed in the open-

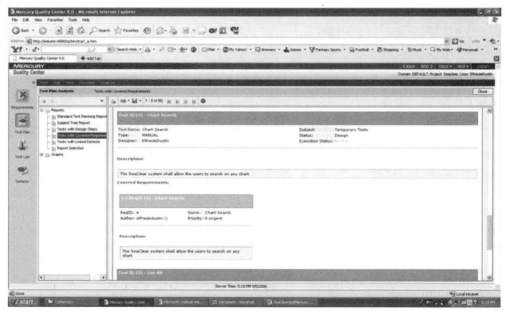

Figure C-2   HP's Test Director example: tests with associated requirements report

source community are also becoming very popular and can address the needs of many programs. The open-source tools are always being updated and can be located on many of the popular open-source sites such as OpenSourceTesting.org and SourceForge.net. For example, FitNesse is a software development collaboration tool that also allows for tracking requirements and defining acceptance tests. There is also the Open Source Requirements Management Tool, which you could evaluate to see if it fits your needs; see http://sourceforge.net/projects/osrmt/.

C.2 Unit Testing Frameworks— Example Evaluation

In this section we'll evaluate an open-source unit testing framework. For the purpose of this example, Java has been chosen as the target language. Of the available frameworks designed for Java code we will examine two: JUnit and JTiger.

How to Evaluate and Choose a Framework

While evaluating these two frameworks we will follow these steps:

1. Identify the tool requirements and criteria (the framework criteria).
2. Identify a list of tools that meet the criteria (JUnit and JTiger).
3. Assign a weight to each tool criterion based on importance or priority.
4. Evaluate each tool candidate and assign a score.
5. Multiply the criterion weight by each tool candidate score to get the tool's overall score for comparison.

Table C-2 shows an example list of unit test framework evaluation criteria. Based on these criteria, we derive weights for the importance of each feature to the overall framework criteria; the more important the criterion is to the stakeholder, the higher the assigned weight (ranging from 1 to 5). Then we rank the target frameworks, also from 1 to 5, based on how closely each of the criteria is met by the framework. Weight and rank are then multiplied to produce a final score. Features and capabilities of candidate frameworks are then compared based on the resulting score in order to determine best fit for the client.

Table C-2 Unit Test Framework Evaluation Criteria

Criteria	Weight (1–5)	JUnit		JTiger	
		Score	Value	Score	Value
Price	5	5	25	5	25
Documentation (availability, amount, etc.)	5	5	25	5	25
Support (forums, mailing lists, etc.)	5	5	25	2	10
Multiplatform support	1	5	5	5	5
Licensing	4	5	20	5	20
Common IDE integration	4	4	16	3	12
No external dependencies	4	5	20	5	20
Test results reporting functions	5	3	15	5	25
xUnit Compatible	5	5	25	5	25
Total			**176**		**167**

For the purpose of this example we will be working with a client that is looking to introduce unit testing to its software development process for the first time. That said, there are three premier Java unit testing frameworks available: JUnit, JTiger, and TestNG. All three offer a substantial set of functionality for unit testing Java code. JUnit has been a force in Java unit testing for some time so it is an obvious choice for a beginner. JTiger was developed by Tony Morris with the intention of overcoming the author's perceived JUnit shortcomings. Therefore, it seemed to be a valid competitor for JUnit. TestNG, developed by Cédric Beust for similar reasons, wasn't evaluated because it is based on JUnit and is therefore quite similar.

Price: JUnit and JTiger both have the advantages of open-source, such as no licensing fees and free support, and therefor we are not tied to a single vendor.

Documentation: Ample documentation is necessary when integrating a new tool, especially in this example case in which the client is unfamiliar with unit testing. Both frameworks have adequate documentation available online to facilitate the frameworks' integration.

Support: As important as documentation is to launching the integration effort, so is support important for understanding the tool itself. JUnit was found to have an edge over JTiger in this respect. JTiger has an Internet relay chat (IRC) channel dedicated to users of the framework, but that is the extent of its online support. JUnit has Web forums hosted by JUnit.org as well as an active Yahoo group dedicated to users of the framework. Also, there is a JUnit section in the Eclipse IDE (a commonly used open-source IDE) help documentation.

Multiplatform support: Since the client's target language is Java in our example, cross-platform support is implicit. A lower weight was assigned to this criterion based on the assertion that all Java unit test frameworks will inherit from the language.

Licensing: Both JUnit and JTiger are licensed under the Common Public License (www.opensource.org/licenses/cpl1.0.php). This license is similar to the GNU General Public License but is intended to prevent contributors from charging fees for content versions to which they've contributed.

Common IDE integration: The ease of IDE integration with the framework is important to the client's development community. Software developers are more apt to become accustomed to using a tool that plugs into their IDE than they are to one that does not. In this example the client has adopted Eclipse, which is one of the more popular Java IDEs, as its development environment. Eclipse comes bundled with JUnit by default. JTiger currently has no direct method for integrating with Eclipse.

No external dependencies: Neither JUnit nor JTiger requires an external library to be installed. Minimizing, or eliminating, dependencies helps to reduce the tool's footprint.

xUnit: JUnit publicizes its membership in the xUnit unit testing framework group. Although there is not a direct mention of it on the JTiger Web site, it appears that it also follows this pattern. The xUnit idea was originally developed by Kent Beck for Smalltalk (www.xprogramming.com/testfram.htm). Frameworks that are a part of the xUnit family are expected to provide the following components:

1. Test fixtures, used to create a state in which multiple test cases are executed

2. Test suites, an aggregate of tests associated with the same test fixture

3. Test execution, with initialization and cleanup capabilities and producing test results

4. Assertion mechanism, a means to determine the success or failure of the unit under test

Selecting a unit test framework that sticks with this pattern gives some confidence that a minimal set of functionality will be provided.

Community: JUnit is hosted at SourceForge.net, which is a predominant site for numerous open-source projects. SourceForge gives direct access to several project details/statistics such as activity percentile, number of bugs (open/total), and repository activity. It is currently being maintained by developers numbering just over a half dozen.

JTiger releases are self-hosted. Its Web site does not provide the specifics about the project that are presented for JUnit.

Features: An advantage that JUnit has over JTiger is the readily available add-ons. These extensions can allow for targeting a specific scope for unit testing such as database applications (DbUnit, www.dbunit.org/) or Java Enterprise Edition applications (JUnitEE, www.junitee.org/).

A plus for JTiger is its reporting functionality. The output can be in HTML, XML, or plain textual format. This could prove useful in the event that a unit test results artifact is a requirement for one of the stages in the client software development process model.

Conclusion: In our example case the history behind JUnit led to its advantage over JTiger. It has been widely used throughout the Java development community and has won the Java World Editors' Choice Awards (ECA) for the "Best Java Performance Monitoring/Testing Tool" in both 2001 and 2002. It is this longevity and success that make for a rich resource repository that is conducive to the introduction of a unit testing framework. Since the target client is unfamiliar with unit testing frameworks, these developer resources are key.

C.3   Configuration Management—Example Evaluation

Configuration management (CM) is a critical part of any system development effort. CM in the technology realm can be defined as "the control or management of modifications made to software, hardware, or documentation throughout the development and lifecycle of a system." CM can be broken down into three subcategories:

1.   Software configuration management (SCM): source code management and revision control

2.   Hardware configuration management (HCM): management of hardware/device releases

3.   Operational configuration management (OCM): management of the configuration items (hardware, software, and documentation) within a technology infrastructure

We were concerned with the SCM paradigm. SCM can be thought of as a process or set of activities put in place to track the evolution of software items in the development of a system.

Benefits of Software Configuration Management (SCM)

At a high level, a good SCM implementation should provide

1.   A secure repository to store artifacts, using authentication and authorization

2.   A stable yet robust workspace

3.   The ability to take a snapshot of the baseline at incremental project milestones and "tag" it with a known identifier

4.   The ability to revert to any of these "tagged" repository snapshots at any time for reproducibility and redeployment of a software build

5.   The ability to allow for simultaneous updates/changes to artifacts in the repository; i.e., a controlled environment for having multiple developers modify the same file at the same time. There are two main approaches that SCM products take toward solving this issue via its concurrency model:

   a.   Merge: Any number of users may write to a file at any time. The master repository may spit out a "conflict error" if a user attempts to check a file into the repository that is not based on the latest revision. The user may then investigate and then merge local changes manually or have the system attempt the merge.

   b.   Lock: One user at a time is allowed to write to a file. The master repository hands out locks one at a time. A user must give up the lock for another user to edit the same file.

6.   The ability to audit and control changes to components

More specifically, for our example we needed

1. A tool that adhered to the GNU General Public License (GPL) licensing model and was open-source

2. Compatibility with Linux and C/C++. We didn't want to have to install a proprietary compiler to build/set up the SCM software. Our developers know C/C++ and Linux well, and having an SCM system written in a proprietary language would diminish the purpose of the open-source paradigm since it would hinder our ability to modify the source if needed.

3. Seamless integration with a defect tracking tool

4. Eclipse and IDE support

5. A quick learning curve for developers

6. Wide support in the community. There is nothing worse than "Googling" a question about a problem you're having with a particular piece of software and getting only seven responses—and they're all in another language!

The SCM Tools Evaluated

We ended up evaluating a number of different products to support our company's SCM needs. Plenty of vendors offer very good SCM solutions, but many of them could be eliminated immediately for not satisfying a particular need. Since we were mainly interested in the open-source community, our options were quite a bit narrower. After researching the available products, we identified the list of features that we considered important and examined four tools with these features in mind. The four chosen packages were

- **CVS:** Dick Grune
- **Subversion:** CollabNet Inc.
- **Mercurial:** Matt Mackall
- **Bazaar:** Canonical Ltd.

Features

Below you'll find a list of the features that we considered, a brief explanation of each feature, and a description of how each tool addressed the feature. Many of the supporting applications referenced here are not fully elaborated on as they fall outside the scope of this writing.

- ***Ease of use/learning curve:*** Is the SCM package intuitive and overall easy to use? After all, the developers will be interacting with it many times per day. Is there a steep learning curve?

  Subversion, CVS, and Bazaar seemed to be at the same level of "ease of use": relatively easy. Many Web site reviews pointed to Mercurial as the more difficult of the SCM tools. Subversion had the largest "head start" here, however, since some of us on the team had prior experience with it.

- ***Licensing:*** This refers to the license model for the application. Licenses can be free or paid.

  All of the evaluated tools were free.

- ***Fully atomic commits:*** When a commit occurs, an atomic commit ensures that all the changes are made or none at all. Non-atomic-commit systems run into trouble when, for example, during a commit of a bunch of files, a network connection is lost. The repository is then put into an unknown and unstable condition. An atomic commit system would ensure that if a network connection was lost before the entire commit finished, none of the commit changes would make it into the master repository.

  CVS was the only tool that did not fully implement the atomic commit model. This was a big minus in the CVS column.

- ***Intuitive tags:*** This describes whether meaningful, human-readable tags can be given to a particular revision, e.g., "Latest Release 2.3 to DoD Customer for Contract No. XYZ.123."

  All tools used intuitive tags. Subversion's implementation of a tag has been criticized as being more of a "cheap copy" but still satisfies our needs in this area.

- ***Web-based interface:*** Some packages come with a built-in Web interface. A Web interface allows for the posting of data to a Web site for audits/ analysis.

  Subversion comes with an Apache 2 module built in. It also offers seamless integration with Trac, an open source defect tracking tool (see Section C.4 for more details on Trac).

  Mercurial comes packaged with a Web server.

CVS allows for the integration of csvweb and ViewVC.

Bazaar can be used with any simple Web server along with webserve, loggerhead, or Trac.

- *Development status:* Is the application still being aggressively developed, or is it simply maintained with occasional bug fixes incorporated? An application that is being aggressively developed is usually the best supported. The developers of these applications are constantly adding new features and bug fixes. Since the world of technology is constantly changing, these applications tend to address the latest needs of the development community better than those apps that are less actively developed.

  Bazaar, Mercurial, and Subversion are all actively developed.

  CVS is more or less in a maintenance phase. New features are no longer being added.

- *Programming language:* This is the language the tool was written in. It can be important in the open-source community when you plan on modifying the source of the tool you're using.

  CVS and Subversion are written in C; Bazaar, in Python; and Mercurial, in Python and C.

- *Stand-alone server option:* Some SCM applications come with a stand-alone server process. This server allows for quick uptime and installation when a full-featured Web server (e.g., Apache 2) is not needed or available. These stand-alone servers are very scarce on features and are usually considerably slower than their full-featured counterparts.

  All tools we considered seem to have their own version of a stand-alone server.

- *Efficient binary file support:* Some SCM tools treat binary files as simple text files, whereas others recognize binary files as such. The merging and tracking algorithms of the latter group of SCSs are designed for this and thus are much more efficient in handling binary files formats.

  Subversion uses a "binary diffing" algorithm, which theoretically makes it just as efficient with binary files as it is with text files.

  Bazaar handles binary files but there is no mention of the efficiency in the documentation. They're assumed to be handled as text files.

CVS handles binary files poorly.

Mercurial is said to handle binary files well.

- *Symbolic link support:* This is the ability of the SCM implementation to allow symbolic links to be put under source control. Opinion seems to be split whether this feature is a nice convenience or represents a hole in security. We wanted to err on the side of security.

  CVS was the only tool that did not support symbolic links.

- *Repository model:* Typically, there are two main models that SCM tools implement. The first is the *client-server* model, in which the server maintains the master repository and each user keeps a local copy of the repository on his/her development machine. Changes made to local copies must be "checked in" to the master repository for the changes to propagate to other users. The second is the *distributed* model, in which users hold entire "peer" repositories, with version history, on their local machines along with their working copy.

  CVS and Subversion implement the client-server model.

  Bazaar and Mercurial implement the distributed model.

- *International support:* This means both multilanguage and multi-operating-system support.

  Subversion and Bazaar are internationalized.

- *File renaming:* This is the ability to rename files while maintaining their version history.

  All packages except CVS supported file renames.

- *Merge tracking:* A system that supports merge tracking remembers the changes that have been merged between each branch and will include only the appropriate changes (missing changes) when merging one branch into another.

  Subversion and CVS do not support merge tracking; Bazaar and Mercurial do.

- *Stand-alone GUI:* Some SCM packages come with stand-alone GUIs, relieving the developer of the need to memorize command-line arguments and formats.

  All the tools offer some sort of GUI front end. These solutions seem to vary in terms of ease of setup and use.

- ***Speed:*** The speed describes the efficiency of the tool's branching, tagging, and commit algorithms. Also, a big factor affecting the tool's overall response time is whether it's written in a compiled (e.g., C/C++) or interpreted (e.g., Python) language.

  Subversion and CVS seemed to have an advantage here, as they're written in C, whereas Bazaar and Mercurial are written in Python. Our analysis was simply based on a comparison of compiled versus interpreted language. The overall speed of any SCM tool is dependent upon the algorithms used.

- ***IDE support:*** This describes whether the tool has smooth integration with IDEs, e.g., NetBeans, Eclipse, Visual Studio, etc.

  All the SCM applications offer a variety of IDE integration options. All of them integrate well with Eclipse, which was one of our main needs.

- ***End-of-line (EOL) conversion:*** This indicates whether or not the SCM tool can adapt the EOL characters for files so that they match the EOL-specific method for the OS in which the tool is used.

  Bazaar was the only package that did not support EOL conversions.

Comparison Table

We assigned a weight and a score value to these features to come up with Table C-3.

Conclusion

As a result of our analysis, Subversion came out on top. Besides the features listed above, one very important fact remained: Our developers had experience with this application in prior jobs. This was a big factor in determining ease of use. Picking the right tool for any job is difficult, and you need to balance the benefits against the liabilities. In this instance we had to weigh the following questions:

- Do we want a feature-rich application even at the expense of ease of use?

- Do we go with something that everyone knows and can start using immediately, or do we look for something new, and possibly better? Will the schedule allow for this "trial" period?

- Do we want a free product for which the support is based on arbitrarily searching the Web for answers, or do we want to spend the cash on a licensed product for which the support will be formal?

Table C-3 Comparison of SCM Tools

Criteria	Weight (1–5)	CVS		Subversion		Mercurial		Bazaar	
		Score	Value	Score	Value	Score	Value	Score	Value
Price	5	5	25	5	25	5	25	5	25
Ease of use/ learning curve	4	4	16	5	20	3	12	4	16
Licensing	5	5	25	5	25	5	25	5	25
Fully atomic commits	5	1	5	5	25	5	25	5	25
Intuitive tags	5	4	20	4	20	5	25	5	25
Web-based interface	3	4	12	5	15	4	12	5	15
Development status	5	2	10	5	25	5	25	5	25
Programming language	4	5	20	5	20	4	16	4	16
Stand-alone server option	1	3	3	3	3	3	3	3	3
Efficient binary file support	4	1	4	5	20	4	16	2	8
Symbolic link support	5	1	5	5	25	5	25	5	25
Repository model*	5	5	25	5	25	3	15	3	15
International support	2	1	2	5	10	1	2	5	10
File renaming	5	1	5	5	25	5	25	5	25
Merge tracking	2	1	2	1	2	5	10	5	10
Stand-alone GUI	2	5	10	5	10	5	10	5	10
Speed	5	4	20	5	25	3	15	3	15
IDE support	5	4	20	5	25	5	25	5	25
End-of-line conversion	4	5	20	5	25	5	25	1	4
Score			**249**		**370**		**336**		**322**

* The scores assigned to the repository model do not indicate an absolute advantage of one over another. We scored the client-server model higher than the distributed model since all of our developers had experience with this model.

- Do we want a "tried-and-true" product with known suitable features, or do we put our trust in an "up-and-coming" product with the potential of monumental enhancements over our older product?

- Can we afford to pick a tool that may not be the best choice because it integrates with another one of our tools? Can we afford to go back and reevaluate our prior choice of tools to accommodate this one?

Balancing the benefits against the liabilities of a tool is an important factor in any tool choice. In our experience, there is nothing more valuable than having a team that is aware of the current options. People, for example, who read technical journals, discuss new technologies with coworkers, and are generally interested in their field will have a much better shot at picking the right tool at the beginning of a project, when it's the cheapest. Needing to change to another implementation of a tool in the middle of a project can be detrimental. This could happen if needs/requirements change but should not happen as a result of ill-informed management from the beginning.

C.4   Defect Tracking—Example Evaluation

In this section we suggest how to evaluate and choose a defect tracking tool. Two of the top open-source tools met our criteria, and here we compare them: Bugzilla and Trac.

How to Evaluate and Choose a Defect Tracking Tool

When tasked with evaluating defect tracking tools for a client, we follow steps 1 through 5 described in Section C.2, How to Evaluate and Choose a Framework.

Table C-4 shows the example list of defect tracking tool evaluation criteria, with an assigned weight and rank, using Trac and Bugzilla as examples. We assigned a weight based on feature importance to each criterion—i.e., the more important the criterion for ourselves or the client, the higher the weight (from 1 to 5)—then ranked the various tools based on how closely each tool criterion was met by the tool. Weight and rank were then multiplied to produce a final "tool score." Features and capabilities of candidate tools were then compared based on the resulting tool score in order to determine best fit.

Table C-4   Defect Tracking Tool Evaluation Criteria

Criteria	Weight (1–5)	Bugzilla		Trac	
		Score	Value	Score	Value
Price	5	5	25	5	25
Allows for import/export	5	5	25	5	25
Allows for database synchronization	5	3	15	4	20
Customizable workflow	5	4	20	4	20
Open API to allow for "other" tool integration	5	4	20		0
Supports access to various users via the Internet, intranet (i.e., a distributed system, not client-server/stand-alone)	5	5	25	5	25
Tool is secure	4	3	12	2	8
Authentication and authorization	5	5	25	5	25
Audit trail	5	5	25	5	25
Advanced reporting facility: generates defect reports, both predefined and modifiable/customizable, that support progress measurements and trend analysis (possibly using SQL queries to add additional customized reports)	5	5	25	5	25
Supports the metrics we need to produce	5	5	25	5	25
Allows for adding project-specific attributes, i.e., is customizable to allow for additional categories and custom fields	5	5	25	5	25
Allows attachments of all types, i.e., files (screen prints, other artifacts, etc.) can be attached to defect reports	5	5	25	5	25
E-mail: automatic notification to the responsible party when new defect is generated or when defect state changes	3	5	15	5	15
Supports multiple platforms	3	5	15	5	15
Total			**322**		**303**

You can generally narrow down the field from the scores of defect tracking tools to a smaller subset that meets your high-level requirements; in our case, this meant we needed to look at only two open-source defect tracking tools. Open-source might not be an option for you, and your subset would not include those.

This section contrasts Bugzilla and Trac as an example of how defect tracking tools could be evaluated. Coincidentally, Bugzilla is widely used by the open-source community (e.g., Mozilla, Apache, and Eclipse) and was selected "Testers' Choice" by the readers of *Software Test and Performance* magazine, announced in the December 2007 issue.

Trac and Bugzilla both meet the advantages of open-source:

- No licensing fees, maintenance, or restrictions
- Free and efficient support (though varied)
- Portable across platforms
- Modifiable and adaptable to suit individual needs
- Comparatively lightweight
- Not tied to a single vendor
- **Licensing**

  Trac is distributed open-source under the modified BSD license (http://trac.edgewall.org/wiki/TracLicense), a "commercially friendly" license sometimes known as a "copy center" license (i.e., take it to the copy center and copy it). It permits changes to be made to source code and kept or distributed commercially with few restrictions.

  Bugzilla is covered by the Mozilla Public License (www.mozilla.org/MPL/), which is sometimes described as a BSD/GPL hybrid. This so-called weak copyleft license requires copies and changes to source code to remain under the MPL, but permits such changes to be bundled with proprietary components.

- **Support**

  During our Bugzilla and Trac evaluations, our questions were often answered within minutes, solving any issues we ran into from the simple to the complex.

  In our experience working with commercial tool vendors, support is usually more complicated. It can take days before a support specialist addresses an issue, and there is sometimes an extra cost or annual maintenance contract to be kept current.

- **Adaptability**

Trac is written in Python (www.python.org). First released in 1991 by Guido van Rossum, this dynamic object-oriented programming language can be used for all types of software development. It offers strong support for integration with other languages and tools, comes with extensive standard libraries, and can be learned relatively quickly by the average developer. Versions of Python are available for Windows, Linux/UNIX, Mac OS X, OS/2, and Amiga, as well as for Palm and Nokia (Symbian) mobile-phone operating systems. Python has also been ported to run on Java and .NET virtual machines and is used at organizations as diverse as NASA, Rackspace, Industrial Light and Magic, AstraZeneca, Honeywell, Symantec, and many others.

Bugzilla (www.bugzilla.org), in its current iteration, is written in Perl. Perl (www.perl.org) is a stable, cross-platform programming language first released by Larry Wall in 1987 and borrows from C, shell scripting, AWK, sed and Lisp, according to Wikipedia. It is used for many projects in the public and private sectors and is widely used to program Web applications of all stripes. Perl is a high-level programming language with an eclectic heritage. Perl's process, file, and text manipulation facilities make it particularly well suited for tasks involving quick prototyping, system utilities, software tools, system management tasks, database access, graphical programming, networking, and Web programming. These strengths make it especially popular with system administrators and CGI script authors, but mathematicians, geneticists, journalists, and even managers also use Perl, according to a history posted at trac.edgewall.org. And with the release of Bugzilla 3.0, Trac and Bugzilla both now allow for modification and customized fields.

- **Community**

Trac is hosted at Edgewall.org and maintained by a community of developers who collaborate on projects based on Python. Edgewall.org is perhaps best known for Trac.

Bugzilla is hosted at Bugzilla.org and is among the many projects administered and maintained by the Mozilla Foundation, which is probably best known for its Firefox browser.

Bugzilla versus Trac

As defined by their respective Web sites, Bugzilla is "server software designed to help you manage software development." Trac is "an enhanced wiki and issue tracking system used for software development projects."

Trac is not an original idea. It owes much to the many project management and issue tracking systems that came before. In particular, it borrows from CVSTrac. The project started as a reimplementation of CVSTrac in Python and an entertaining exercise; it toyed with the SQLite embeddable database. Over time, the scope of the endeavor broadened, a goal formed, and it was brought on its current course.

Both Trac and Bugzilla offer browser-based defect tracking with multiuser access, attachments, e-mail integration, import/export capability, custom fields, authentication and authorization, reporting, and audit trails.

Once we had narrowed our investigation to these two tools, we started comparing features beyond their basic capabilities. Some of their major pluses and minuses are shown in Table C-5.

- **Installation on Windows**

    Most open-source defect tracking tools are cross-platform-compatible, but until its later releases Bugzilla focused less on the Windows environment. Windows installation is a Trac strength, and Trac gets a plus for this feature. Trac installs and runs on Windows without a hitch.

    There is currently no Bugzilla "bundle" install for Windows, whereas Trac has a "bundle" install, which makes Trac the easier install; installing Bugzilla on Windows requires more work.

Table C-5   Bugzilla and Trac: Pluses and Minuses

Criteria	Bugzilla 3.0	Trac 0.10
Installation on Windows	−	+
Ease of use	+	+
Features such as project management, other tool integration capabilities	+	+
Customizable workflow	+	+
Security	+	−

- **General installation**

  We found the Trac installation to be seamless and straightforward and were up and running within a couple of hours. Bugzilla, on the other hand, is a bit more difficult to install and maintain; there are many more components to install.

  We also liked the fact that Trac can run as a stand-alone Web server, in addition to a Web server such as Apache, whereas Bugzilla cannot run stand-alone, but always requires a Web server, such as Apache.

- **Ease of use**

  Once installed, both tools are easy to use, both Web interfaces are straightforward and intuitive, and therefore both deserve a plus in this category. Trac is more lightweight and can be used with little overhead; Bugzilla has many more components that can be used.

- **Features such as project management and other tool integration capability**

  Trac is a project management tool that integrates wiki, defect reporting (or PTR) tracking, and SCM "out of the box":

  - *Wiki server:* A wiki is a type of Web site that allows users to easily add, remove, or otherwise edit and change some available content; i.e., it is a "Web 2.0" technology. For example, the wiki could be used as a project management tool or provide a quick project status overview when the user first logs into Trac.

  - *Issue tracker:* You manage not only the defects here, but also any other issues that are associated with a project.

  - *Integrated with Subversion (CM):* Subversion is an SCM program used in software development—an improved CVS (another popular SCM tool). See Section C.3 for more detail.

  Subversion is another open-source CM tool and seems to be the up-and-coming version control tool. The goal of the Subversion project is to build a version control system that is a compelling replacement for CVS in the open-source community.

  Trac seamlessly integrates with Subversion, whereas Bugzilla requires another tool to integrate with Subversion called scmbug. Another option for the Bugzilla/Subversion integration would be to contact www.it-projects.com.

Trac's unique implementation includes a wiki, so each Trac page can be modified by the user.

Trac is lightweight and its plugins and available components integrate seamlessly, but Bugzilla offers more add-ons and utilities. If you are looking for a large number of features and components, Bugzilla gets the plus; on the other hand, if you are looking for lightweight and seamless integration, Trac gets the plus.

- **Customizable workflow**

  The goal of any defect management process is to resolve all defects quickly. Independent of the defect tracking tool chosen, a process should be followed to ensure consistency and accuracy in the way defects are logged and tracked in the tool. Therefore a workflow is necessary to ensure that a defect follows proper procedure and does not get lost during the release cycle. Having a customizable workflow is an important consideration when evaluating a defect tracking tool.

  Trac allows for advanced ticket workflow customization using plugins, which is a feature we prefer to Bugzilla's current option, where by default the workflow is hard-coded, and customized Perl code would be required. However, upcoming versions of Bugzilla are supposed to allow for customized workflow; for that reason Bugzilla and Trac both get a plus. Figure 9-2 outlines the Bugzilla defect tracking lifecycle/workflow.

Conclusion: Security Is Job 1

According to Bugzilla's maintainers, "The current developer community is very much concerned with the security of your site and your Bugzilla data. As such, we make every attempt to seal up any security holes as soon as possible after they are found." A list of the security advisories issued with each release that included security-related fixes is provided on the Bugzilla home page. "This is almost every version we've ever released since 2.10," reads a statement indicative of the recent attention being paid to security matters.

When we asked the Trac development team about its attention to security, we got this response: "I cannot give a complete answer, but what I know is that we actively look at code we have from multiple angles to see if there's a potential abuse." We are concerned about such a lax position toward security.

In the case of this evaluation, lax security was a deal breaker. And because of the attention to security that Bugzilla developers have paid of late, the project's longevity also played a major part. After all, Darwin's theory of survival of the fittest also plays a role in the open-source arena. And the more active the community, the longer an open-source tool has been around, generally the bigger the user space, and the better the chances are that security issues have been uncovered and addressed.

C.5   Security Testing

Existing security testing tools have been proven useful in the secure development and security verification of various systems and components. This section provides a summary of the types of security testing tools available and the requirements each tool meets, and maps vendors to each security tool. Typical antivirus software, network sniffers, and intrusion detection and firewall software are assumed to be in place. Security testing tools complement those existing tools.

Table C-6 summarizes one example of security testing tool requirements. Each of the requirements listed in this table can be further broken down into detailed requirements.

Many security testing tool solutions are currently available, and a comparison of their available features to the example security testing tool requirements are mapped in Table C-7. (*Note:* Security test tool requirements highly depend on your systems engineering environment.)

Table C-6   Example of Security Testing Tool Requirements

Requirements Number	Example Security Tool Requirement
1	Allows for testing source code for any type of vulnerability
2	Allows for testing test binaries, i.e., software executables, for any type of vulnerability
3	Allows for detecting issues specifically related to real-time systems, such as deadlock detection, asynchronous behavior issues, etc.
4	Allows for creating a baseline and regression testing any type of patch for newly introduced vulnerabilities
5	Allows for providing assurance that already verified source code hasn't changed once it is built into an executable

(continues)

Table C-6   Example of Security Testing Tool Requirements *(Continued)*

Requirements Number	Example Security Tool Requirement
6	Helps a tester find the trigger and/or the payload of malicious code
7	Provides information about the binary such as which local system objects are created
8	Can be applied during the software development lifecycle and can check software for vulnerabilities in software in various stages
9	Provides a minimal amount of false positive or false negatives, i.e., the effectiveness of the tool has been statistically proven
10	Is able to handle foreign source code, i.e., is able to handle foreign language comments, etc.
11	Shall be cross-platform compatible (i.e., Solaris, Linux, VxWorks, etc.)
12	Is compatible with various development languages, i.e., C, C++, Java, etc.
13	Is able to scale to test source code or executables of various size, i.e., up to millions of lines of code
14	Shall not leave any footprint, i.e., any changes to the SUT, to assure security testing tool does not adversely affect code
15	Shall generate useful diagnostic, prognostic, and metric statistic

Security tools that meet the requirements in Table C.6 are various static analysis and dynamic analysis tools, and fuzzers or penetration testing tools, which can be used at the source code and/or binary and executable level.

Static Analysis versus Dynamic Analysis

Program analysis can be categorized in two ways[3] according to when the analysis occurs.

1. *Static analysis* involves analyzing a program's source code or machine code without running it. Many tools perform static analysis, in particular compilers; examples of static analysis used by compilers include analyses for correctness, such as type checking, and analyses for optimization, which identify valid performance-improving transformations. Also, some stand-alone static analysis tools can identify bugs or help visualize

code. Tools performing static analysis only need to read a program in order to analyze it.

2. *Dynamic analysis* involves analyzing a *client program* as it executes. Many tools perform dynamic analysis, for example, prowlers, checkers, and execution visualizers. Tools performing dynamic analysis must *instrument* the client program with *analysis code*. The analysis code may be inserted entirely inline; it may also include external routines called from the inline analysis code. The analysis code runs as part of the program's normal execution, not disturbing the execution (other than probably slowing it down), but doing extra work on the side, such as measuring performance or identifying bugs. Static analysis can consider all execution paths in a program, whereas dynamic analysis considers only a single execution path. However, dynamic analysis is typically more precise than static analysis because it works with real values in the perfect light of runtime. For the same reason, dynamic analyses are often much simpler than static analyses.

Also consider running tools like Perfmon in parallel to show how an application uses system resources without the need for instrumentation.

Source Analysis versus Binary Analysis

Program analyses can be categorized into another two groups, according to the type of code being analyzed.

1. *Source analysis* involves analyzing programs at the level of source code. Many tools perform source analysis; compilers are again a good example. This category includes analyses performed on program representations that are derived directly from source code, such as control-flow graphs. Source analyses are generally done in terms of programming language constructs, such as functions, statements, expressions, and variables.

    Source analysis is platform- (architecture and operating system) independent, but language-specific; binary analysis is language-independent but platform-specific. Source code analysis has access to high-level information, which can make it more powerful; binary analysis has access to low-level information (such as the results of register allocation) that is required for some tasks.

2. *Binary analysis* involves analyzing programs at the level of machine code, stored either as object code (pre-linking) or executable code (post-linking). This category includes analyses performed at the level of executable intermediate representations, such as byte codes, which run on a virtual machine. Binary analyses are generally done in terms of machine entities, such as procedures, instructions, registers, and memory locations.

One advantage of binary analysis is that the original source code is not needed, which can be particularly important for dealing with library code, for which the source code might not be available on systems.

Application Footprinting

In addition to static and dynamic analysis, a useful way of detecting vulnerabilities on binaries is application footprinting, which is the process of discovering what system objects and system calls an application uses. Application footprinting uses similar inspection techniques to network footprinting, but focuses on just one application. It will help determine how that application receives inputs from its environment via operating system calls. It can help determine what OS objects that application is using, such as network ports, files, and registry keys.

Fuzz Testing or Penetration Testing

Fuzz testing[4] or fuzzing is a software testing technique often used to discover security weaknesses in applications and protocols. The basic idea is to attach the inputs of a program to a source of random or unexpected data. If the program fails (for example, by crashing, or by failing inbuilt code assertions), then there are defects to correct. It should be noted that the majority of security vulnerabilities, from buffer overflows to cross-site scripting attacks, are generally the result of insufficient validation of user-supplied input data. Bugs found using fuzz testing are frequently severe and exploitable bugs that could be used by a real attacker. This has become even truer as fuzz testing has become more widely known, as the same techniques and tools are now used by attackers to exploit deployed software. This is a major advantage over binary or source auditing, or even fuzzing's close cousin, fault injection, which often relies on artificial fault conditions that are difficult or impossible to exploit.

Threat Modeling—Prioritizing Security Testing with Threat Modeling

After the previously described techniques—dynamic and static analysis, footprinting, and penetration testing—have been implemented, the results need to be evaluated. Threats need to be evaluated, then ranked and mitigated according to the ease of the attack and the seriousness of the attack's potential impact.

Table C.6, which describes at a high level the example requirements that a security testing tool needs to meet, lists requirement number 6 as "Helps a tester find the trigger and/or the payload of malicious code." Using threat modeling, potential security threats are hypothesized and evaluated based on an understanding of the application's design. Threat modeling is further described in *The Art of Software Security Testing.*[5]

Automated Regression Testing

Automation has proven very effective during regression testing. Automated regression testing can verify that no new vulnerabilities have been introduced to previously verified functionality. In addition to those included in Table C.7, there are numerous other automated software testing tools that can aid in verifying that a patch or update didn't break previously working functionality—and/or allow for verification that previously secure functionality still is trustworthy.

Wireless Security Assessment Tools

An increasing number of testers need to verify the security of wireless clients. KARMA[6] is a set of tools that assess the security of wireless clients at multiple layers. Wireless sniffing tools discover clients and their preferred/trusted networks by passively listening for 802.11 probe request frames. From there, individual clients can be targeted by creating a rogue access point for one of their probed networks (which they may join automatically) or using a custom driver that responds to probes and association requests for any service set identifier. Higher-level fake services can then capture credentials or exploit client-side vulnerabilities on the host.

In summary, numerous security testing tools are available to meet various requirements. It is important to evaluate a security testing tool based on your specific systems engineering environment.

Table C-7 Various Security Testing Tools and Features

Testing Tools	Type	Features	Pros	Cons	Example Vendors	Satisfies Table C.6 Tool Requirement
Test tools for binaries	Profilers, checkers, memory leak detection tools, binary code scanners	Runs on binary/executable Tests code during runtime Code is instrumented to allow for runtime evaluation	Doesn't require source code; can be run on binaries Typically excels at detecting dynamic memory corruption, resource leak, and threading defects Pinpoints precisely what went wrong in a given execution trace of the code Produces relevant results. One advantage that binary code scanners have over source code scanners is the ability to look at the compiled result and factor in any vulnerabilities created by the compiler itself. Furthermore, library function code or other code delivered only as a binary can be examined.	Requires test cases; tied to test suite; test is only as good as tests that were designed/executed; this can result in false negatives Can be slow when trying to cover all paths; potential performance implications that mask bugs (nondeterministic) Defects are discovered later in the software development lifecycle	*Open-source:* Valgrind (www.valgrind.org) *Vendor-provided:* Rational/IBM Purify (www.ibm.com), http://samate.nist.gov/index.php/Binary_Code_Scanners	2, 8, 9, 10, 12, 14, 15
	Application footprinting	Runs on binary/executable; process of discovering what system calls and system objects an application uses	Will provide information about the binary such as which information the application accesses over a network or which local system objects are created	Bugs are uncovered late in the SDL	lsof on UNIX; or strace/ktrace/truss on UNIX; ProcessExplorer on Windows	7

Category	Tool	Description	Pros	Cons	Tools / References	
	Fuzz testing tools and techniques (also called penetration testing)	Fuzz testing or fuzzing is a software testing technique often used to discover security weaknesses in applications and protocols	Useful for performing a black-box assessment of a network, server, or application	Bugs are uncovered late in the SDL	Peach Fuzzer Framework (http://peachfuzz.sourceforge.net/)	2
Test tools for source code	Static code analyzers	Tests code during compile time. Analyzes source code for possible vulnerabilities. Can also find unused code	Can detect a wide range of coding flaws. No test cases required to find problems. Much better coverage because it analyzes the entire code (without test cases), which can result in more test coverage. Faster and many more possible outcomes/ results. Bugs are uncovered very early in the SDL	Source code needs to be accessible. False positive problems. Output can be very superficial if it doesn't understand how your software is built from the source code. Often difficult to provide the entire picture of all the code (sometimes only looking at a code file at a time). Based on heuristics that don't necessarily apply	*Open-source:* Splint is open-source version of Lint (http://splint.org). *Vendor-provided:* PRQA (Programming Research, www.programmingresearch.com/) or Coverity (www.coverity.com)	1, 3, 4, 6, 10, 11, 12, 14, 15

C.6 Automated Software Testing Framework (ASTF)—Example Evaluation

Our initial approach to automating testing had us looking at developing our own ASTF. As we defined the ASTF requirements further, it seemed less and less cost- and schedule-effective to do that. We decided to look into the open-source and commercial communities in search of a tool that satisfied all or most of our requirements. It was unrealistic to try to find a tool that would account for everything, so we looked for a "framework" that would address the high-level requirements that we defined:

- Launch applications or processes in parallel or in series.
- Support multiple platforms and OSs.
- Have a test manager capability that will allow for selecting, monitoring, executing, and modifying test cases and test data.
- Provide a way to capture test case results running on a single machine or in a distributed environment.
- Provide a way to create test cases for execution.
- Support a distributed test environment.
- Support high-level languages.
- See Appendix D and this section for further details on our ASTF requirements

This was the minimum set of requirements to make automation feasible. Most complex systems under test are multinode or distributed; therefore, it was key to find a solution that worked in a distributed environment. For our initial evaluation we selected an open-source framework called Software Test Automated Framework (STAF; http://staf.sourceforge.net/index.php). STAF is an open-source framework developed by IBM and available as open-source for other companies or individuals to use. "The Software Testing Automation Framework (STAF) is an open source, multi-platform, multi-language framework designed around the idea of reusable components, called services (such as process invocation, resource management, logging, and monitoring). STAF removes the tedium of building an automation infrastructure, thus enabling you to focus on building your automation solution. The STAF framework provides the foundation upon which to build higher level solutions, and provides a pluggable approach supported across a large variety of platforms and languages."[7]

STAF is actively supported and is being used by projects such as the Linux test project (http://ltp.sourceforge.net/). STAF provides many features we need, but does not meet every single need, yet the fact that it's open-source makes it easy to add customized features to it.

When we talk about an automated testing tool, we could mean one tool that does everything or a group of tools that fulfills the testing requirements. It's been our experience that no one tool does it all. Instead, you begin with a test tool framework and add capabilities or new tools as new requirements dictate. We generally try to stick with open-source products, but we are certainly not limited to them. For our purposes, most problems can be solved with an open-source product or set of products and added in-house development. Here we detail the items that we have found to be essential for an effective ASTF.

Test Case Development

Every ASTF will need to allow for test case development and execution. STAF provides an XML service (STAX) that allows you to write your test cases using XML and Python. This allows the test cases to be lightweight and easy to understand. The ASTF needs not only functional tests, but also performance tests, security, and so on. (See the section "Scalable" on page 310 for more details.)

High-Level Languages

The automated test tool should support well-known high-level languages such as C/C++, Java, Python, etc. You want to avoid having to train your development team in a proprietary language specific to the ASTF or integrated tool.

Platform Support

In the ever-increasing complexity of systems, multiple-platform support is very important. You should pick a tool that supports a large list of operating systems and hardware platforms. STAF supports a broad list of OSs.[8] This weighed heavily in our selection of STAF over any other open-source and even commercial products.

Open-Source

As explained in the overview, our initial approach was to create our own proprietary solution. Before you go down that path, we advise that you come up with an exhaustive list of requirements. Then take those requirements and search for open-source products that fulfill all or most of them. If not all requirements are met, you can add your own capabilities to an open-source solution using in-house development skills. The following services were available from STAF without any cost to us. They fulfilled some of the requirements that we had and we could build upon those.

- Internal STAF services
  - **Process:** Allows you to start, stop, and query processes
  - **Variable:** Provides a method for maintaining configuration and runtime data (variables)
- External STAF services
  - **Cron:** Calls into STAF services at a specified time interval (Java)
  - **E-mail:** Allows you to send e-mail messages (Java)
  - **Event:** Provides a publish/subscribe notification system (Java)
  - **Log:** Provides a full-featured logging facility (C++)
  - **STAX:** Provides an XML-based execution engine (Java)
  - **Zip:** Provides a means to zip/unzip/list/delete PKZip/WinZip-compatible archives

This is a subset of the services that are provided. It's intended to show the types of services that are available and have been in development for years. So the advantages of tapping into these resources are immense. For a complete list of services, go to http://staf.sourceforge.net/current/STAFGS.pdf.

Cost

This identifies any costs for licensing or hardware that needs to be purchased for a commercial or open-source product; licenses are "free" for open-source, but other costs will be involved and have to be considered. Our experience shows that there is no such thing as a free tool (TINSTAAFT). Even open-source products have to be maintained and come with a cost. See the "Conclusion for ASTF" section on page 311 for more details on open source.

Multiple Process Management

In any test environment there is a need to start and stop processes. A *process* is defined as an application or executable file that needs to be executed to carry out a test, whether it's a simple test case running a single process on one machine or running increasingly more complex test cases. The ASTF will need to manage the processes execution. When searching for test automation tools, make sure that this feature is available. For our test framework, STAF provides a service called Process, which allows you to invoke calls to the STAF demon telling it to execute a process either locally or on a remote machine.

Capturing Test Case Results

A key feature of any ASTF is reporting results of the test. It becomes increasingly tedious and difficult to manage in a distributed environment. It is best to look for a tool that has accounted for logging results in a distributed environment. The results should be timestamped and contain the host that logged the entry along with project-specific data. Another concern is the format in which the test results are captured. CSV format or some other standard format is recommended. STAF allows for those formats.

Support of Distributed Environment

We have touched on this quite a bit already. It is *very* important that the ASTF picked support a distributed environment. Most tools work well on a single machine, but it's important that it function in a distributed environment as well. The following are some key features to look for:

- Launching processes on multiple machines. You will need to manage at a test case level which processes to execute, where, and when.

- Logging results back to a central location. You want to avoid having to retrieve multiple log files from different machines. You then have to worry about trying to combine them. This feature should be accounted for in the test tool that you pick.

- Provide some kind of notification service or function. It is sometimes necessary to communicate between applications that are developed to carry out the test.

- STAF provides shared variables, which allow multiple processes to access the same variables across machines.

Future Execution Time

It is often desirable to execute tests at a future time. For example, CPU-intensive tests may be run off shift. This gives the test director the ability to schedule a test to run in the future. STAF provides a service called Cron that meets this need.

Scalable

It is vital that the ASTF scale as test programs become larger and larger. It's not unreasonable to have hundreds if not thousands of test cases for a given project. What we have found in our testing is that it is desirable to group tests and run them from one selection. For example, you may have 90 tests that are required for the project. You can select the 90 test cases individually every time, but it's more desirable to select one test case batch that executes all 90. Another use of this feature is for grouping tests. There may be, say, five tests that are run for each regression test. You would want to provide the capability to the tester to group test cases 1, 2, 3, 6, and 9, for example, and call it "regression test." So when the tester wants to run the regression tests, he or she can just select that set of tests to run.

Additionally your ASTF needs to be able to scale to allow for integration of various testing tool types (such as the ones described in this appendix) and to allow for support of the various testing types, such as those discussed in Appendix B. STAF/STAX provides that integration and scalability.

Footprint on SUT

Although it is important that the ASTF scales as needed, can handle concurrency issues effectively, and is secure, it also has to perform efficiently. See Appendix B for those types of ASTF testing considerations. You should be aware of any performance issues or footprint the ASTF leaves on the SUT. Regardless of the size of the ASTF, it should be lightweight, have no impact on the SUT's performance, and be light on memory and CPU usage.

E-mail

An e-mail feature is a "nice to have" but is helpful to the test team. It can be used to send test execution results to the members of the test team or to notify the team of failures that require immediate attention. For additional ASTF requirements, see Appendix D for our ASTF case study.

Conclusion for ASTF

It is important to identify all of your ASTF requirements before deciding which direction to take. Having a set of well-defined requirements makes the search for a solution that much easier. (A sample set of requirements and evaluations is shown in Table C-8.) We have found that the open-source products available are generally sufficient to satisfy the requirements. Here are some advantages to selecting an open-source solution that we have experienced:

- They are usually well supported with bug report systems that can be searched, active discussion forums, and plenty of online documentation.

- The source code is available. We can't emphasize enough the importance of having access to the source code. You are not tied to releases of a product, and you can control what features are added and when.

- Most of the requirements that you come up with have already been accounted for. The open-source product is the product of a team that went down the path already.

- They support a lot of different platforms and are usually at the leading edge of technology.

There are many tools available for automated software testing that can be integrated into the ASTF or run stand-alone; for example, Visual Studio Team System's Test Edition comes highly recommended if you are looking for code coverage tools for a Microsoft .NET application. It is a module/add-on that comes with VSTS and it offers excellent unit testing and code coverage for .NET applications. If you are specifically testing in a J2EE environment, a couple of tools worth mentioning are LISA from ITKO (see www.itko.com/site/products/lisa/j2ee.jsp) or QAWizard by Seapine Software (www.seapine.com/qawizard.html).

Table C-8   ASTF Evaluation Criteria—Sample Set

Criteria	Weight (1–5)	Tool 1		Tool 2	
		Score	Value	Score	Value
Allows for test case development	5	5	25	5	25
Uses high-level language	5	3	15	4	20
Cross-platform support	5	4	20	4	20
Open-source	5	4	20		0
Cost if not open-source	5	5	25	5	25
Multiple process management	4	3	12	2	8
Capture test case results	5	5	25	5	25
Support of distributed environment	5	5	25	5	25
Scalable	5	3	15	5	25
Performance	5	3	15	5	25
E-mail	5	5	25	5	25
Test manager feature	5	5	25	5	25
And more. For additional criteria, see, for example, www.sqaforums.com/attachments/ 347896-ToolEvaluation.pdf, taken from *Automated Software Testing*,[9] or Terry Horwath's sample test tool evaluation criteria at www.lakefolsom.com/whitepapers/ TestToolEvalCriteria.pdf.					

Automated Test Tool Example: Testplant's Eggplant

As part of our ASTF development efforts we needed to integrate an automated GUI testing tool, or capture/playback tool. One of the major requirements in our GUI testing efforts is that the test software should not impact SUT applications and configuration. We have researched all available tools on the market that meet this criterion and found Testplant's Eggplant to be the only vendor-provided tool that meets it.[10] There is a freeware solution (not yet open-source at the time of this writing) called VNCRobot, but since it is a freeware solution the code is not available for modification.

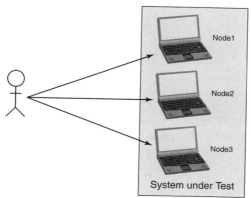

Figure C-3   Typical manual test scenario

Testplant's Eggplant takes advantage of the VNCServer technology.

Figure C-3 illustrates the typical manual test scenario. The test engineer manually kicks off a test using three SUT boxes.

1. Click menu X on node1.
2. Verify within ten seconds that window Y is displayed on node2.
3. Change some value in drop-down list Z on displayed window.
4. Hit OK on displayed window.
5. Verify that confirmation window is displayed on node3.
6. And so forth.

Figure C-4 illustrates how this manual scenario is converted to an automated scenario using a capture/replay (C/R) or capture/playback tool.

1. Capture/playback tool allows for automation of the previous "manual" GUI testing tasks.
2. Tool acts as a VNC client.
3. SUT consists of multiple OSs running on varied hardware.
4. Via X forwarding, not every node requires a running VNC server.
5. Tools allow image comparison, object comparison, and text comparison.
6. Tool may "play back" or execute its own comparison code.

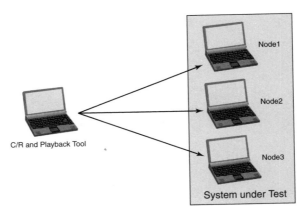

Figure C-4   Typical automated test scenario

Here is a typical automation script using Eggplant:

```
Connect to node1
Find Image for menu X and Click
If (imageNotFound (menuX){
logError("menu X not found")
}
Connect to node2
Find expected window Y image within at most 10 seconds
If (imageNotFound (window Y){
logError("window Y not found")
}
Find image for drop down list Z and Click
Click new value from list
Find image for OK button on window Y and click
Connect to Node3
Find image of confirmation window
If (imageFound(confirmation window){
log("Confirmation Window Found")
}
Else{
logError("Confirmation Window Not Found")
}
```

Figure C-5 shows how Eggplant can connect to the SUT using VNCServer.

1. VNC Server Running on System under Test
   - Fast/responsive but you now have process running on target hardware

2. XForwarding/NO VNC Server Running on System under Test
   - No test process (VNC server) running on target hardware but this method can be potentially much slower with severe network bandwidth hit

Figure C-5 Comparison of VNC Server running on SUT to VNC Server forwarding, not running on SUT

As mentioned, one of our major requirements was that the GUI testing tool cannot be installed on the SUT; therefore, this solution is ideal for our environment. There are some caveats, however:

- **VNC server on target hardware**
  - A proprietary OS may make running a VNC server too difficult.
  - There is a performance hit; however our tests show very minor CPU/memory usage, although usage can vary.
- **Network bandwidth**
  - In the XPolling/XForwarding configuration, the network bandwidth hit could prove too costly.
- **Remote access to target display**
  - Super-secure networks may not allow another machine to touch the network.
  - Ask yourself: Can you ssh/telnet into the target display node and set up the appropriate X configurations (e.g., "xhost +", "X forwarding," etc.)?

- **Unconventional display hardware**
  - The display that the user normally interacts with may be difficult to interact with via the software, e.g., touch panels.

We have found that Eggplant meets our current baseline GUI testing needs, and enhanced it using in-house development, as needed.

C.7 Other STL Support Tools

Small tool utilities can be helpful and streamline our efforts to automate software testing, and many such support tools and utilities are available. This section lists some tools worth looking at that have also been proven valuable in our automated testing efforts.[11] You may also wish to review the discussion of advances in AST technologies in Chapter 1, Section 1.3.

- **SIW (System Information for Windows):** Gathers hardware and software information
- **Crimson Editor:** Portable text editor, has code formatting and color shading
- **7-Zip:** Archive tool
- **CCleaner:** System cleanup tool
- **RegEx Builder:** A tool to verify regular expressions
- **WinDirStat:** Shows you file and directory size graphically
- **WinMerge:** Open-source file comparison/diff tool
- **duplicate_finder:** Will search and report on duplicate .dlls and .exes found on a system
- **InCtrl5:** Tool for tracking installations with new, deleted, and modified files
- **WmC File Renamer:** Self-explanatory—bulk file renamer
- **CmdHere:** For Windows XP, opens DOS prompt through file manager
- **Filezilla:** Open-source free ftp program
- **Virtual test environments support:** For your test environment the use of VMWare is worth a look; see www.vmware.com/, where they explain,

"Virtualization essentially lets one computer do the job of multiple computers, by sharing the resources of a single computer across multiple environments. Virtual servers and virtual desktops let you host multiple operating systems and multiple applications locally and in remote locations, freeing you from physical and geographical limitations. In addition to energy savings and lower capital expenses due to more efficient use of your hardware resources, you get high availability of resources, better desktop management, increased security, and improved disaster recovery processes when you build a virtual infrastructure." For an open-source version, take a look at www.virtualbox.org/, which provides VirtualBox, a free virtualization hosting program.

- **Example test data generators**
    - GNU-licensed; http://generatedata.com
    - NIST; compares test data generators; have their own to tool FireEye; http://csrc.nist.gov/groups/SNS/acts/documents/comparison-report.html
    - Matlab; www.mathworks.com/matlabcentral/
    - Pairwise.org; http://pairwise.org/tools.asp
    - IBM Intelligent Test Case Handler, an Eclipse plugin for creating test configuration data subject to coverage criteria; see http://alphaworks.ibm.com/tech/whitch/download
    - Open-source; Test Vector Generator (TVG) provides a software tester with GUI to generate combinatorial test vectors based on the input-output relationship, N-way coverage, or randomly; see http://sourceforge.net/projects/tvg/

- **Example test case generators**
    - IBM Telelogic Rhapsody ATG
    - Teradyne TestMaster
    - Conformiq Test Generator
    - T-VEC

- **Software that allows for video recording of test activities, such as duplicating a defect**
    - Camtasia
    - Testplant's Eggplant; comes with its own built-in movie recording capability

—   For Visual Studio 2010, Microsoft plans to include the ability to record the full screens of what testers are seeing, as well as data about their machines.[12]

Additionally, for a frequently updated list of available tools, see www.qadownloads.com/Tools/.

Self-testable or Autonomic Computing

We've mentioned that automated software testing can be perceived as a paradox: using software to test software. Software testing might change somewhat in the near future with the rise of autonomic computing, a trend we are following closely and will be involved in to some extent.

Self-testable or autonomic computing[13] is a tool or method we felt is worth mentioning here. Autonomic computing (AC) is an approach to self-managed computing systems with a minimum of human interference. The term derives from the body's autonomic nervous system, which controls key functions without conscious awareness or involvement.

Dynamic self-configuration, self-optimization, self-protection, and self-healing features of autonomic systems require that validation be an integral part of them. This new view of computing will necessitate changing the industry's focus on processing speed and storage to developing distributed networks that are largely self-managing, self-diagnostic, and transparent to the user.

This new computer paradigm means the design and implementation of computer systems, software, storage, and support must exhibit these basic fundamentals from a user perspective:

- **Flexible:** The system will be able to sift data via a platform- and device-agnostic approach.
- **Accessible:** The nature of the autonomic system is that it is always on.
- **Transparent:** The system will perform its tasks and adapt to a user's needs without dragging the user into the intricacies of its workings.

So what does it mean for an SUT environment to be autonomic? It means that systems are

- Self-configuring, to increase IT responsiveness/agility

- Self-healing, to improve business resiliency
- Self-optimizing, to improve operational efficiency
- Self-protecting, to help secure information and resources

Currently research efforts on AC are under way at MIT, Princeton, UC-Berkeley, and IBM, to just name a few research organizations and universities.

Notes

1. See Dustin, *Effective Software Testing*, item 31 on "Types of Tools Available," updated from original Table 3-1, "Test Life-Cycle Tools," in Dustin et al., *Automated Software Testing*.
2. E. Dustin, "Software Testing Starts When the Project Begins." See www.csc.com/features/2003/165.shtml.
3. http://valgrind.org/docs/phd2004.pdf.
4. www.hacksafe.com.au/blog/2006/08/21/fuzz-testing-tools-and-techniques/.
5. Wysopal et al., *The Art of Software Security Testing*.
6. www.theta44.org/karma/index.html.
7. http://staf.sourceforge.net/index.php.
8. http://staf.sourceforge.net/getcurrent.php.
9. Dustin et al., *Automated Software Testing*, 90–93.
10. www.testplant.com.
11. For some of the tools provided here, see related discussions started by Tony Davis on www.sqaforums.com.
12. http://news.cnet.com/8301-13860_3-10052412-56.html.
13. www.research.ibm.com/autonomic/ and http://www-03.ibm.com/autonomic/pdfs/AC_Blueprint_White_Paper_4th.pdf

Case Study: An Automated Software Testing Framework (ASTF) Example

In this appendix we will summarize a case study of how we successfully implemented an automated testing framework, using mostly open-source tools.

Using the guidance given in Appendix B, we first define our requirements; for the purpose of this case study they were as follows:

- Support applications[1] running on multiple distributed computers.

- Support applications developed in different languages.

- Support applications running on different types of OSs.

- Support applications that have GUI and those that do not (for example, message interface testing).

- Support applications that use different types of network protocols such as TCP/IP, DDS, CORBA, etc.

- Support the integration of multiple commercial testing tools from different vendors (as new or better products emerge).

- Support testing without having to install the ASTF on the same computers as the SUT.

- Allow for test input data to be inserted in one or more applications using existing application interfaces. Application interfaces include GUI, message-based, command-line, and file-based.

- Testing scenarios to be supported include individual applications or components, and coordinated and concurrent interaction with multiple applications or components.

- Test software should not impact SUT applications and configurations and should require a very low footprint.

- Be able to capture/document test results at both the test step and test case levels.

The framework additionally needed to provide the following capabilities:

- Select and execute one or more (batch) tests to be run at a specified time.

- Verify that the system configuration is valid prior to test execution.

- Provide the status of test execution:
  - Test run percent complete
  - Pass/fail status

- Generate a searchable electronic log of test results.

- Provide an automated analysis of test results and generate the appropriate reports.

- Document test results per test case in the RTM.

- Prefill a trouble report for review and analysis before submitting it to defect tracking tool in the event a test step fails.

Figure D-1 describes our initial high-level framework concept.

Our goal was to implement open-source tools using the automation framework concept described in Figure 6-6. The distributed environment supported by the framework was similar to that shown in Figure D-1.

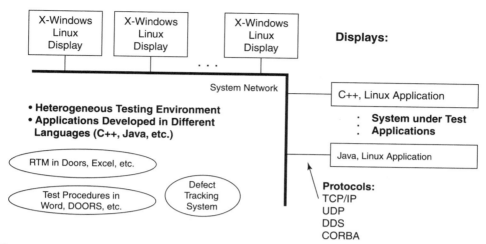

Figure D-1 Distributed environment supported by framework

D.1 Key Design Features

Our framework design consisted of the following key design features:

- We used a single design/approach to support testing at the system level and on individual applications.

- The goal was to leverage commercially available automation test tools and open-source tools and products to the maximum extent possible.

- We planned for ongoing insertion of automation test tools and products from multiple vendors (to be able to use the best tools and products as the market changed).

- The test suite had to be scalable and portable.

We then searched for a framework that would provide automation tasks as defined in Figure D-2, i.e., a framework that would provide for automation startup, system setup, test case execution, test case output analysis, test case cleanup, results notification, and automation completion.

For each automated test, the test execution needed to be managed or coordinated. We found, among other tools, that Software Testing Automation Framework (STAF) met our needs.[3] We could manage the test case execution through STAF-provided services. How we evaluated STAF/STAX and the

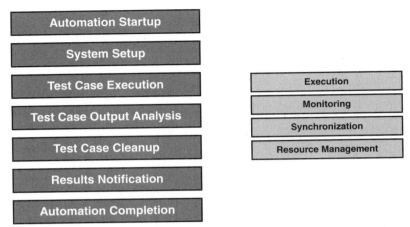

Figure D-2 Automation tasks[2]

requirements this automation framework needed to meet are described in detail in Appendix C.

We determined that end-to-end automation would be possible using STAF/STAX; see Figure D-3.

We also determined that STAF/STAX could meet all our needs related to a central test manager (see Figure D-4), central to the automation framework.

Additional features to those provided by STAF-STAX were required and in-house design, architecture, and development were needed. See Figure 6-7 for the sample design we came up with.

Figure D-3 End-to-end automation with STAF/STAX[4]

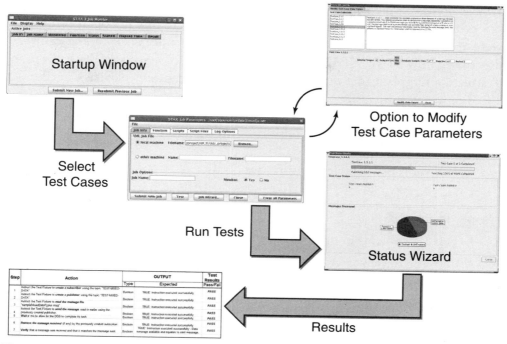

Figure D-4   Test manager central to the automation framework

D.2   Test Manager

This is generally the central feature of the test automation tool. Here, which test cases and the number of them to be run are selected, or the timing of when the batch test file is to run is dictated. This feature of ASTF should have the following minimum set of requirements:

- Allows test case development and modification
- Allows browsing of test cases to be run
- Allows selection of test cases to be run
- Allows monitoring of test case execution
- Allows for statusing of test case execution, including how many steps are complete, how many are left, how many tests have been run, and their pass/fail status
- Allows an operator to bring up historical test case runs and reports

We used STAF, which comes with a test manager GUI called STAXMon. It did not provide all of the features described above, but because it's open-source we were able to add the needed features easily. See Appendix C for more details describing how STAF/STAX met our framework needs. See also the section on Testplant's Eggplant that describes how it met our capture/playback needs.

For message interface testing we needed to implement additional code. Here we looked at automatic code generation: When writing automation test code (code to verify the SUT), consider autogenerating code, because it

- Provides predictable test software
- Is scalable
- Is portable
- Fixes problems in one place
- Can be reused across projects
- Cuts down on development time per project, which makes automating tests more feasible

D.3   More on Automated Test Case and Test Code Generation

We generated automated test case code and automated framework code.

For example, the automation framework code generated code that glued the SUT interface code to the test framework. A software interface could be a DDS middleware or a simple Multicast layout. We generated software interface code from various input formats, i.e., IDL, C-style headers, etc.

Although many test case generation tools are available, we didn't want to be tied to a vendor-provided solution and therefore developed this functionality in-house. For automating test case code generation, we implemented the following: Each step in the test case procedure had associated code generated to execute its behavior. A standardized test case format facilitated automated step procedure extraction. Here XML was used to define the extracted test step information as input into the autogeneration process.

Additionally, we enhanced an out-of-the-box capture/playback tool with additional capability; as the test engineer, for example, "clicked" on a GUI to record a test step, automated code was generated behind the scene, based on keywords.

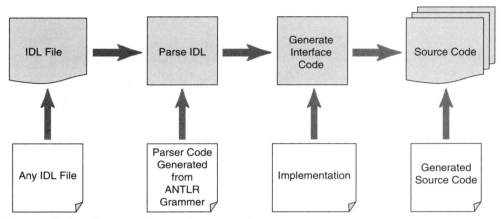

Figure D-5 Automation code generation concept

StringTemplates provided for a common code set as well as project-unique sets. Figure D-5 shows the automation code generation concept.

Tools used for this automated code generation effort were (as already described in Chapter 1)

- **ANTLR** (www.antlr.org/)
    - Works off of grammar files; several common languages' grammar files are available for download (e.g., IDL, C)
    - Generates lexical analyzer and parser functionality in Java (other languages are supported as well)
- **StringTemplate** (www.stringtemplate.org/)
    - Uses ANTLR; developed by the same team
    - Provides pluggable templates; code can be generated in multiple languages without modification of the autogen code
- **JAXB** (https://jaxb.dev.java.net/)
    - XML to Java object binding based on XML schema
    - Generates Java classes used to interpret XML data

D.4 Results Reporting

Our goal for results reporting was to keep it as generic as possible and independent of actual decision making, whether we used a data parser as depicted in Figure D-6 or an application reporting actual results from a test run.

Our lesson learned was to report actual results only to simplify autogeneration of source code. We put comparison logic in a separate utility and were then only concerned with comparing expected results (text, integer, etc.) with the actual results from the test run, as described in Figure D-7.

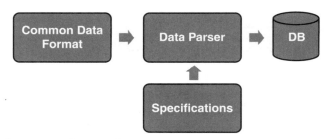

Figure D-6 Automated reporting

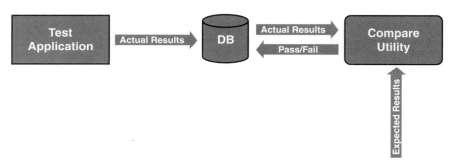

Figure D-7 Reporting modularity

D.5 Automated Defect Reporting

As we have mentioned throughout this book, it is important to define and adhere to a defect tracking lifecycle. Chapter 9 provides the Bugzilla defect tracking lifecycle example. For our defect tracking tool, for the purpose of this case study, we selected Bugzilla. As part of our case study, we also automated the defect reporting. Our framework allowed for filling in most of the information needed for a software trouble report, and we used information gathered from the test run to provide a detailed trouble report. This helped developers re-create failures. We decided not to directly populate the defect tracking database with the failures, but instead reported the potential failures to an intermediate output that would allow a reviewer to review the defect before submitting it automatically, with the click of a button, to the defect tracking database. The types of information about the failed test steps we were tracking as part of this effort were

- Test case name and step number
- Test case step detailed information
- Requirement that failed
- Test data used
- Description of failure, which can include a screen print of the error and more

We considered adding "priority"; however, this would work effectively only if priority was considered in combination with "severity." For example, a high-priority test case failure could become a high-priority defect, but with low severity. Using priority as a predefined field stand-alone wasn't effective, because a high-priority test case run could result in a low-priority defect.

Notes

1. *Application* here refers to either the SUT or the AUT.
2. www.staf.sourceforge.net.
3. Ibid.
4. Ibid.

Contributing Authors

Scott Bindas is the software development manager at Innovative Defense Technologies. The focus of the software team has been to deliver an automated software testing framework incorporating various open-source, vendor-provided, and IDT-developed software solutions. Prior to joining IDT, Scott worked at a major defense contractor as a principal software engineer. In that role he was responsible for the software design, development, and testing of applications for Navy submarine programs. Scott holds a B.S. in computer engineering from the University of Massachusetts, Dartmouth.

Marcus Borch is a software development technical lead at Innovative Defense Technologies developing automated software testing suites, responsible for designing and implementing test modules to automate various types of software testing ranging from functional testing to system-level testing. He has worked for a major defense contractor as a software engineer for more than eight years. He graduated from SUNY New Paltz, New York, cum laude with a degree in computer science.

Vincent Vallarine is a senior software engineer implementing automated testing solutions at Innovative Defense Technologies. Vinny began his career at a major defense contractor after receiving his B.S. in computer engineering from the University of Rhode Island in 1999. At the defense contractor he worked as a software engineer responsible for designing, implementing, and testing software for Navy Combat Systems. He also earned an M.S. in computer science from the University of Massachusetts, Dartmouth.

Index

Page numbers followed by a t or and f indicate a table or a figure, respectively.

A

American National Standards Institute (ANSI), 19
ANSI. *See* American National Standards Institute
API. *See* Application programming interface
Application programming interface (API), 96
Application under test (AUT), 5
The Art of Software Security Testing (Wysopal, Nelson, Dai Zovi, Dustin), 303
AST. *See* Automated software testing
ASTF. *See* Automated software test framework
ATG. *See* Automated test generator
ATLM. *See* Automated testing lifecycle methodology
ATRT. *See* Automated test and retest
AUT. *See* Application under test
Automated defect reporting, 329–330
Automated software test framework (ASTF), 101, 105, 116, 129, 146–149, 216–217
  case study of, 323f
    key design features, 323–325, 324f
    test code generation, 325–326, 326f
    test manager, 325–326, 326f
  coverage, 182–183
  customer review, 183–184, 183t
  effective development, 169–170
  peer-review
    all components review, 173
    automated test code review, 178–181, 178f, 179f–180f, 181f
    software lifecycle and, 170–172, 172f

    test cases review, 173–176, 174t, 175t
    test data review, 176, 177f
    test logic review, 175, 175t–176t
  requirements, 182–183, 182t
  testing of, 167–184
  traceability, 182–183
Automated software testing (AST)
  advances of, 8–11
  automated test case code generation, 10
  automation payoff, 101–128
  automation standards, lack of
    cross-platform compatibility, 95
    ease of automation, 94
    plug and play, 95
    product availability, 95
    product interchangeability, 95
    product interoperability, 95
    testing capability, 95
  benefits from, 15
  black-box testing, 12
  business case, lack of, 97
  capture/playback equating, 80–81
Automated software testing (AST)
  challenges for, 24–26
  code reuse, library concept of, 91
  coding standards, 89
  complexity, 7
  configuration management, 242–245
  cost reduction, 26–38
  criteria for, 7, 33–34
  defects, finding of, 82
  defect workflow, 37
  definition of, 4–5

Automated software testing (AST) *continued*
   document test cases, 88–89
   enhanced defect reporting, 13
   error status/correction monitoring
      analysis, 36
      closure, 36
      defect entry, 36
      recurrence, 36
   failures and pitfalls, 69–97
   functionality of, 24
   functions of, 23
   gray-box testing, 12–13
   immediate reduction, schedule, 77
   immediate test effort reduction, 76
   implementation of, 209–222
   implementation requirements, 6, 6f
   improvements for
      advanced test issues focus, 44
      build verification (smoke test), 43
      concurrency testing, 49
      configuration compatibility testing, 44
      defects, reproduction of, 45
      distributed workload, 49
      documentation, 48–49
      endurance testing, 47
      "lights-out" testing, 45–46
      manual testing and, 45
      multiplatform compatibility testing, 44
      mundane tests execution, 44
      performance testing, 46
      quality measurements, 47–48
      regression testing, 43–44
      requirements definition, 46
      stress testing, 47
      system development lifecycle, 48
      system expertise, 45
      test optimization, 47–48
      traceability, 48–49
   increased testing precision, 13–14
   initial test effort increase, 28
   investigative testing, improved ability to
      do, 13
   as manual tester activity, 81
   mission criticality, 8
   mitigating factors for, 37–38
   myths and realities, 74–83
   object naming standards, 91
   Object Management Group's Interface
      Design Language , use of, 89

open architecture standards, 86–87
open-source components and, 9
open-source products, advantages, 92
"perceived" vs. "actual" quality, 72
phases of, 211
   phase 1, 212–215, 233, 236–237, 239–
      240, 242, 244, 252–253
   phase 2, 215–216, 234, 237, 240, 243,
      244–245, 253–254
   phase 3, 216–217, 234, 238, 240–241,
      243, 245, 254–255
   phase 4, 217–218, 218f, 235, 238, 241,
      243, 245, 255–256
   phase 5, 218–219, 235–236, 238, 241,
      243–244, 245, 256
process checklist, 251–256
process management
   adherence, 220–221
   performance, 220
production support, 15–18
program correction, accuracy of, 17
program management, 232–236
progress development, 187–206
quality assurance, 244–245
report creation, 37
research reports for, 25–26
results analysis, 33–35
risk, 8
sample test tools standards
   application program interface, 96
   capture feature, 95–96
   integration, 96
   modularity, 96
   reporting, 96
   scripting language, 95
   test data, 96
   test tool output, 96
schedule, 7
skill sets requirements, 230f
   ASTF architecture, 227
   ASTF implementation, 226–227
   automated generation of code, 228–229
   libraries, 227–228
   modular script development, 227
   modular user interface, 227
   perceived progress, 224–225
   reusable functions, 227–228
   soft skills, 231–232
   version control, 228

software development, 72, 239–242
software development, lack of, 83–91
software quality impact
    benefits, 39–41
    effective test time, 41f
    metrics for, 39
    model projection, 40f
specific program components, support of,
    16–17
STAX (STAF engine) and, 7
STAF (Software Test Automation
    Framework) and, 7
standard documentation format, 87–88
standards assessments, 20f
    application, 19
    development standards, 19
    step-by-step process, 19
STR (Software Trouble Report) triage,
    support of, 17–18
systems engineering, 236–239
system test automation, focus on, 82–83
technology, 7
testability, building of
    class name, 84
    host name, 84
    messages, 84–86
    method name, 84
    process ID, 84
    timestamp of entry, 84
test case procedure code, 10
test coverage, 79–80
test data generation
    breadth, 29–30
    conditions, 31–32
    criteria for, 32
    depth, 29
    execution data integrity, 30–31
    scope, 30
test execution, 32
testing lifecycle phase, 7
testing programs, factors for, 25
testing recipes, 5–8
testing recommendations, 89–90
testing time reduction, 26–38
test plan generation, 74–75
test tools for all, 75–76
timelines, 7
tool evaluation

    longevity, 93
    past experience, 93
    requirements, 93
    user base, 93
    tools for use, 77
    troubleshooting, support of, 16
    universal application of
        compatibility tests, 78
        limiting factors, 78–79
    virtual quality gates, 219–220
    white-box testing, 12
Automated test and retest (ATRT), 97, 169,
    221f
Automated test generator (ATG), 9, 88–89
Automated test strategy
    approach identification
        test case development, 139–143, 141f
Automated testing lifecycle methodology
    (ATLM), 69, 209, 210f
Automated testing tool
    cost, 308
    criteria for, 311t
    distributed environment, support of, 309
    e-mail, 310
    future execution time, 309–310
    high-level languages, 307
    multiple process management, 308–309
    open-source
        external STAF services, 308
        internal STAF services, 308
    platform support, 307
    scalable, 310
    test case development, 307
    test case results, 309
Testplant's Eggplant, 312–315, 313f, 315f
AST environment/configuration
    automated CM, 153–158, 154f, 156t–
        158t
    clean, 150–151
    functionally equivalent, 151
    predictable, 151
    repeatable, 151
    test configurations, 151–152, 152f, 153t
automated software test framework
    architecture, 148, 148f
    design components, 148, 149f
    requirements, 146–147, 147f
automation effort analysis, 135–136

Automated testing tool *continued*
  base automation requirements on
    budget, 138
    customer needs, 138
    highest to lowest complexity, 138
    highest to lowest risk, 137
    personnel, 138
    time, 138
  budget considerations, 134–135
  defect tracking, 164
  expertise considerations, 134–135
  general comments, 129–130
  Jfeature requirements, 163, 163f
  manual procedure to automation, 143–144
  repetitive tasks and, 136–137
  reuse potential for module analysis, 136
  RTM (Requirements Traceability Matrix)
    update, 161–162, 162f
  schedule considerations, 134–135
  scope and objectives, 132f
  step-by-step approach, 134
  strategy document, 131
  test case development techniques, 145
  test case hyperlink, 160, 160f
  test case templates, 160
  test code generation, 144–145, 145f
  test objective, definition of, 138–139
  test procedure documentation, 144
  test requirements, based on risk
    complexity, 135
    failure probability, 135
    impact, 135
  tests for automaton, criteria, 133, 133f
  test steps updates, 161, 161f
  support requirements
    ASTF framework, 105
    AST process requirements
      budget, 113
      corporate culture and, 113
      development process, 114
      effort level, 112
      phased solution, 113
      responsibilities, 114
      roles, 114
      schedule, 113
      technology choices, 113
      testing phases, 112
      testing team, 113

AUT/SUT requirements
  scope, 104
  system understanding, 103-104, 104f
  data requirements, 105-107
  design documents, 115
  hardware requirements, 110-111, 110t
  interviews, 118-120
  knowledge base, increase of, 120
  legacy application
    effective development process, 124
    existing application, 123
    single version, 123
    update on exiting application, 124
  manual testing procedure, 114
  modifiable test data, 107, 107f
  prototypes, 115-116, 117f
  RTM implementation
    example of, 125f, 126t-127t
    information in, 125
  software requirements, 111-112, 111t
  test environment, 108-112
    preparation activities, 109-110
  unmodifiable test data, 107

B

Beck, Kent, 272
Beizer, Boris, 26
Black-box testing, 12
Boolean result, 174, 175t
Bugzilla tracking lifecycle, 217, 218f, 294–295
Business case
  automation justification, 55–65
  business needs identification
    development time savings, 59–60, 60f
    diagnostics time savings, 62–63, 62f
    efficiency need, 53–54
    evaluation time savings, 62–63, 62f
    execution time savings, 61–62, 61f
    speeding up need, 53–54
    testing cost decrease need, 54–55
    test team member skills need, 55
  definition of, 51–52
  environment setup time savings, 57–58, 59f
  other considerations for, 67–68
  purposes of, 52
  risks for
    adequate skills, lack of, 66

difficult-to-automate requirements, 66
new technology, 66
short time-to-market, 66
ROI considerations
intangible automation savings, 64
lab equipment requirements, 63
metrics, 65
personnel requirements, 63
test case maintenance, 63–64
ROI estimation, 55–56
test automation savings, 57, 57f, 58f

C

Cardholder information security program
(CISP), 18
CCleaner, 316
CISP. *See* Cardholder information security
program
CM. *See* Configuration management
Code coverage testing, 269–271, 270f
Concurrency testing, 263f
tools for, 265
types of, 264
Configuration management (CM), 242
benefits of, 285–286
example evaluation, 284–292

D

DARPA. *See* Defense Advanced Research
Projects Agency
Darwin, Charles, 298
Database design document (DDD), 115,
138–139
Data distribution service (DDS), 151
DDD. *See* Database design document
DDS. *See* Data distribution service
Defect tracking
adaptability, 295
Bugzilla vs Trac, 296, 296t
community, 295
ease of use, 297
installation, general, 297
licensing, 294
support, 294–295
Defect tracking
tool, choice of, 292, 293t

Windows, installation on, 296
workflow, customizable, 297
Defense Advanced Research Projects Agency
(DARPA), 87
Dijkstra, Edsger, 264
Discrete Mathematics and Its Applications
(Rosen), 79

E

Enhanced defect reporting, 13

F

Foxit Reader, 316

G

Gamma, Erich, 272
Google Test Automation Conference (GTAC
2008), 11
Graphical user interfaces (GUIs), 5, 71, 76,
78, 83, 89–90, 136, 289
Gray-box testing, 12–13
GUIs. *See* Graphical user interfaces

H

Hardware configuration management
(HCM), 285
HCM. *See* Hardware configuration
management
Healthcare Portability and Accountability Act
of 1996 (HIPAA), 18
HIPAA. *See* Healthcare Portability and
Accountability Act of 1996
How We Test Software at Microsoft (Page/
Johnson/Rollison), 145

I

IDD. *See* Interface design document
IDL. *See* Interface design language
Increased testing precision, 13–14
Initial test effort increase, 28
Interface design document (IDD), 115
Interface design language (IDL), 10
Internet relay chat (IRC), 283

Investigative testing, improved ability, 13
IRC. *See* Internet relay chat

K

Kan, Stephen H., 200

M

Mean time to critical failure (MTTCF), 39
Mean time to failure (MTTF), 39
Metrics and Models in Software Quality
    Engineering (Kan), 200
MTTCF. *See* Mean time to critical failure
MTTF. *See* Mean time to failure

N

National Institute for Standards and
    Technology (NIST), 9–10
NFRs. *See* Nonfunctional requirements
NIST. *See* National Institute for Standards and
    Technology
Nonfunctional requirements (NFRs), 257

O

OA. *See* Open architecture
OCM. *See* Operational configuration
    management
Open architecture (OA), 86
Operational configuration management
    (OCM), 285

P

Perceived progress, 224–225
Performance testing, 266f, 267f
    CPU utilization, 268
    garbage collections, 268
    test results variance and, 268
    total memory usage, 268
    total thread execution time, 268
    use of, 267
PIM. *See* Platform-independent model
Platform-independent model (PIM), 9
Platform-specific models (PSMs), 9
Problem trouble report (PTR), 132. *See also*
    System trouble report (STR)

Progress development
    actions, tracking of, 192
    AST metrics, 193f
        automated software testing ROI, 204,
            204f
        automation index, 196–198, 197f
        automation progress, 198, 198f
        categories of, 193–194
        common test metrics, 205t
        defect density, 201
        defect removal efficiency, 203–204, 203f
        defect trend analysis, 202, 202f
        definition of, 193, 194
        features of, 194–196
        test coverage percentage, 199–200,
            200f
        test progress, 199
    constrains, examining of, 189
    defects, tracking of, 192
    integrity safeguard, 190–191
    internal inspection, 189
    issues, tracking of, 192
    risk mitigation strategies, 190
    root cause analysis, 205–206
    schedule and costs
        communication, 191–192
        definition of, 191–192
        tracking of, 191–192
    technical interchanges, 189
    walk-throughs, 189
PSMs. *See* Platform-specific models
PTR. *See* Problem trouble report

Q

QoS. *See* Quality of service
Quality of service (QoS), 139

R

Reflexive User Interface Builder (RIB), 89
RegEx Builder, 316
Requirement management (RM), 132
    automating management, 278–281
    definition of, 276
    manual RTM example, 279t
    test director requirements, 280, 281f
    traceability and, 277
    use of, 277

Requirements traceability matrix (RTM), 17, 124–127, 130, 159, 213, 215–216, 217
Results reporting, 328, 328f
Return of investment (ROI), 4, 8, 27, 38, 55–56, 63, 82, 94, 136, 194, 212, 217, 239–240
RIB. *See* Reflexive User Interface Builder
RM. *See* Requirement management
ROI. *See* Return of investment
Rosen, Kenneth H., 79
Rossum, Guido van, 295
RTM. *See* Requirements traceability matrix

S

SCM. *See* Software configuration management
SDD. *See* System and software design document
Security testing, 299t–300t
   application footprinting, 302
   automated regression testing, 303
   buffer overflow, 258, 258f
   code analysis, 260
   fuzz (penetration) testing, 302
   source vs. binary analysis, 301–302
   SQL injection vulnerability, 259–260, 259f
   static vs. dynamic analysis, 300–301
   threat modeling, 303
   vulnerability, 258
   wireless assessment tools, 303, 304t–305t
Service-oriented architecture (SOA), 5
SIW. *See* System Information for Windows
SLOC. *See* Software lines of code
SME. *See* Subject matter expert
SOA. *See* Service-oriented architecture
Soak testing, 261–262
Software configuration management (SCM), 284
   features of
      development status, 288
      ease of use, 287
      efficient binary file support, 288
      end-of-line (EOL) conversion, 290
      file renaming, 289
      fully atomic commits, 287
      IDE (Integrated Development Environment) support, 290

      international support, 289
      intuitive tags, 287
      licensing, 287
      merge tracking, 289
      programming language, 288
      repository model, 289
      speed, 290
      stand-alone GUI, 289
      stand-alone server option, 288
      symbolic link support, 289
      web-based interface, 287–288
   tool comparison, 291t
Software lines of code (SLOC), 72
Software testing automation framework (STAF), 306
Software testing lifecycle (STL), 4, 52, 130, 275
   other tools for
      CCleaner, 316
      CmdHere, 316
      Filezilla, 316
      Foxit Reader, 316
      InCtrl15, 316
      RegEx Builder, 316
      test data generators, 317
      virtual test environment support, 316
      WinDirStat, 316
      WmC File Renamer, 316
      7-Zip, 316
   Self-testable (autonomic) computing, 317–318
   System Information for Windows (SIW), 316
STAF. *See* Software testing automation framework
STL. *See* Software testing lifecycle
STR. *See* System trouble report
Subject matter expert (SME), 66, 116, 246
System and software design document (SDD), 115
System Information for Windows (SIW), 316
System trouble report (STR), 15. *See also* Problem trouble report (PTR)

T

TA. *See* Test automation
TC. *See* Test conductor

Test automation (TA), 132
Test conductor (TC), 9
Test execution data integrity, 30–31
Test management (TM), 132
Testplant's Eggplant, 312–315, 313f, 315f
TM. *See* Test management
Trac, 294–295
    definition of, 297
    integrated with subversion, 297
    issue tracker, 297
    wiki server and, 297

U

Unit testing, 273f, 274f
    assertion mechanism, 272
    frameworks
        common IDE integration, 283
        community, 284
        criteria for, 282t
        documentation, 282
        evaluation method, 281
        features, 284
        licensing, 283
        multiplatform support, 283

        price, 282
        support, 282–283
        xUnit, 283
    test execution, 272
    test fixtures, 272
    test suites, 272
    use of, 271

V

VE. *See* Virtual environment
Verification and validation (V&V), 25
Virtual environment (VE), 108
Virtual machine (VM), 49
Virtual network computing (VNC), 90
VM. *See* Virtual machine
VNC. *See* Virtual network computing
V&V. *See* Verification and validation

W

Wall, Larry, 295
WASS. *See* Web application security standards
Web application security standards (WASS), 18
White-box testing, 12

Addison Wesley

 PRENTICE HALL

SAMS

Tools, Techniques, and Resources for Effective Software Testing

Critical Testing Processes
Plan, Prepare, Perform, Perfect
Rex Black
978-0-201-74868-0

Software Testing
A Guide to the TMap Approach
Martin Pol, Ruud Teunissen, Erik van Veenendaal
978-0-201-74571-9

Effective Software Testing
50 Specific Ways to Improve Your Testing
Elfriede Dustin
978-0-201-79429-8

xUnit Test Patterns
Refactoring Test Code
Gerard Meszaros
978-0-131-49505-0

Software Testing
Second Edition
978-0-672-32798-8

test-driven development
A Practical Guide
David Astels
978-0-131-01649-1

The Art of **Software Security Testing**
Identifying Software Security Flaws
Chris Wysopal, Lucas Nelson, Dino Dai Zovi, Elfriede Dustin
978-0-321-30486-5

TEST-DRIVEN DEVELOPMENT BY EXAMPLE
Kent Beck
978-0-321-14653-3

 **informIT**

Safari Books Online

For more information and to read sample material, please visit informit.com.

Titles are also available at safari.informit.com.

FREE Online Edition

Your purchase of *Implementing Automated Software Testing* includes access to a free online edition for 45 days through the Safari Books Online subscription service. Nearly every Addison-Wesley Professional book is available online through Safari Books Online, along with more than 5,000 other technical books and videos from publishers such as, Cisco Press, Exam Cram, IBM Press, O'Reilly, Prentice Hall, Que, and Sams.

SAFARI BOOKS ONLINE allows you to search for a specific answer, cut and paste code, download chapters, and stay current with emerging technologies.

Activate your FREE Online Edition at www.informit.com/safarifree

> **STEP 1:** Enter the coupon code: WUCGKEH.

> **STEP 2:** New Safari users, complete the brief registration form.
> Safari subscribers, just log in.

If you have difficulty registering on Safari or accessing the online edition, please e-mail customer-service@safaribooksonline.com